O AND I

To Linda, may she find
a few meaningfull words here.

Schwab

XMAS 2011

O AND I

There Are Bridges between the Seen and the Unseen

ALFRED SCHWAB

iUniverse, Inc.
Bloomington

O and I
There Are Bridges between the Seen and the Unseen

iUniverse books may be ordered through booksellers or by contacting:

iUniverse
1663 Liberty Drive
Bloomington, IN 47403
www.iuniverse.com
1-800-Authors (1-800-288-4677)

Because of the dynamic nature of the Internet, any web addresses or links contained in this book may have changed since publication and may no longer be valid. The views expressed in this work are solely those of the author and do not necessarily reflect the views of the publisher, and the publisher hereby disclaims any responsibility for them.

Any people depicted in stock imagery provided by Thinkstock are models, and such images are being used for illustrative purposes only.
Certain stock imagery © Thinkstock.

ISBN: 978-1-4620-2894-8 (sc)
ISBN: 978-1-4620-2896-2 (dj)
ISBN: 978-1-4620-2895-5 (ebk)

Printed in the United States of America

iUniverse rev. date: 06/09/2011

CONTENTS

Introduction

The author was married with two sons, a house in the country with pool and apple trees, two cars, two dogs, and a terrific job with IBM. He coached Little League and Youth Soccer, planted a hundred trees and bushes on his land, and was reasonably happy.

In other words, he was—and still is—pretty much a regular guy. He participated in the office football pool, played soccer on an IBM team for older guys, belonged to a poker group that played mostly for bragging rights, loved cutting nature paths through his wilderness areas, spent too many hours on his garden tractor, wielded his chain saws with gusto, rooted for the Mets and Jets, etc. etc.

He was satisfied with his lot in life—except for an occasional uneasy feeling that he had no idea what was going on, that there must be a reason why things are the way they are, that 'luck' is not an explanation for anything, that the events of our lives may not be mere coincidences, and so on.

And then the events documented in this book began to unfold, changing his reality forever.

He wants to share these experiences and hopes that others will find a few nuggets in these pages that will make them wonder about who we really are and where we come from.

O

1 When the Student Is Ready

It was a quiet evening. The kids were in bed, my wife Linda was at a meeting. I was sitting at our dining room table, scribbling down ideas about some metaphysical points my fellow deep-thinkers and I discussed that day at work. We loved developing elaborate theories about every conceivable mystery—from consciousness to life after death to where we humans fit into the order of things, and even the size of the universe. Nothing was safe from our intellects. Diagrams appeared on blackboards to "explain" the latest theory. Dreams, aliens, destiny, gods—everything was fair game.

Our German short-haired pointer, Odin von Schwab, was stretched out on the kitchen floor watching me with big warm brown eyes. As I returned his gaze absentmindedly, he took my apparent attention as an invitation to get his head scratched, got up, and walked towards me. I resumed looking at my notes, with my hand out to receive his head—we had done this before.

A moment went by before I became aware of a gentle splashing sound. I glanced up, and there was my always-well-behaved Odin standing by one of my most treasured possessions: the Encyclopedia Britannica, leather-bound, in its fine oak cabinet. His right hind leg was ominously raised, and, oh God, he was calmly peeing on that repository of human knowledge!

My shock and disbelief boiled up into rage. As I flew out of the chair, my intent had nothing to do with higher understanding or evolving consciousness. But, incredibly, the rage was snuffed out the very next instant by two things: the look on the dog's face—an expression of such unconcerned satisfaction, so inappropriate for the occasion; and a rush of ideas about the possible meaning of what I was witnessing.

I stood there, speechless. Slowly I turned my head and looked at my diagrams and words on the notepad, then back to the dripping leather covers. There were vague thoughts about cleaning up, but instead I plopped back into my chair and mumbled something. Odin was back in the kitchen, doing his circling ritual to find the perfect orientation for lying down. All was again quiet and peaceful.

But not inside me.

I spent a lot of time in the days that followed thinking about Odin's 'lesson.' Of course, I did not suddenly stop intellectualizing about the secrets of the cosmos, no, that was too much fun, too dear to me. But taking my mental constructions seriously—no, that time was suddenly over. For how could I even begin to explain a reality wherein something grabs the brain of a dog and uses it to tell me that maybe my intellect was merely admiring itself while 'seeing' nothing?

Since then, the ideas and events this book presents have hammered, chiseled, melted and otherwise reshaped my beliefs so completely that I have trouble recalling what they once were.

Doing something different

When Mexican families celebrate a birthday, they hang a piñata from the ceiling, stuffed with toys and candies. The birthday kid is blindfolded, twirled around, and given a stick that's long enough to reach the piñata. The kid swings the stick wildly, hitting many objects to squeals of laughter, until he or she strikes a lucky blow and the piñata, made of paper, bursts open and the treasures spill out.

I think we're like those birthday kids as we move through our lives. We experience events but are only partially aware of their meaning. Deeper levels of meaning get collected and stored in some inner piñata, where they ripen in time into new understandings. Then, one day, some event, large or small, 'breaks the piñata' and we are showered with new insights and beliefs, ready to be tasted and played with—but yet already strangely familiar.

At the time this all started, I was a designer and developer in systems programming at IBM. I liked the work. I love logic. My degree is in math, with additional courses in electrical engineering and computer science. I still have my slide rule, leather sheath and all. I used to wear it proudly on my belt to show those fuzzy-brained, liberal-arts types at CCNY which of us had the functioning gray matter.

I was submerged in the design and development of IBM's large operating system. My brain feasted on the flow charts covering my office walls. Fueled by a dozen cups of coffee and two packs of Camel Filters, I worked ten to twelve hours a day, and I was not alone: hundreds were immersed in this technical subculture. After a couple of years of this, the shrinks in the area were overworked, families suffered, the operating system was hugely successful, and we programmers were happy.

I liked my life. I was married with two sons, Michael and John, a house in the country with pool and apple trees, two cars, two dogs, and that terrific job. I coached Little League and youth soccer, planted a hundred trees and bushes on our land, and was satisfied—except for an occasional uneasy feeling that I had no idea what was going on, that there must be a reason why things are the way they are, that 'luck' is not an explanation for anything, that the events of our lives may not be mere coincidences, etc.

And then my body rebelled. My diabetes was out of control. I was thin and weak, and when I finally dragged myself to a doctor, she told me that if I wanted to see my sons grow another year older, I had better change my ways immediately, and drastically. That is, I had to stop abusing my physical systems and start taking much better care of them. Then she sent me to get a psychological profile done (oh shame). The analyst concluded that I didn't need his services, but if I didn't broaden my interests and get more involved with something outside my job, I would soon find myself on his couch.

I was humiliated and upset. And scared silly.

Well, I already knew of something I was interested in, and so did my wife. A few days after relating all this to her, she enrolled me in a course at the local community college that offered a grab bag of topics truly different from programming: ESP, reincarnation, UFOs, angels, shamanism, etc. Oh boy! This was not the same as playing philosophical games about the meaning of life with old friends in my safe office. I felt so self-conscious and uneasy about sitting there among 'those people' that I coerced one of my colleagues-in-logic to sit there with me!

I happily confess that I soon found myself enjoying the course. I read the recommended books, and scores more. I couldn't get enough, and when someone suggested we continue meeting after completion of the course, I signed up. Every Monday night we got together and talked and talked and talked.

Preparation

One Friday afternoon on the way home from work I stopped at my favorite bookstore to look for an Eileen Garrett book somebody had suggested. I couldn't find it, but with a cigarette dangling from my lips and my eyes burning and watering, I enjoyed my leisurely search.

I settled on a book for weekend reading and started toward the cash register when I remembered an ashtray I had seen sitting on a low divider wall in the back. I went to put out my butt and there, next to the ashtray, I saw a book entitled *The Seth Material* by Jane Roberts. I read the front cover, then the back, then the table of contents, feeling a strange excitement building in my belly. I put back the other book (I'm wonderfully housebroken, not like the slob who left Seth by the ashtray), paid for Seth, and rushed home hoping to find some time for reading. The weather god made it pour on Sunday so that my soccer team's game was canceled, my wife took the boys to a birthday party, and everything was perfect.

By the time I got to the Monday night meeting, my brain was swimming in Seth's ideas. I paid little attention to the voices droning on around me. It was hot and I was tired and all I wanted to do was feast on the incredible ideas about our reality presented by the nonphysical entity called Seth. Yes, nonphysical, invisible! An outrageous concept, but to me inexplicably acceptable, even natural.

I was glad when the meeting ended. Should have stayed home and continued my reading, I was thinking. I mumbled good nights all around, got into my car, and was about to drive off when a woman from the group came to my window and stood there in such obvious distress that I asked her what was wrong. Did she want to talk?

Hello

She had been reading *Crack in The Cosmic Egg* by Joseph C. Pearce until about 4 a.m. one night when she fell asleep with her hand and pen lying on her open notebook. When she woke up, she found the notebook covered with words and symbols, and when she exclaimed, "What the hell?" her hand moved the pen and wrote out an answer.

She was convinced she had cracked, so to speak. She ran to a shrink, took pills, cried in fear and frustration—but the writing continued. Finally, since no harm was evident, healthy curiosity won out, she relaxed, and was soon engaged in lively conversations, much like Jane Roberts was channeling Seth! In secret, of course. She wasn't about to tell somebody and get ridiculed—until she got this message one night: "Go share this with Schwab, he'll understand." No way, she protested. She hardly knew me. But the need to tell *somebody* became too powerful, and so there we were.

If I hadn't just read the Seth book, I would have found a way to cut short the conversation and hurry away. Especially when my name was mentioned. Instead, I assured her that she wasn't a bit crazy, gave her the book and told her that this weirdness was entirely normal and, in fact, immensely exciting and potentially much more informative than all these books etc.—was that me saying those things? How smart and wise I had become in just one weekend!

She invited me to meet this 'contact.' I agreed immediately, and enthusiastically. Thoughts of special knowledge, of being chosen, of secrets revealed—all kinds of notions danced in my head. There were some qualms, too. Something about 'this is nuts,' but that faint thought had no chance.

We arranged to meet at a diner. I brought a pen and a thick notebook, and a belly full of anticipation and butterflies.

What would you do if you had an invitation from such a source to ask about any subject your excited mind could think of? Wouldn't you go a little berserk for a while? I did. I came to that diner armed with a long list of questions. Never mind that there were doubts about who or what 'he' might be, whether he was some mysterious 'other' at all or a voice from normally hidden regions of the psyche (which would be just as amazing, anyway)—answers were forthcoming, and that's what mattered. The following is just a sample of my onslaught of questions:

Who are you?
Why are you doing this?
Who killed JFK?
Is there life after death?
How long will I live?
Are UFOs real?
Who am I?
Will there be a cure for diabetes?
Who will win the Super Bowl?
Who built the Giza pyramids?

Most of these he readily answered, as you will see.

I asked for a name. Here's how that went.

"Listen, I would very much like to use a name when I address you. I don't know why exactly, but it would make me more comfortable with the idea of communicating with you. Do you have a name? Please."

"No, not in your sense. But for you, here is one I will be happy to answer to: Or-if-I."

"Or-if-I?? Or if you what? Never mind. I'll leave out the dashes, and so Orifi it is."

O

2 Getting Acquainted

And so it went for many months. We became a fixture at the diner. I wrote questions and Orifi patiently indulged me.

"When my scribe reads the words of my written questions to you, what do you actually get? My words or her mental translation?"

"Neither. I actually get your thoughts before they are words, before she sees or hears them."

"You get my thoughts directly? Before they become words?"

"Of course."

This little piece of news, after many safe, third-party conversations, rattled me, and I hesitated to test it. But, of course, I had to. I wrote a list of explicit questions of the type that do not call for lengthy discussion (for example, where was Atlantis?), then flipped to the next page in the notebook and asked my scribe to get me answers—without first reading the questions.

The answers flowed out of her pen without hesitation, concise and to the point.

I sat up straight and stared at the air around me, wide-eyed and unfocused, shivering a little somewhere inside. Is every thought we have, I wondered in alarm, known to a whole cheering section of consciousnesses? I was not comfortable with this idea.

No, this isn't all there is

"Relax, Schwab. Yes, people have difficulty relating to other, less sensory (that is, of the physical senses) areas of being. Yet, know that when you look at ordinary life and shout, 'This can't be all there is!'—you're right: what you are seeing is not all there is. When you limit yourself to what is seen, you limit the depth and scope of your experience. But relax and you will see the true reality. Everyone will, eventually. It's not something you must push for or make happen. It simply is, and your life will show you that it is.

"How will it do that? Will I need some drastic lessons??"

"When your focus shifts, as everyone's will, this 'other' reality will be in the foreground of your awareness. Just relax and don't look for something different, hoping it will be 'better.' Look to what you have in this physical place as a vehicle for guiding your focus to that other reality."

"I like that. These are good words to say to me. I like my physical 'place,' even if my curiosity about this other reality is huge and I love talking about it endlessly. That's the extent of my involvement with it, you know—talking, speculating, and, yes, daydreaming a little. There is nothing concrete. You know the saying, 'If I can't hit it with a hammer, it ain't real?' That's how my mind works. I think this may be a problem."

"It is no more than a reflection of your present need to see physical proof and repeated verification. It is good that you want physical proof. It is good that your desire for such proof is so relentless. If you didn't have this desire, you wouldn't be human. If you didn't admit to it, you'd be dishonest. And if you didn't resent this need of yours, you wouldn't be pressing to balance yourself by fulfilling it. Please relax."

"Yes, you're right, I wish I didn't need it so much.

That reminds me: I've been coming across sentences in the books I'm reading that are almost identical to things you said to me a few days before. That always startles me so. Are you feeding me verification pills? How do you do that? Do you know in advance what I will read? Seems such a little thing to be paying attention to."

"It's just that I see it as you will. 'Will,' however, applies only to your time-determined system of reality. I simply see it, not before or after anything. It just is!"

"What? Not before or after anything? Orifi—there's so much I don't know. Is your reality like that? Is there ignorance where you are?"

"Of course! Universal is universal. How else could we meet like this? I must grow to live, as you must. And what do I know of your physical sensations? I have never taken physical form. If I see your reality more clearly than you do, it is only because I am outside the system myself."

> *I must grow to live, as you must.*

"I don't understand that.

You have never taken physical form? One 'takes' physical form? You mean it's a choice?

So fascinating. And so exciting, because I see the possibility that you will teach me some breathtaking things that I can then pass on to others. I confess that I have always had this dream, this desire hidden in some unlit corner of my psyche, to be able to teach some uplifting truths or something. No use trying to hide this secret, since you prowl my mind anyway. I am now convinced of this, although not yet reconciled to it. Anyway, what do you say to this?"

"How can you presume to teach what you yourself have not done? How can you dream of showing others a reality you do

not know yourself? If, in fact, you did know it, you would have no desire to teach. You would know and understand that it is within each person that real learning happens. Yours is not a mission to teach but to learn, to consciously participate in your own glorious rebirth. Science may well be the best tool available to you to reach that goal."

"Rebirth? Science? Now there are two fellows that usually don't live in the same neighborhood! You will explain rebirth to me one day? You must know that some of the humans who incessantly use that word make my skin crawl. And maybe you can try to avoid adjectives like 'glorious'?"

"Relax. There is a time to gather, and you are gathering. Aside from information, you gather strength. Who knows, maybe some day you might write a book about our conversations . . ."

"I love your words. Even when you contradict yourself. You just said that I'm not here to teach but to learn. Let somebody else write books."

You don't own ideas

"Sharing is not the same as teaching.
Remember, never disturb yourself by trying to follow my 'train of thought.' Very often I don't have one! It is only human contention that I must. It will suffice that you simply content yourself with grasping my fleeting ideas as they flash across the mirror of your mind. Don't even try to capture them, or hold them, or examine them. Just let them fly through your mind as they will."

"And how do I do that? How do I grasp an idea unless I hold it for awhile and chew on it and examine it?"

"No, Schwab, you needn't hold a thought or an image, or try to make it your own, in order for it to work its power for you or

through you. You be the wire, my ideas the electrons running through it.

Again, these ideas I present are, very much like love, only meant to pass through you, not to be owned or saved or used or hoarded by you. They need always to be in motion to be real. Any idea (or love) that isn't, is a stagnant unreality."

"Makes no sense to me. I really love some ideas, and I'm happy that I have them in my mind. They are my companions."

"Yes, and you collect them like trophies. The good ones you try to claim as your own. Not until you realize, or admit, that these come only through you, will you understand inspiration. Without a steady flow of inspiration out of the 'great beyond' and into the minds of men, the silence of the empty page would be deafening. The novelist, the doctor, the teacher, the poet, and yes, the scientist, all find themselves flooded with ideas—and even if these are not new, they are at least seen in a new fashion.

Truly there is nothing new, but there are infinite new ways of viewing what is old. You need to ponder this."

"There is nothing new? What does that mean? Every day is new, every moment is new. What do you mean?"

"Unique, but not new.

This very moment, this one right now, is eternity. Explore each instant in time with serious patience and lighthearted love. Therein, eternity will show its face to you, for it is contained in every breath you take, in every smile that escapes you, in every tear that trickles down your cheek. The beautiful, unique combinations of factors that join forces in each second, or any part thereof, are not repeated in the same context, ever."

"Beautiful words, O. Each moment is eternity? Wow. So what moves through time? My perception? Something moves. I get older. I am confused. You are tying my thoughts into knots. Where is the moment when I will understand all this?"

"There is, of course, no one moment of truth; each and every moment has the potential of revealing its own truth to you.

Truth does not necessarily hit you between the eyes. Sometimes it is what you humans think of as very slow in coming. Ideas are more likely to seem like the proverbial light bulb turning on inside your mind, while truths are more likely to osmose themselves into your total being, your real existence, slowly (in your terms), often over many Earth years. This often makes you very impatient, which is one of the most serious detriments to human learning."

"Ah yes, impatience. And now that I have you available, it grows daily. Is there a cure?"

Be total
"You need now to take time for total aloneness whenever you can. It is essential for replenishment. Don't withdraw into a shell, just be total."

"Be total?"

"When you are with someone, be there, and when you are alone, be alone.

To be means to focus, and to focus simply means to do one thing at a time, and while you do that, do only that if you wish to do that fully.

Be laughing when you laugh,
Be thinking when you think,
Be working when you work,
Be playing when you play,
Be loving when you love, and, of course, to promote love, the natural place to begin is by loving your Self—not your ego or your id, not your body or your mind, not the reality of your dreams, but the spirit of life that lives in the center of your Self.

Be with your Self and you are with that spirit. Just be to be. If this sounds cryptic, it will not once you have had the option to move that mountain and

> *Seek a conscious and constant companionship with your personal god.*

experienced the lack of separation between that and this, here and there, you and me, God and all."

"This is all too much for me to absorb. These words move something in me, but I wish I knew what to do with them.

And what is this God business? I'm sure I don't know what you mean by that."

"It is a word of your language, not mine. I can only use the words you make available to me.

Schwab, let's forget semantics. I say again: trust your own inner wisdom and you are in fact putting your trust in God, or your life's spirit, if you prefer. It is within you that it functions, and you needn't die to live with it."

"Fine. But please remember that words like God make me uneasy, and it will take me time to get over this.

Go beyond time

And why, by the way, do such mental changes take time? I want to change on the spot, when I decide to change, not Earth years from now. Yes, I do get impatient with this process. Doesn't everybody? Do you think it might be fruitful to explain to me why it takes time to adjust my brain, my beliefs, my fears, or whatever is involved?"

"Time is irrelevant in the process. Your thoughts are the deciding factor, that is, whether they are spirit-directed or material-directed. You will learn eventually that there is no impatience outside of time, and when you learn to go beyond time at will, you will not even recall what impatience feels like."

"Go beyond time!? You drive me crazy. And I can't imagine *ever* forgetting what impatience feels like."

"Be patient."

Be still

"To seek silence in the midst of noise should be your immediate goal. Great things take form in silence. Listen to your own inner need for silence and the productivity of quiet. There is truly something breathtaking to be discovered within you, but it can only be revealed to a still mind. Even when you can't retire from your noisy, hyperactive world, you can learn to separate from it and retreat inward to a place of calm and stillness. You don't have to create this place, it is always there. You simply need to learn how to get there.

You'll be shocked at your own physical and mental endurance once you have learned to take mini-vacations of a minute or less as often as you feel a need for them. Don't be trapped by outer noise and confusion. The place of stillness always waits. Go to it. Just stop and go within. Use it."

"Just like that? Just go to it and use it? Orifi, this sounds like a wonderful thing to do, but I have no idea how I might go to this place, nor 'where' inside me it might be. And you know that I don't, so why tell me?"

"You will learn about accepting things on faith, about believing. It is essential."

Of belief and faith

"Believing centers in the heart and functions out of the intuitive aspect of the right lobe of the brain. Knowing is simply a computed by-product of learning in the rational function, or through the left brain lobe."

"I have no control over the intuitive aspect. It is a mystery to me. I know it's there, but I am trained to live in that other lobe. So if developing faith is something that the rational mind is not involved with, then how do I develop it?"

"You don't. It is a natural product of the growth process and happens of its own.

Also, you must achieve a place in your beliefs where you find a balance between the flexibility that allows you to learn, and enough solidity so that your beliefs are growing from within and need no exterior verification from anyone."

"That, believe it or not, makes sense to me. Even though 'growing from within' is one of those statements that sounds so good but, in truth, is merely a bunch of words to me. I just hope it's happening."

"You know that it is. Why do you pretend that you don't know? Trust your own feelings, Schwab.

Here is a simple truth about beliefs in your reality: If it happens, then you believe; or, if you believe, then it happens. Both statement and converse are true."

"If I believe, then it happens? Maybe where you are. I have to think about this. But can't I work on this 'balance,' for instance, with my rational mind at all?"

"No. Prayer is a better method. It can take you where mere words never could. You can make the happening occur by prayer if it comes from the heart and not from the head."

"By prayer? Fine. I've read that in a hundred places. But, for whatever reason, prayer has not been part of my repertoire for a long time, probably since I was a good little altar boy eons ago, happily singing those Latin words in my sweet little voice. Do you know about that? Yes, of course you do, you simply see what is! I can't get used to that idea. So you were there? Did you by any chance implant something in my receptive little head then that has made me wonder about the moon and the stars to this day?!

Don't bother trying to understand

Seriously, O, there are times when I would much rather just stop all this craving for information, this desire for learning. It seems like a disease in my head sometimes. I'm always trying to understand this world I live in. And not getting very far."

"Please stop trying to understand. You will go very far under your own new systems before you understand how they work. Understanding is no more than a by-product of fully sensing reality. You can gain a lot of experience within your reality without ever understanding any of it.

Those advertisers of yours would be in the poorhouse if only the people who understand how TV works were allowed to view it."

"Funny. And a good point. But I will never stop trying to understand. Never. Never ever. It's in my DNA."

"Of course, but sometimes you need to give it a rest. Now is such a time. Keep yourself busy with tasks that are physical enough to tire your body to release tension, which might otherwise chain your spirit to your body at night when it needs to soar as a counterbalance to the heaviness of your awake hours."

"Wow. A mouthful. I mean, I have no experience, no framework, to help me understand this."

Stop judging yourself

"Yes, I know. If you could understand my point of view better, you would see many things more clearly. I cannot give you my point of view, however. I can only show you, and I can't do that unless you come willingly."

"Consciously I am more than willing, as you well know, but deep inside somewhere I must not be. I suspect that I don't know what it means to be willing, and, further, that my conscious willingness is nothing more than my ego lusting for some grand experience. What do you say to that?"

"I say just because your ego is in the way sometimes is no reason to believe that it is the only thing in you. You are most definitely beyond egocentric, but occasional regressions are natural in outgrowing any imbalance.

Seeing beyond ego, beyond gender, beyond even capabilities, changes the world you see, and most especially the way you see the people in it."

"I don't know, Orifi. Sometimes all my actions seem connected with my ego's search for food. It's discouraging. Whenever I look at why I do what I do, it always seems to involve my ego."

"Self-judgment blocks the relief of tension that is necessary for movement in a positive direction. In short, don't waste energy on self-recrimination when you have so few of the essential facts available to you.

Unfortunately for you at the moment, you have not accepted that you must construct your own reality. It is beginning to dawn on you, though. Don't worry too much about judgment for the time being, as your life is running on automatic for now. Relax."

"Running on automatic? What does that mean?"

"It means you're on the road now, Schwab. No turning back. And if there is a time when you don't want to continue, you will still be on the road. Enjoy."

"What road? There is a road? I like that, for some reason.

But I wonder what I'm going to run into on that road. I've been reading some books lately that have to do with 'paths' of all kinds, and some of these I think I would rather not travel."

"Do you savor caution over curiosity? Safety over adventure? Remember, the entire gamut of human experience is yours for the taking."

"The entire gamut? Fine, that means that I can choose the gentler parts of the gamut, right? That's what I will do."

"When the forces deep within the earth gather and shift and need a form of release, a volcano somewhere erupts to ease the pressure. As the hot, molten masses move, they have no way of escape save the move upward, bursting forth from the crust of

> The fruit is ripening on the vine.

the earth. Likewise, forces of life that move within every living soul have no place to move save upward, as such is the law of life. As the volcano has no need of knowing that it is the vehicle through which energy at a given moment finds balance, so it is not necessary that an individual consciously pursue this upsurgence. He/she needs only to offer an avenue through which balance might be restored."

"This has something to do with my road? Doesn't sound gentle. Powerful symbology. Can you be more specific? What are you talking about?"

Change is in the air

"The time is nearing for a major change in the human drama. Each psyche is being prepared, in a way that it can comprehend, for great changes that are in the process of becoming. Since not every psyche, of course, can accept these things on a conscious level, a futuristic projection of the new reality is being sent to each individual on whatever level he/she is most capable of understanding it.

Yes, the fruit is ripening on the vine. Change in physical reality is at hand, as you know. In fact, your mind has been extremely busy lately managing far more than your earthly plans. You must remember that your mind cannot function in all its aspects through the physical brain, and emphasize them all. Confusion would follow."

"As I know?! I don't know anything of the sort. Who is sending projections? And who is in charge of the part of my mind that is too big for my brain to handle? You are overloading me, but I love it. More. After all, so much stuff has already spilled over the rim of my filled brain, more will not be noticeable."

The reason for your journey

"Your human minds can handle much more than you can even imagine. Relax.
When your conscious equals your subconscious, you will have reached your real selfhood—and that is, of course, the reason for your journey.
Believe me when I say that it is not essential that you understand what is happening or why, only that you should have awareness that the process is happening."

"If you say so. So this road you say I'm on, it leads to my 'real self?' I've been reading about this concept and have often used the term in conversation, but you know that I have no idea what it means. And yet there's a longing in me when I think of some 'bigger' and more 'real' me. How I hope that I will meet it some day and see what 'I' really am. Isn't that odd?"

"Wishful thinking has probably had more profound results in your world than you could ever imagine.
No one comes from elsewhere, no one is going anywhere. The key is in the here. To really be there, you have to have really arrived here. Sink your roots deeply where you are."

"Again I don't know what you mean. Something inside me responds to these words, accepts them, is warmed and thrilled by them—but I don't know what they mean."

"You will. Remember, it has all been said before and will be said again eternally. I am not the first who has said these words and I will not be the last."

"Fine. And can I tell you something? It comforts me that you don't claim to be some unique oracle."

"It is such healthy, fertile, happy soil you have provided for our seeds."

"What?!?"

Remember, you are eternal.
You are not your body,
you are not your mind,
you are not your opinion of yourself,
you are not the opinions others hold of you,
you are not your Id,
you are not your ego . . .

O

3 Dreams Return

I hadn't remembered dreams for years. Maybe I didn't believe they were worth remembering. Too confusing, too flaky. But now, seeing that the invisible was not dead but alive with intelligence, I longed for my own inner voices, and dreams were the only inner voice I had ever personally experienced. I wanted them back.

So I put a notebook and pen on my night table and waited. Weeks passed, but there was nothing. I gave up, then tried again for months, then gave up again. And then, maybe a year after meeting Big O, conscious memory of dreams returned.

What an experience a dream can be—so rich, so surprising, so totally unpredictable, sometimes with an obvious message, often incomprehensible.

Dreams proceeded to play a vital role on my journey. They filled me with happy wonder at the ingenuity and wisdom of the designer. They kicked me in the butt whenever I allowed myself to believe that I was eternally stuck in concrete. They persisted in reminding me that no matter how uninspired and bored I may feel, there are mysterious things going on inside. Not on Arcturus or in some holy man, in *me*!

Of course, there were things to complain about. Why all this elaborate symbology? Why not words? I know, words are unnecessary in the realm of thought, but couldn't an exception be made just for me, to help me understand better? Are you listening, dream maker? No, I don't mean that you should replace your magnificent symbology with words, no, I love your stuff. What I'm suggesting is to add a running commentary, maybe.

Dream: The owner

I was walking with some friends on the apple orchard road near our house. It was dusk. Suddenly somebody yelled something and pointed to the sky and there, no more than a hundred feet up maybe, was some kind of flying object. It was slowly descending as we stood in amazement and mounting unease. I couldn't believe it was landing, but it was. Three struts came out of its bottom as it set down only fifty feet or so in front of us right in the middle of the road. My fear changed to excitement and curiosity and without a word I walked towards it. My friends shouted at me to stop, but I yelled back 'no way' and walked right under its belly. It seemed to be no more than twelve feet in diameter. Not a huge craft.

I was standing under it, wondering what to do next, when I noticed a hole in the underbelly, about the width of my hips. The next thing I knew I was inside a tube, wriggling and struggling to get up into the interior. Suddenly my head popped out into a large round room, and I stared in disbelief: There were normal-looking humans sitting on normal-looking console chairs facing instruments and displays all around the room. They were busy and ignored me. Then some guy looked my way, gave me a friendly smile and said, loudly, 'Good to see you, Schwab.' Others looked over and said something in greeting and then continued with their tasks.

I was shocked and speechless. They knew my name. And why were they human? My mind was racing, trying to take it all in, trying to draw conclusions. It was working like it normally does, when I'm awake.

Then a tall guy with lots of curly red hair got up and came over to where I was still sticking out of the floor from my shoulders up. He invited me, laughing, to come on in, and then wanted to know if I was interested in a tour. Was I ever. So he showed me around and talked about various gadgets and then led me to another room (I swear the thing seemed bigger on the inside than on the outside) where the propulsion unit was. I was fascinated and fully aware that if I could remember what I was seeing, it might be of tremendous value to all of us later. Not to mention what it would do for my bank account. That's what I was thinking as he talked about the row of five or six huge crystals that were glowing brightly under what looked like a plexiglass dome. Then he asked me with a sort of good-natured grin, 'Would you like to meet the owner?'

My stomach knotted up and my heart jumped into my throat, but I nodded and said, 'Yes, I would.'

He seemed pleased. He turned to the wall behind him and picked up a small figure that was lying there on what looked like a bookshelf, then turned around again and held it out to me. I stared at what appeared to be a doll made of some clay-like material, seemingly lifeless. It had a normal body, maybe a foot and a half long, with arms and legs where they should be, but there were no facial features, only geometric shapes, mostly boxes, formed by slight ridges in the material.

I looked up at my friendly guide with doubt and confusion, asking the silent question, 'This is the builder of this craft?'

He nodded and said, 'Here, you hold him.'

Before I could agree, he unceremoniously shoved the form into my arms, turned around, and walked away.

What happened next is hard to put into words, partly because it was so strange and also because it all happened at once, not sequentially. It's frustrating to tell it one word at a time. I have the urge to pile all the letters of the description onto one spot on the paper.

As I stood there awkwardly holding the thing, looking at the face, the ridges began to move. I felt movement in the arms and legs. My mind was flooded with a sensing, a knowing, an awareness of the presence of such enormous intelligence and understanding, something so far advanced in science, in everything—and filling me with a surge of such immense love that my entire system was overwhelmed. I was close to tears as warm molasses flowed through my belly, where it is remembered to this day.

Then I awoke. Jerking up into a sitting position and staring at my arms, I expected to find 'it' there, and was deeply disappointed to see them empty.

Whatever you need ...

"Orifi, speak to me! Was that a dream? Felt so incredibly real."

"How many times did you wake up to move away from it? This holds for you the answer."

"What? I don't know. I do remember stages, or phases, of awareness or something, if that's what you mean."

"Yes, dreams that sort and categorize wake you up only once, but deeper dreams force you to wake up as many times as you are levels removed."

> *Whatever you need to come home will be there as you need it.*

"Whatever that means. And why am I remembering now?"

"You have always dreamt and traveled as everyone does to some degree, but you now need to know where you go, so you learn to remember. What you need, whatever you need, to come home, will be there as you need it."

This statement has been a companion ever since. Sometimes, when I rage against unpleasant circumstances, whether personal or general, I drag it into my mind and then look at those circumstances again. Although this can cause consternation (as in: what? I need this?), it is always sobering. Sometimes, when very fine things are going on, the statement walks into my mind of its own and reminds me of its message. I don't know whether anything has changed my thought processes more than this little statement has—'whatever you need will be there as you need it.'

"And who or what provides me with what I need?"

> *Don't look for life after death, look for life before death.*

"*Life exists on many levels. You are not alone. I know it is still difficult for you to conceive of this.*"

"Yes, it is. Although, since I have always professed to believe in 'life after death,' as they say, I must have believed in some kind of invisible world of consciousness all along."

"*Don't look for life after death, look for life before death. Look right now.*"

O

4 Colleagues

"Help me find it, OK?

I can't seem to get enough of you, Orifi. I love these conversations. But I can't help wondering why you are doing this. Why are you available? Don't you have anything better to do? I'm serious."

"The work that must be done is not by you alone. I work here."

"*Must* be done? What do you mean? And where is here? Ah yes, that's something I wonder about, too. I know you're not in a physical place, so your answer probably won't mean much, but indulge me—where are you?"

"I live near blue."

"You live near blue? What, or where, is that? I don't know why, but for some stupid reason I like that answer. Never mind. Please continue."

"I have, you could say, sensed my mission and am anxious to begin. In the future—'the whole of this,' as I prefer to put it—there will be times when you will feel as if you are waiting for me. I know you picture me somewhere in space waiting for you to organize and begin to work effectively, but I am in fact studying your thoughts and actions of late with great enthusiasm—as well as

your reactions to me and to what I relate to you. Relax. Let's spend time unraveling some inappropriate senseless sensing now."

"Senseless sensing? If you mean confusion, then by all means, let's unravel, full time. But first, I'd like to ask again: how exactly do you know about me, about the people I know, about the thoughts I think and the dreams I dream?"

"I add what basic knowledge I have gained to the information I gather from your mind and come up with a judgment."

"That doesn't help a whole lot. Except that it implies that this mind of ours must be some piece of work, largely unknown to our conscious selves."

"Indeed. Specifics, specifics now, please, or give me the floor."

"Gladly."

"Keep going until your seeds germinate, please."

"What?"

"Work out the ideas that are beginning to crystallize in your mind until they do just that and you can look at them."

"What ideas do you see in my mind that are crystallizing? I wonder now whether there are any ideas in this mind that should be crystallized. That's what you have done to me.
And suppose I do want to 'work out' the notions that are floating around in there, how do I proceed? Where do I begin?"

"I think you can be more specific, and therefore far more helpful to your own process, once you have some background. Any information I could offer you now, when you are in a sense like an empty slate, would mean less than what you may arrive at, whether right or wrong, towards an eventual understanding of the multifold relationships involved here. It is not something

easily translatable to your realm or it wouldn't be sent as a life's work for you to elaborate upon. It is your job to reach conclusions here."

"Life's work?? I don't know if I like that term. Has a religious flavor. Makes me uneasy."

"Yes, I know. Forget it for now."

I am not the final word

"I am not, as I stated, in any sense the final word, but only another point of view to add to your own so you can make your decision to act or not to act a more appropriate one. I do not decree your fate. I only report what I perceive, which in my realm is more appropriately considered just plain thought. In short, I can tell you what I think based on the information I have available to me. As you function still within time, my information seems prophetic to you."

"Yes it does."

"Likewise, however, answers I have already received from you, few as they are, make you almost seem that way to me because they explain the tangible, physical aspect of universal reality, of which I know nothing.

I do not liken you to a prophet perhaps only because you approached me first."

"That's totally unfathomable. Explain."

"Our thoughts landed on the same topic, at the same time, on numerous occasions. But then, just that once, your imagination accounted for the possibility of me—and we met."

"Have mercy. Go on."

"*Not by my answers, but by your processes, I am learning, too.*"

"That's so hard to accept. You seem to know everything. The idea that you're learning from us . . .

Anyway, explain to me what you know about this multilevel mind we apparently have. It seems to contain an awful lot more than we are aware of on a conscious level. I wonder whether you can see this difference between what we have access to and what is apparently there. Can you? It is important, because I may not be aware of what you think I am aware of."

"*Very well taken, since this is the crux of the very real problem I face in communicating with you. I see the mind as the totality of itself and no, I cannot perceive the separation, although it quite apparently exists, since what I know you know you may not have usable knowledge of. This can make things extremely difficult sometimes, since it takes us on side trips of sorts where I must reprove that I am not playing games, as you call it.*"

"Well put."

"*It is time. We are all overdue for some horse-sense explanations with and to and for one another. Anyone functions better when no energy is spent in useless defense, or in wonder of wondering. Yes, it is equally important to me that we face and overtake these small hurdles so we will have a bondtype strength between us when the bigger ones present themselves—and these are ahead of us.*"

"How reassuring. What big hurdles!? I know you're not going to tell me, and I'm not sure how that would work, anyway. I've been thinking about that. If one knew what hurdles lie ahead, then wouldn't one do everything possible to avoid them? But then the pre-knowing would have been false . . . You need to explain this to me one day. So confusing.

Just don't forget the point about you seeing the totality and me seeing only a teeny part. And is that why you start so many remarks with 'Remember . . . '? Very annoying, sometimes."

"*Remember, Freddie, forgetting is not part of my reality. I simply see what is.*"

"I'll try to remember that."

The physical is your arena, not mine

"*And remember, it is not because of my arrival into your life that you will pursue this work, but actually in spite of that arrival. While I will function as a colleague, I cannot offer you pat answers to problems that involve a relationship that transcends or overlaps out of the pure thought realm. In short, you must grapple with aspects that overlap into your physical reality, because I cannot. Here you will steer the ship and I will be, in a sense, a passenger.*"

"Pursue what work? You are getting me all worked up, full of anticipation and restlessness. How I would love to work with you on some tangible project. The idea drives me crazy. But I think maybe you should steer that ship."

"*You are not obligated to give socalled correct or true guesses, any more than I can be. You can, however, reason and respond with the information you have available to you, much as I can. You don't have to continue down any path that is bringing you to a blank state or an immovable mental block, but do at least attempt to continue in a forward direction.*
Don't worry about the exact meaning of my words or instructions, as there is in fact no literal translation. Just work. Take it for what it means to you and work with it. Work, work—work is fun."

"Yes, work is fun. But what work are you talking about? Are you waiting for me to guess? Everything I know seems guesswork based on the guesswork of others."

"*A hypothesis is an educated guess. A law is a hypothesis that has been made to work. This law is then elevated to the status*" of universal simply because it works, even though it only works because it was made to work to prove the hypothesis that was constructed to prove the guess."

An infinite number of realities

"I like that. Sounds true.

But if that is so, then there must be an infinite number of possibilities of anything. Each guesshypothesislaw group is one possibility out of an infinite number? And a collection of these makes up our physical reality?"

> *You are the architect of your reality.*

"*Yes indeed! And you are the architect of your reality, and can share that reality when you can show others. Infinite possibilities exist. Let5 your natural inclination help you pinpoint one method over another. This is important, since a focused interest will take you more efficiently to the realization of your goal.*"

"OK. I see that you are going to keep reminding me that you know something about some 'goal' that I have. In my conscious mind I am not aware of any 'life's work' kind of goal. I have my share of both lofty and kooky daydreams, for sure. Doesn't everybody? So let's put that subject aside. It makes me uncomfortable."

Dream: Going to school

I found myself urgently trying to get to some class in a big city. I was late, and nothing was going right. I waited impatiently for a bus, then raced through a crowded subway station to get to my train, which was late, then slow. I became more and more frantic. My progress was like molasses, and there was so little time. When I got off the subway, I found that I had to walk a couple of very long blocks. When I finally reached the big, very old-looking stone building, I felt great relief—until I realized that I didn't know the room number! I ran down long hallways, retraced my steps, tried other directions, nothing. Panic was just starting to grab me when I suddenly knew that I was standing in front of the right door. I took a deep breath and gratefully leaned my head against the door for a little rest. But then I realized how late I was, and new reasons for panic filled my head: What did I miss? Will I be able to make it up? Will they let me in at all?

I knew that I had to get into that class, though, fears or no fears, and so I gathered some courage and opened the door as quietly as I could. There was a large room full of busy people, writing and reading and occasionally looking up to somebody in front who was lecturing. Nobody paid any attention to me! I had the impression that it was normal for people to come in at any time and get whatever they could out of the class. I tiptoed to an empty seat nearby, put some papers in front of me, and happily began listening.

After I woke up I had no memory of the teacher or any hint as to the subject matter. This was frustrating, but the idea that I was sitting in classrooms in my dreams was comforting. It occurred to me that the conscious state might not be the only one we learn in—and what a good thing that would be.

O

5 Exercises

"I will give you specifics now on some work you should begin. Exercises of this sort will ultimately enrich all of your thinking because they will convert easily to the solution of some very basic human problems. Our goal includes devising a science through which the condition of being human can be more adequately understood."

"That's our goal!? That's the 'work' you've been alluding to?"

"Yes, Schwab, part of it. And remember that these exercises are not 'busy work.' Knowing you, you will at times suspect that they are.

Ultimately, this work will provide you with both a trust in your own unconscious judgments and a consistent language with which to communicate with your own subconscious mind.

There is a method to my madness, so bear with me for a while. This is supposed to be fun, so keep it light and in the background."

"I'm chomping at the bit. Let's see the specifics."

Exercise: 500 white circles

"You need a sheet of black paper, a sheet of white paper, and a simple hole puncher. We will learn about the amazing capabilities

of your human brains and how easily they can be trained to translate unconscious information to you in a conscious form.

Punch out 500 white circles.
Drop random amounts against a background of black paper.
Glance at them and guess how many there are.
Make a quick judgment, not an analytical one.
Make ten tries per day for ten days.
Keep a record.
Place your guess in one column and the actual figure, after counting, in another.

When you have developed confidence with a small amount of circles, we will use a large amount.

Exercise: Dice

You need a pair of dice. We will explore probability and chance. Later, time will be more understandable to you.

Use the dice as you have used the dots. Just record at first. Record 8 sets of 800 rolls each, with no mental participation, no wishing.
Express a mental wish or preference for one number over all others. Again 8 sets of 800 rolls each. Then compare. Don't analyze.
Keep the dice on your person for one full week. Repeat #2. Compare differences, if any.

If you don't do octet samples each time, you simply will not have enough numbers to show any clear or repeated tendency or pattern. Probability does not support the use of this pattern, but in those cases you already know what will happen, you just want to see it.
Be sure to keep absolutely accurate records if you hope to see a pattern emerging. Try not to hope for a result in one direction or another, since you could adversely affect the results by so doing.

Remember that if you think you see a pattern emerging and secretly hope to help it along, you may possibly get information that is opposite from the intended.

Begin by simply guessing. Record exact results for a few weeks. Next begin to wish for one number and only one number. Record these results in a column next to the others for easy comparison. Do not proceed from this point until you have scored above chance by wishful thinking.

Now, forget your special number and wish for a different number with every roll. Record results. These must ultimately be analyzed or they will be useless, but we will save that for later. Also, you might play this game and the paper puncher game with your children and notice the difference between their results and yours.

Later, when we do far greater numbers and file the results for computer analysis, we will need this early background to understand our own tests.

Consider that we are doing a unit of work on improving our guessing skills by performing drills of sorts. Incorporate our study into your daily life. Whenever you can guess at something and get immediate feedback about accuracy, do it. Examples: how much gas your tank will take, how much you weigh, what your grocery bill will be, etc... You might keep a record of these random guesses also.

Try to see the process

It is important that you understand the words themselves, but try to see what I am attempting to show you. Look for the greater view, the process within the exercise. See the small sample we use, and also see the larger truth reflected therein.

This work is tedious, I know, and you may consider it overly simplistic, frivolous, corny, perhaps even obvious—but I simply cannot tell you, it is imperative that I show you. To tell would accomplish little."

I plunged into these exercises with enthusiasm. It was something concrete that I could do, something real and physical. And I found the stated goal so very appealing: to learn to communicate with my own subconscious, and to trust its messages.

But, you know, it isn't much fun, after all, to pick up 347 little paper circles again and again. Frustrations built up—not the least of which was the thought that there was a lot more going on in my subconscious than recording numbers and looking for patterns; my conscious self, the hard working circle counter, was unaware of these inner happenings, unaware of any 'language' being constructed, and stretched in vain to get messages from the subconscious. Over time, I wearied of the work.

O

6 Intermeshed Continuums

"Tell me more about my 'arena,' this physical reality, and its infinite possibilities. Infinite, of course, is true for all arenas, not just my beloved Earth. You know that this is one of my pet subjects, and that I'm dying to get some jewels of information about it from you. As far back as I can remember, the idea that this should be the only planet with life on it always seemed absurd to me. Infinite possibilities? Yes, that is more satisfying.

I suppose that's one of the reasons why I accept *you*, don't you agree? After all, you're just one of those infinite possibilities.

So indulge me, while I count little paper circles, and talk about those short gray guys. Let's start with this: I assume that different types have been here?"

"Yes indeed, there are many different types of 'visitors,' of infinite varieties, in both the physical and nonphysical sense, as you understand it. In the mind realm there are myriad levels of activity on earth, simultaneously present and interacting upon one another. Many of these minds are alien, and, of course, invisible to humans, and therefore often misread as anything but what they in fact are, that is, alien mind forces. What seems most difficult to the human mind is to conceive of, or picture, what cannot be seen.

Physically speaking, life expresses itself in an infinite array of sizes, shapes, forms, and designs. Beings at similar levels of activity, however, are not necessarily similar physically. So remember, a dragon fly could be an alien. Many things could be—how would you know?

You will never recognize alien life, even if you do encounter it, unless you are totally consciously aware of the variety of expressions that radiate from all things, carbon or otherwise, living or not.

Those parallel universes you sense are not so much parallel as intermeshed with one another, and they exist in infinite continuums on Earth as everywhere in the universes."

"Scotty, beam me up! Infinite continuums intermeshed. How I love it. You must tell me much more about this, you Invisible Beauty. Forget spiritual goals and all that. Tell me about intermeshed continuums for the rest of my days.

Now answer this biggie: Why do they come here? Why do they bother with us?"

"They would all like to aid your ancestors in checking your progress, but they send whoever is in the area, or, more likely, whoever is involved in studying your progress because of their own interest."

"Checking our progress? What's so interesting about our progress? What do you mean, our ancestors? Our ancestors are from elsewhere?"

About the root home of our psyche

"Yes. Earth life began spontaneously, but intelligent life was indeed planted. You have read the futuristic viewpoints of some who have speculated on this possibility and presented it to the general public. I, however, do not speculate. I simply state."

"How was intelligent life planted? Did some visitors interbreed with earth life? Why? Did the earth have some effect on them?"

"Yes, indeed. Your Earth has, to them, a very strong magnetic field. It caused the physiological, thus psychological, lowering

of the axis to the pelvic region (as with the other 'animals' of Earth), which in turn caused those most physiologically weak, or susceptible to the magnetic force, to interbreed with Earth animals. Eventually there was no true breed. But the only other choice for the aliens was death from energy imbalance caused by the strength of the magnetic force. Within a few generations, all chose life in this form over extinction."

"And eventually they completely forgot?"

"Yes, they lost their natural eye strength and lost all conscious memory of the higher physiological axis of power."

"Eye strength?"

"Energy of total mind, pulsating in waves outward. It's an integral part of all psi phenomena, and because of it, you will gain some essential physics background for materialization and dematerialization—or conversion, if that is simpler for your mind to handle. You will need to understand the mechanics involved."

"Orifi, my beloved guru, I know you say many things just to get certain emotional reactions from me, to get me to think and feel in new ways, or to annoy specific thought patterns in my head. You are a scoundrel, and I love you for it. What ego dreams are you scheming to dissolve now? Is this somehow connected with this goal business?"

"Yes, intimately connected, in that humanity needs to be reoriented toward the upper axis and all of the powers that lie therein. Mankind needs the spark that will eventually return it to the level where your alien relatives were on their first arrival on Earth. Then there will be little threat of interbreeding causing the same lowering."

"Great. Then they'll be able to do all the interbreeding they want, just for the fun of it? What do the females of their race look like?

Seriously, if these ancestors, these kinfolk, should ever return to Earth, wouldn't they seem like gods to us again? So wouldn't associating with us be sort of pointless for them? Even if we have evolved somewhat since they saw us last?"

"No, as they will, of course, understand the far-reaching implications of their mission."

"Mission? I thought they just check on our progress? Now they have a mission? And another thing: why didn't they just leave if Earth was such a danger to their survival?"

"They knew exactly why they were here, Freddie, as they know now why they are returning. Remember infinite continuums, and the difficulty of translating from the timeless to the time-locked—and that there is no coincidence."

"Yes, I remember. But I have to ask more time-locked questions. This topic is such a delight for me. I just don't care that I'm getting a warped picture.

So our 'home' is actually on some tiny pinpoint up there in the night sky? Wow. If they took us there now, would that place seem very alien to us, instead of like home? Just a sentimental thought."

"Yes and no. It would probably seem strongly familiar, much like the sensation of flight is so familiar to most of you."

"Are those who wonder about these things near remembering their lineage on a conscious level?"

"Sometimes, yes. Their unconscious drive to search is sometimes a homesickness of sorts for the root home of their psyche."

"Root home of their psyche? Love it.

But isn't our ancestors' reality very different from ours, Orifi? And if so, how do they find our reality in this brew of infinite realities?"

All minds speak the same language

"Mind functions above, although in some cases, such as yours, as a part of, physical reality. The communication you could and would experience is direct in the sense that it is mind to mind, "universal" in the universal sense of the word. Upon meeting, your minds are mutually capable of instant understanding of the basic reality of the other's mind. This is true in any instant where minds "meet" in a physical dimension such as yours."

"Mind to mind? So why do we have to meet physically before we can communicate in this way? And why, by the way, do they have to come here to check on our progress? Does mind, in their case, also 'function as a part of physical reality?'

And aren't you in touch with these guys? So you have been familiar with physical existence all along? Isn't our human reality just another type?"

"Yes, but I am newly introduced to this entire physical realm. I know their reality only since I became acquainted with your reality. But, again, this is extremely difficult for me to translate out of timelessness into the pastpresentfuture system that you still think within."

"Okay, fine. I will never understand timelessness.

A few curiosities

Let me stick to simpler aspects of this gorgeous topic. For instance, thinking about our origin and history, those stories about Atlantis and Mu come to mind. Did they really exist?"

> *You need the clearest sight to see what is right before your eyes.*

"Indeed, both existed. Reruns from both still live. Those with close to conscious realization remember in a sense and believe, others do not."

"Reruns? That's funny. Where were they?"

"Mu, southern Pacific. Atlantis, mid-Atlantic."

"Yes, that's what some books claim. But why are there no physical traces?"

"Traces are in much of what you call your technology."

"You're kidding. They had PCs and word processors? Seriously, is it true that Atlantis was more advanced than the ancient civilizations we're familiar with?"

"Atlantis was the peak of that Aquarian age, and America will be in this one."

"*That* Aquarian age? You mean ages are repeated?"

"Yes, in cycles, endlessly. It is math. Math is consistent. The time between ages is 24,000 years."

"Wow. Mind boggling. But how does 'endless cycles' agree with the idea of evolution of species? Isn't evolution a linear process?"

"No, only in the lowest vibratory level, that is, in the physical aspect of existence."

"Fine. Can I ask another million questions? How far is the nearest inhabited planet?"

"Not far. Saturn."

"What!? Who/what inhabits it? Something recognizable?"

"Yes."

"I mean, can we see them?"

"*Not with your eyes, but with instruments patterned after mind.*"

"Oh, too bad. That will be a while yet. Are there any who are like us somewhere out there? Besides our ancestors?"

"*Yes. Not the same eyes, but similar. They've been to Earth, too.*"

"Did any of them have something to do with building the original pyramids?"

"*Your ancestors did. The pyramids, alone on Earth, simulate energy flow and pulsation on the planet that is the home of Earth intelligence.*"

"Fascinating. Those sweet interbreeding ancestors built them? Can I ask how? With big muscles or advanced technology?"

"*They used Hertz reversal, which is a way of using the pattern of the energy of sound to move physical objects. This was common at one time, but fell into disuse because of the politics of power of that day.*"

"How did they use that pattern?"

"*Sound was directed at an object, along the energy lines that for different substances are always the same, such that the energy inherent in the sound pattern (its note) lifted the object.*"

"What kind of sound? How did they generate it? Teach me, and I'll never bug you for the lotto numbers again."

"*A piano, a harmonica, a flute, a violin, a human voice with perfect pitch, etc. etc., can be the source. Even some birds' songs. In this case, monks chanted and stones rose.*"

"Incredible. Can we learn how to do this again!? You're making me crazy."

"Have you forgotten 'infinite possibilities?' What does that mean to you? Ask yourself. Of course it can be learned again. Anything can."

"All right, fine. It's just too much, sometimes. What secrets do the pyramids still contain?"

"The energy flow therein is in itself the secret. In a pyramid humans can get a sensory reaction to that other, higher axis by the interaction of form-contained energy and gravitation."

"Mathematical secrets?"

"No, just a reality of form interaction. It is a measurable universal, but not within your math system."

"Explain form-contained energy. The form of physical things has significance?"

"Yes, all physical forms have their own unique pattern of vibrational interaction with their surroundings, be those immediate surroundings energy or matter. Combinations of forms, which you call design, change that interaction. For instance, if you take a circle, which spreads energy evenly, and top it with a cone, which focuses energy, you have focused energy in a concentrated, although evenly distributed, area."

"So it's more concentrated, so what."

"So the interaction with the environment changes."

"I mean, how does this effect show itself? Can we detect it? Are there practical uses for this?"

"*Would it be practical to see through metal walls? Endless possibilities.*"

"Hmm. How about some gadgets?"

"*How about a form vacuum cleaner that works on a principle similar to your present ones, i.e., region-of-higher to region-of-lower pressure, only from region-of-higher to region-of-lower energy! No wires, no noise.*
Or a heart pacemaker, built by form alone, to tune into a given exterior pulsation. Then there would be no need for an operation to replace the cell, but one could instead just replace the cell in the exterior pacesetter, etc., etc. Could go on and on."

"God, I love it. One day we must grab my tools and build something, OK?"

A hello maybe?

There were many acres of apple orchards in the valley behind my house, bordered by woods and quite a respectable little mountain chain curiously named Hussy. I loved taking long strolls late at night deep into the rows of well-tended trees, musing either about some words of the Big One or about some woes and shortcomings and problems of my life—those poor trees, the thoughts they had to listen to.

Sometimes, when they got tired of some particularly intense whining, they would call on their allies, the deer, to put a stop to it. Can you imagine walking among trees on an overcast, dark night, deep in thought, and then have some apple-munching deer wait until you're ten feet away before exploding out from under their tree with those strange barks they make when alarmed?

On this particular night, I was almost back to the house after a pleasant hour or so among the trees, engrossed in some mental business as usual, when I suddenly felt that prickly somebody-is-staring-at-you sensation on my neck. I froze, then wheeled around—and found my eyes glued to a round, milky-white object in the sky. It was hanging there about a hundred feet above the trees, no more than a few hundred feet away. My mind went into overdrive searching for an explanation—a plane: no, it's not moving; the moon: no, I can see Hussy Mtn. behind and above it; a helicopter: no, there's no noise, and it's a round white ball (maybe ten to fourteen feet in diameter).

There was a tingling in my belly as I ran out of possibilities and dared to consider the incredible: it must be *them*! No, stop it, get a hold of yourself. But what else can it be? With that thought I relaxed, straightened my shoulders, and with some bravado said in my mind, "All right, at least give me some sign, dammit." The instant I said that, the orb rose straight up maybe ten feet, then dropped down twice that distance, then rose back up to its original position. It looked like a deliberate sign, a kind of 'hello.' I stood there rooted to the ground, overwhelmed, and completely speechless. But there was no fear, only wonder. I was happy, if that makes any sense. Because, somehow, I *knew* in that moment that they had really, truly waved to me. Such a nice, tame, little, nonscary, unremarkable wave, and yet so enormous.

After about twenty seconds the object began moving away, slowly, keeping to the same elevation until it reached the end of the valley. Then it rose up and disappeared behind a low point of the ridge.

I don't know how long I stood there. I just didn't want to leave. After some time I sat down, appreciating the cool grass and solid earth under my bottom.

This little encounter really scrambled my brains. But my reaction to it, now that I can look at it from the vantage point of distance in time, was weird: I didn't do *anything*. That is, I didn't tell anybody, I didn't go shouting from the rooftops, nothing. My innards were

> *You are the architect of your reality, remember?*

enormously stirred up and I did try to integrate this experience into my view of things, but what else could I really do with it? As the weeks passed and life went on, my thoughts gradually settled back into their habitual patterns, and soon I hardly thought about it any more. Isn't that astonishing? I just keep doing what's comfortable and familiar, no matter what! I find that astonishing.

I did, of course, run to my all-knowing one, bubbling with excitement and demanding details. He said that they had indeed waved to me and that they now had my 'frequency' and could find me whenever they needed to. Very matter-of-fact, ordinary, practical information, you know? Like giving somebody your phone number . . .

I went slightly nuts. Then I wanted to know why they didn't just stop being cute and land and take me for a little ride. I meant it, too. He said they didn't think I was ready, which didn't sit well with my ego, and then this:

"You must first know them on all levels of consciousness."

"Orifi, that means I don't have to start packing my travel bags any time soon. That's discouraging. Although, I must admit, it makes a lot of sense. What would be the purpose of meeting openly if all I could do is stare at them with open mouth and big round eyes? Too sad. How the hell am I going to know them on all levels of consciousness? There better be a lot of learning happening on my inner levels.

Wait. I just had a disturbing thought. Did you mean me when you said 'you' or did you mean everyone? The whole human race must know them this way?"

"Eventually everyone will. But, once again, this is extremely difficult to translate from a time-less to a time-dependent reality."

"Frustrating."

"Yes, it is apparently quite difficult to go from linear to nonlinear thinking. But it must be done if you want to begin to understand any of your reality.
To be there, be here. I kid you not."

O

7 Intermeshed Bodies

"In fact, anything that is or ever will be real to you or for you is simultaneously from within and from without. You must conceive of this so-called duality nondualistically if you are to understand any of the reality of your universe—and you must understand, then believe, then live accordingly!"

"And how am I going to get that understanding? Out of the blue? If I am aware of anything, it is that my understanding of my universe needs some help. Mostly, I know that I need some way to clear out, or bypass, what I have accumulated all these years. I need new approaches, new methods. Or maybe I don't know what I need? This is a tall order."

Peeking out from a reflection

"Relax. You have me now, and I will offer you some new points of view.
Here's a little exercise for you to try: Stare into a mirror, then shift your consciousness, or, rather, allow it to travel, to the image of you, until you are looking at yourself with your image, instead of the other way around. Know that this is the reality you live in within your physical shell."

"I can look at myself from my image? Then where am I? Not in my 'physical shell?' But if I am in my image in the mirror, then I am everywhere? Be nice to me . . ."

"Strange, you human spirits. You are so coated that you often fail to recognize your own selves when faced with them. But then we, too, have our nonuniversal ways that distinguish us from other intelligences."

"What is coated? How can I be faced with my own self? How many of me are there looking at one another? Am I a reflection looking at an image? A mind that imagines me?"

"Are you different from that of which you are made?"

"And what am I made of? Mind?"

"No no no, your mind is a tool of your spirit."

"We are made of spirit?"

"Of course."

"I don't know what spirit is, Orifi. Do you know that? The word is so common, used in so many ways—and yet I have no idea what it is. Can you tell me first how this physical shell I am aware of fits into the scheme of things? I have read of other bodies, or levels, of man, such as the astral. Is there such a thing? Please explain."

The five bodies of man

"Yes, indeed. Man consists of five intermeshed bodies: the physical, the astral, the causal, mind, and spirit. These correspond to specific levels of density and vibration of light.
There is a connection between the macro—and microeffects of light and every life process. Analyze light's parts, or energy

separations, that are perceived as color. See light in everything. See the negative effects of its lack. Capture it when it happens of its own in your mind. Study its form, its direction, its motion.

Light is the meeting point of all energy. Intelligence on every level can be known there. Create it in your mind—and you understand all of creation."

"Whew. Too much. I hope it 'happens of its own.'

What's the causal level?"

> *Spirit rules matter, always.*

"The causal level contains all interrelationships that exist between mind and matter, between time and space. More on all this later."

"I hope so. But why don't we know these things? Why don't we know our selves? I still think that's bizarre.

And why do we choose to go through this physical experience, in which we have so little awareness of who we are? There are delights, but also plenty of the opposite. Why? Are we only here within this reality to learn how to escape from it?"

"This question you pose is a poignant one—and you thought you were just making a random search for important-sounding questions."

"Thanks. Can I have an answer?"

"Like every experience you will ever have from here to eternity, the physical experience is adding tremendously to your personal growth and understanding. The process of becoming physical, then understanding the physical level, then learning to detach from it, then learning eventually to separate from the physical reality, is an awesome one. It cannot be understood by any given statement or experience; it can only be conceived of in stages as it unfolds."

"Wow. Well, I know I have successfully completed step 1, that is, becoming physical.

As I try to digest what you tell me, the difference between your understanding and my own seems so huge; it's just too much. I don't like feeling stupid. I think we humans are a strange race. Beautiful and wonderful in many ways, but mostly stupid. Don't you think so? Are there other races like us?"

"The human race is no more or less stupid than any other. You would do well to concentrate on the beautiful and wonderful, since concentrating on the incredible stupidity will get you absolutely nothing. Marvel at what you have. What you don't have can't help you, although it can't hurt you, either. Forget it.

In general you are much more like others than unlike them, but specifically speaking, the converse is true. Just as, generally, a dog and a man both need air, water, food and sleep, while specifically their habits and mental capacities are grossly different."

"So we are to them as dogs are to us? Great. I feel reassured, comforted."

"I speak of your conscious self, not your vast real self. Forget it for now."

> Marvel at what you have.

"All right. I just feel overwhelmed by this vast picture of our nature that you have been painting for me. I love it, but it also makes me, this conscious me, feel small. The more you tell me, the smaller I feel. Shouldn't it be the other way around? Sometimes I catch a glimpse of myself sitting there stretching my brain to reach for new understanding, at times quite impressed by my reach. It reminds me of that ant that crawled up an elephant's leg with lust on his mind. You know of that story? We have such wonderful stories, you should be jealous."

We are not alone

"Relax. Whenever you feel discouraged, remind yourself of this truth: we are not alone. By we I mean you and I and every

conscious mind extant anywhere. A dimension of reality exists wherein constant, conscious camaraderie flows freely between all minds! You need not envy that state or seek it here and now for yourself. It will come to everyone in the end. It is not something you need seek."

"But I do envy that state! How I would love to be conscious of the fact that 'we are not alone.' Such a wonderful statement, but all I have is my willingness to accept it."

"We are indeed all connected with the universe. The lines between us all would startle even a mathematician."

"Great. But I don't see any."

"I know. I tell you this so you can relax and forget it for now. I tell you also so you have something to look forward to."

"I appreciate it. But I don't know about relaxing. I want to reach out and touch just one of those lines."

"I say again: No one anywhere exists alone, disconnected from the total spirit that is life. Even after what you call life ends, the possibilities for connection are limitless. From where you are, you could never understand the instantaneous nature of such a flow of information!

This reality is no different now than ever, only the level of consciousness on which it functions changes, that is, it depends on where you find yourself on the upward spiral, and where humanity finds itself on its upward spiral. Only certain people's personal spiral reflects accurately the whole human condition at any given point in the progression.

Knowledge is never lost. It only fulfills itself on different levels of life's consciousness at different periods of what you call history."

"I don't know what to say to all this. I need to chew on these thoughts. My head is spiraling—I mean, spinning."

Beyond the mighty lion

"Should you sleep the deep, unconscious sleep of the mountain lion, you would glory in a silence so complete and enveloping that any remembrance of what sound even is would escape you, seemingly forever. But by making this connection with silence on such a purely instinctual level you would forfeit the culmination of human history that has delivered you into this very moment.

When man awakens in an instant in time, his experience is far beyond that of the mighty lion, partly because of his very self-consciousness. The lion can witness an event, but only man can experience a miracle. The lion remains one with nature, but only man is capable of inspiration. The lion marks off his territory and guards it jealously and proudly. Man's true territory reaches to the far ends of the universe, and beyond."

"You make me dizzy. Will I ever be able to play consciously in this 'territory'?"

"Travel on the eternal sound that is contained within you.
It will carry you into the astral world.
Wake up again to find yourself there
and see the light.
Then travel on the light into the causal world.
Wake up again to find yourself there
and see, yes, see, the thought.
Then travel on the thought
and you will find your self's center in God.
go flow grow
We hear and live and think these words here a lot."

"Where did that come from?? I will never understand this."

Draw on what you will be

"Relax. The pressure for progress in human history and evolution requires not that you live in the past or future, but that

you understand them enough to draw from their vastness. You see, you can draw on what you will be to the same extent that you can draw on what you were. Therefore, whether an experience is one year behind you or one year ahead of you makes very little difference here, in my reality. The experience is a part of you. Perhaps only to a small degree consciously, but definitely available."

"My present is influenced not only by the past but also by the future? I can draw on the future?"

"Now go get some clay."

"Clay? What do you mean?"

"Gray stuff that can be molded dimensionally. Go buy some."

"What on earth for?"

"I will show you. You need to work on space to move out of space."

"To move out of space? Goodie . . . can I use the stuff they use in kindergarten?"

"Get any clay, Schwab."

Dream: The bear

I was running through an old forest of large trees, fleeing from a huge bear that was hunting me. I was trying not to make any sound, often looking back for what I somehow knew was a monstrous beast. I couldn't see it, but I could hear it. Sweating, heart pounding, I ran as fast as I could.

I slid down a small embankment, over ferns and mosses, and came to a stop under a thick bush. I lay still and listened, and sure enough, the bear was closer than ever, crashing through brush like a bulldozer. I knew I couldn't escape much longer. Panic was replaced by resignation, and then by something close to anger as ferocious snorting was getting closer. I felt certain that the bear could somehow sense me and I wasn't going to get away no matter what I did.

There was somebody with me. I couldn't see him, but he was there behind my right shoulder. I felt that I knew him well, but I couldn't quite find a name. I have a vague memory of advice being given. What he could possibly have been advising me in this situation would be interesting to know, but I can't remember.

The bear couldn't have been more than twenty feet away now. I had an overwhelming sense of this huge, primeval, unstoppable force, and I was filled with dread again. I crawled deeper under the bush, head first, trying to hide my feet under ferns and dead leaves, all the while knowing that it was useless. Then I woke up.

For hours I felt the fear in my belly, a very real, physical fear. There was also another feeling, hard to name exactly—something like admiration for such immense, brainless power, almost like a desire to let him maul me so I could lose myself in experiencing that power. And maybe become part of it? Strange. I wondered what the bear symbolized for me. Was it some part of myself that I was afraid to face? Was my bigger self about to gobble up this little self? Or was it just something I was avoiding in real life? I didn't know.

I was also somewhat disappointed by this dream. Didn't I have that glorious meeting with the owner of the craft? And here I was, being chased by a stupid bear. Didn't seem like progress.

O

8 On Spirit

"Why don't you explain spirit to me now. If I am made of it, I'd like to know what it is. Does anybody at this physical level have any idea what it is? You know how our minds are: Once we label something, we act as if we know that thing. Gravity, dreams, atoms, spirit—as long as we have a word for it.

Is it more than some form of energy at some level of vibration?"

"Spirit is indeed higher vibration. It is, in fact, the highest vibration of man. It is not 'more' than energy, it is purer energy.

The highest vibration your physical senses can respond to is light (though your physicists would argue the description of light as vibratory); thus, man likes to visualize to understand. On the mental level many things exist that vibrate at a higher level than light, but these are, of course, invisible. Thus, any conception that is fit into the physical sense understanding is inaccurate.

It is not time to explain further what such things are, but it is a good foundation for you to begin to understand what they are not."

"So everything is energy at different levels of vibration? Our lowvibratory physical plane and our mental activities? If the mind could speed up the vibrations of the physical body, then the body would become invisible to physical senses? And it could then travel around like thoughts? Is that what dematerialization is?"

"Very nearly. But it is not so much a raising of the lower physical vibrations as it is a matter of training the higher vibrations not to need the protective coatings of the lower-vibratory shells you wear."

A coating for the spirit

"Our physical bodies are lowvibratory shells for the protection of our spirits? Protection from what?"

"Yes. In fact, even your mind is a comparatively lowvibratory coating for the spirit, which is so high and fine that it would not function in the physical planes at all without this protection. The protection prevents the spirit from spiraling upward out of the reaches of the physical world.

Once you allow your spirit to 'explore' other realms, you must convince it to return to bring the information back to the physical world. The process is a difficult one of physiology over spirituality."

"I must convince my spirit? But I *am* my spirit! How on earth does that work?"

"This is, of course, the difficulty, because it is a process of temporary reversal, in which the mind's will must exert power of control over its benefactor, the spirit."

"Mind's will? What is that?"

"Will is nothing more than control. Mind's will simply indicates wherein the control rests. It is like a shifting of control from one vibratory level (the spirit) to another (the mind)."

"I have no way of understanding that. As a concept it's easy, but what it might mean . . . I have trouble conceiving of this whole vibratory business. What differentiates me from another human when we are all the same kind of vibration? What makes me an individual?"

"Your spirit is your individuality, yours alone. It is not a collective energy force of some sort. Your mind, on the other hand, is not as individual as you might believe, but a piece of a collective total."

"A shared mind? A supercomputer with nearly six billion logged on users? That's some image. I'll have to chew on this one.

On unfolding

So the four other bodies are all just temporary tools of the spirit? The mind is like a piece of machinery, or a hunk of energy with certain capabilities, assigned to the spirit that is me? And my life experiences cause the spirit to grow?"

"Yes, those bodies only serve your spirit. Your mind is far less a machine than a tool of your true self, the spirit that is you. And you do not, necessarily, use the same 'piece' of mind in each of your many lives.
The spirit doesn't actually grow with added experience, but rather unfolds. Growth insinuates the addition of something. Actually, you only shed new light on what already exists in you."

"Like a vessel with a certain capacity? It never grows in size, but becomes fuller with each experience? And when it is full? Back to its creator?"

> *Be as a vessel waiting to be filled.*

"Yes indeed. But I prefer the more accurate analogy of shedding light on newly uncovered corners, since the vessel analogy again insinuates adding to, which in fact is not the process."

"So when the spirit has unfolded and gone back to its creator, is that the end of it? Does it continue? What does it do after it has unfolded?"

"Try to imagine selfconsciousness and Godconsciousness simultaneously, then you tell me. Remember, logic is a rational game."

"I can't. How can I imagine God-consciousness? Yes, this is just a rational game, but what else can I use? So let me exercise my logic some more: which part of us is aware of the unfolding? The spirit? But the spirit is the thing that is unfolding! You mean it controls its own unfolding? That's a tough one, I must tell you. It knows all of itself and at the same time controls its own unfolding? And for what purpose, if it already knows its entirety?"

"Your spirit only knows its own fullness to the extent that it knows its creator."

"So the experiences it goes through cause the unfolding and thereby the greater knowing of its creator, and therefore of itself?"

"Yes, exactly."

"That has a certain logic to it. But the basic definition does not: unfolding means shedding light on what *already exists*??"

"Yes. Forget it for now."

"All right. Let me continue with my 'logical' questions. Are we all at different levels of unfolding? And is there an average, or mean, level for all of humanity? The Human Unfolding Index, or HUI? Seriously, has the average of all unfoldings of humanity risen to where we now, as you once said, stand ready for an upward leap?"
"Yes."

"Super. I'm ready. Let's leap."

"Do not speak too glibly about your spiritual center, as it is both the blueprint and the essence of your being. Never try to presume control over it.

> *More knowledge in no way insinuates more wisdom.*

And you are awake to the degree that your mind and your senses serve your spirit, rather than counteract or ignore it.

Unimpeded vision will come (has come) in those spaces that you make available to it. Accept the fact that as far as universal knowledge or wisdom are concerned, you can never do more than scratch the surface. You were never meant to. That is reserved for the creator. What is vaster than our experience was planned to be that way. Insight beyond your understanding does not simplify but only complicates.

There is an awe, a sense of wonder, and even a touch of healthy fear involved whenever anyone ventures into the mystical. And trying to emulate or imitate what one finds there is a hopeless task.

The very culmination of your spiritual journey will be in a letting go, not a holding on. It can be a long, tortuous process, and only as poignant or profound as your conscious awareness of it."

"And why am I not more aware? Make me more aware."

"Relax. Alert relaxation is the precursor of all spiritual insight. Relax.

In essence, you are not the captain of your soul, the master of your fate, the chooser of your own destiny. Sorry, you simply are not. I'm not either!"

"You know, your words always make me feel elated, give me a high—but they also leave me restless and anxious. Why?"

"You can't walk till you learn to crawl!"

O

9 On Wisdom

"Don't cling to my words, Schwab, as if they were some kind of panacea. The information I give is free to anyone seeking it, and the channels through which such information can be transmitted are infinite, truly. Relax."

"Wow. To think that all that knowledge is sitting there, and that infinite channels are available for getting it . . . it's just too much."

"But this information is temporal knowledge, as I have already said, and as such will pass with the passing of all things temporal. Its use is to guide you towards discovering wisdom, the real goal of Earth life."

"The goal of our lives here is to 'discover' wisdom? Unfolding means gaining wisdom? Maybe I need a lesson on what wisdom is. I want more knowledge, more hard facts. Who cares about wisdom?"

"It will help you to feel less desperate if you realize that wisdom will eventually fill your being, as all beings, whether you want it or not, whether you care or not. Relax."

"I don't think that I'm feeling desperate. Eager to learn from you, but not desperate. So go on."

Age-old truths

"I say nothing here that hasn't been said many, many times throughout the ages. You write nothing here that hasn't been written in a multitude of ways through a multitude of ages for a variety of reasons. There is nothing new. How often I have said this to you, how easily you have forgotten. For want of excitement you have tried, in vain, to make ageold truths seem like new revelations. When you couldn't disguise them as originals, you became angry or bored, or both."

"I don't remember doing anything of the sort. What are you talking about?"

"I need to begin a dissertation of sorts that is likelier than not to bore you to tears, if just by its repetition alone. I only tell you to point out, up front, that the repetition is a necessary part of this lesson. It is meant to saturate your consciousness with certain principles. Again, don't analyze or even concentrate.

This is important. Simply listen. Do allow yourself to associate the ideas freely with similar ones you may have had and may have considered to be your own originals. Don't be set back—the word 'original' is as deceiving as the word 'new.'

Relax and bear with me. This will be, as all things are, as boring and tedious or as refreshing and stimulating as your attitude allows it to be. Remember, relax, relax . . .

It is written exactly as I say it—over and over, in many places, in many ages. I only repeat it to you again, here and now."

"I'm ready. Let's hear your ancient stuff."

Have faith

"Have that faith that enables you to go forward, to do the seemingly impossible, to move ahead in spite of all the logical reasons why it can't be done. Choose a difficult task for yourself,

one that you may have been avoiding or thinking of as impossible. Change your mind about it, then do it.

What are you seeking, wisdom? Where do you begin, with faith? How can you endure, with patience? How long before you can do the things you want to do, before you get feedback? How much is enough?"

"Great questions. I have no answers, which adds to my impatience."

"Too often, the doer becomes impatient and neglects the task while he looks forward to personal recognition and acclaim. Remember the role of time. It is not always granted to the sower to see the harvest. All work that is worth anything is done in faith."

"Looking for acclaim? Ouch. I'll get over that in time. And I don't understand the last sentence."

"The test of faith is action and perseverance, but also patience.

You can't expect to have an oak tree tomorrow from a seed you planted today. If you really wanted the oak to grow, would you dig it up every so often to see how it was doing? If you really wanted the tree, you would trust in life to do the rest."

"Fine. No one can argue with that, for a tree. But I am not a tree. Is there not some inner place I can peek at to see how I'm doing?"

"Relax. This faith that lets you go forward in the dark is so similar to confidence, to believing without seeing. Don't misunderstand, I do not advocate sacrificing thinking to believing. Instead, I hope you relax to allow a balance and positive, reciprocal action between the two.

All I can give you is knowledge so that you might be prepared to gain wisdom on your own. Knowledge aids in dealing with the material world, wisdom with the intangible. Don't savor knowledge and thirst after it alone because, truly, it is only a temporal tool *that you will ultimately discard with all things temporal. It is a tool by which you use earth experience to gain wisdom. In the realm of the invisible, wisdom is as knowledge is in the physical world.*

Wisdom is of the intuitive function, while knowledge is of the rational function, and one grows deep into the self's center as roots, while the other makes a vibrant array of lifeness akin to foliage on a tree."

"Great image. This all makes sense to me in my 'rational function,' Orifi, because it seems logical, but how do I use this information? What can I do with it?"

"You show no serious lack in grasping the abstract difference between knowledge and wisdom. You do, however, lack the ability to make practical applications of this concept."

"So are you going to give me this missing ability?'"

Enjoy becoming wise

"Listen now.

Honey whets the appetite, and so does wisdom. When you can enjoy becoming wise, there is hope for you. That you may learn wisdom, set your desire on my words. Long for them and you will be instructed. A sincere desire for instruction is always the beginning of wisdom, and concern for instruction is love of her, and love of her is the keeping of her laws.

Wisdom is radiant and unfading and easily discerned by those who love her. She goes about seeking those worthy of her and graciously appears to them in every thought.

Can't you hear wisdom's voice? She stands at every fork in the road, at the door of each and every home.

'Please listen! I have important information for you. Quiet yourself to hear what I say. My words are plain and clear to anyone with half a mind, if that half is only open.'

If you will but look for these very words, you will find them, for they have been written before exactly as I say them. Find where they are and you will have a new insight.

'I existed before the Earth began.
I was before the ocean was.
I was before the mountains and the skies were.
I am wisdom, and I give you common sense and good advice.
I love any who love me, and those who search for me shall surely find me.
Come, you simple ones without good judgment, come to wisdom's banquet and drink the wines that I have mixed.
Leave your foolishness behind and learn how to live, learn to be wise.
I, wisdom, will make the hours of your day more profitable and the years of your life more fruitful.'

"That is beautiful. I can't honestly say that I 'love' wisdom, but tell her that I certainly want to come to her banquet."

"*Remember, wisdom and good judgment live together, for wisdom knows where to discover knowledge and understanding.*

It is always the fool who thinks he needs no advice, while the wise man listens to others. The wise man is glad to be instructed, while the selfsufficient fool falls flat on his face. If you profit from constructive criticism, you will be elected to the wise men's hall of fame.

Wisdom is enshrined in the hearts of men of common sense, but it must shout loudly before fools will hear it. The wise man hungers for truth, while the fool feeds on trash. A wise man doesn't display his knowledge, it is the fool who displays his foolishness.

The advice of a wise man refreshes like water from a mountain spring, and he can draw out the good advice that comes out of the hearts and minds of other wise men. Yes, the ability to give good advice satisfies like a warm meal.

Drink from your own well. Wisdom is a fountain of life to those who possess it. You're not born with it, you are only born with the capacity to have it. To learn, you must want to be taught.

Everyone who asks, receives. Everyone."

"What can I say. You know, part of me (my ego?) cringes with these fancy, poetic, dramatic words, while another part loves them and feasts on them."

"Relax—a relaxed attitude lengthens a man's life.
Remember, he who loves wisdom loves his own best interest."

Thinking about a cicada

When something on my nature walks catches my eye, like the strange stepladder in the webs of angiope spiders, or two ant armies battling to the death on the steps of the front porch, I sometimes stare at the scene with a strong sense that there is a lesson there, that what I think I see is not really what's going on, that it's a show put on to assault my reason—and I look around to see if something is watching me, half expecting to hear a soft chuckling. Maybe staring in total befuddlement at a spider weaving strange designs is the first sign of approaching wisdom? I hope so, because I'm getting good at being befuddled.

There's a cicada that does the following incredible thing: it cuts a hole in a leaf on a tree, then sits beside it and strums its love song. Why? Because the arrangement, scientists have found, amplifies the sound of his mating call and therefore increases the distance at which females can hear it! Can you picture this scenario without getting just a little bit unnerved?

I love thinking about how such behaviors might have evolved. This one I can see clearly. Zillions of years ago one of these guys happened to sit behind a leaf into which a caterpillar or an ant had cut a hole. He paid no attention to this as he sang his lusty song. All over that tree his male relatives were doing the same. After a while, as usual, the girls showed up, each pairing off with her favorite musician. Except for our guy—he was surrounded by adoring females who told him that they heard his song from incredibly far away and that he must be a super sire for sure.

The next morning, with what little strength he had left, he carefully studied his surroundings to see what might have caused his good fortune, because he was well aware that he had done nothing out of the ordinary. The only unusual thing he could think of was that leaf with the round hole in the middle. So he decided to test it. He sat in the same spot again that evening and bingo, again they came in droves. The next night he sat somewhere else, and only one lady showed up. Aha! Blessed with great intelligence, our cicada immediately realized that if he could pass this secret on to his offspring they would, in time, come to dominate this particular cicada tribe, making him the Adam of a new race.

Seriously, I do reflect on how such a system could have developed by chance, in stages. Step-by-step adaptations? He must sit a certain distance from the leaf, the hole must be a certain size . . . never mind. It just won't work unless all the pieces are in place, in their present perfection. Intermediate stages would seem to make little sense.

Such thoughts are, of course, a rational game. But maybe the mere acknowledgment of such mysteries is evidence of a little bit of wisdom?

We are floating in a soup of playful intelligence, and something is forever playing peekaboo with us—look at this, it whispers, look at that, it shouts, here I am—but we don't see. Strange. What kind of system is this? Then, one day, the implausible behavior of an insect hits the consciousness at just the right time, and bam!—eyes open and stare in wonder. And then miracles all around that were hidden through familiarity are shockingly obvious, and everything is unfathomable—every caterpillar with his internal schematic for a butterfly, every dragonfly performing impossible maneuvers, every cicada using his amplifier to boom out his love song.

O

10 I Borrow Your Senses

"How much do you know about my physical world, Orifi? All these thoughts about spirit and wisdom—wonderful stuff, but I feel a touch of sadness when I walk on my nature paths and realize that you can't see what I see, can't hear what I hear, can't smell what I smell . . . or can you? Do you know trees and birds and flowers and water and clouds? Do you know skin, and how the sun feels on it? I wish I could share my physical sensations with you, all of them."

"But you do share them with me. I am able to 'borrow' all of your senses, and therefore tap any and all sensory input that you get, my dear earthling friend. Let me show you by example instead of explaining further: let me describe one of your typical physical summer days."

"That would be super."

Orifi's earth day

"The world grows tame, in control of itself. Shadows deepen. The air is perfumed with honeysuckle. The afternoon sky blushes violently, bloodred, and today's sun, seduced by the sweetness of the horizon, sinks into the ocean's deep abyss.
You sink into a deep meditation. For once this sun finally goes down, you can bid a profound farewell to one more day of your life.

For a while, a mute loneliness is felt for the passing of a day that you will never see again.

The sun now reaches down, its rays giving one last kiss to the sky's foundation. Your mind stirs. Likewise, the early evening is astir, in anticipation of its sweetness. Twilight envelops you like spirit's breath. The leaves on the trees flutter, whispering the secrets of night. Each tree is wrapped in its own rosyblue veil. The blue shadows of evening settle quietly, everywhere. This is the glorious new night that twilight promised you earlier.

The earth has grown cool, blanketed by the night. It rejoices in its privacy, feeling no obligation to divulge its secrets. And you can prepare to drink a different kind of light when the moon and the stars mount the sky. The quiet, still light of the moon, though less intense than sunlight, is still most powerful. It penetrates your very flesh. You can become intoxicated by its rays. The full moon, enormous and mute, begs you to submerge yourself in its light to chance losing control.

The moon is one of the voices of the night. It whispers songs from the roots of the world, tender and melodious.

Listen intently to the night as it unfurls its mighty wings to fly across your consciousness, leaving its mark on your every thought. Listen as the night wind whispers to your heart. Should the moon hide behind some solitary cloud, feel the still, deep darkness, and listen—you may even hear the heartbeat of the universe throbbing right through you. Listen as the night pleads in earnest for you to take flight into the heart of it, leaving sorrows and woes far behind you. It is said that "the darkest hour is just before dawn," a time when night falls into its own deep ravine, not unlike the black holes in the universe.

The night air is damp and sweet as the stars ascend in their assigned patterns to keep a silent vigil over the planet. The sky is so clear, so cloudless, the stars pinpoint themselves against its velvety black backdrop. The starry light bleaches your face a pale white as you stand basking in it.

The splendor of the night is concealed by a cloud momentarily. It soon leaves with the wind, and the moon's glittering light jumps down and kisses the crest of each wave on the water. Feel the cool night air against your face as a quick wind rises, then falls dead still again. The hush is almost excruciating.

Oftentimes, even before the moon sinks behind the horizon, earth's face invites the new day's light to enter there. The sky lightens and brightens gradually, bathing earth in the softening roselight of the dawn. But the sun's encore is never gradual. It is a dramatic bursting forth, always, as it returns, again and again, to perpetually reassure the world that all is as it should be. Light is drawn away from one half of the earth, now willing to share itself with the other half, once again.

The new sun's smile shines warmly on the morning dew. Here is another gift for you: today!"

All this from my senses?

"Wow. You have the makings of a poet—I am smitten!

But I must know: do you really get all that from my physical senses? I find that so hard to believe, because if it's true, then I must not be very much attuned to my own senses!"

"Yes, of course it's true. Where else would I get it from? I have no physical senses, I only see your mind."

"Geez. You 'see' smell, touch, sound, and color in my mind? And how do you see my physical body?"

"I read your energy body. It, of course, corresponds directly to the physical body you have that I cannot see. You in a sense transmit the information your energy body carries."

"So—then you can see things in my physical body that are abnormal? And tell me about it?"

"I can tell you what I see, but there is no normal or abnormal. There is different, and there are degrees of positive and negative."

"A disease is abnormal, isn't it?"

"It is not abnormal. It is a difference noticeable by its different degree of positiveness."

"Same thing. It is important to me to explore this in detail.

What about moods? We are creatures with sometimes big swings in moods, and these affect our behavior in so many ways. The logic brain is often just a spectator to the gyrations of our moods. Can you see moods?"

"Yes. Transmission, but most especially accuracy, changes with moods, which are in fact energy level changes, and therefore can be measured by means such as the galvanic skin response test that so intrigued Jung for this very reason.

Your color changes as your mood changes."

"Color?"

"Yes."

"Amazing. We must look like one of those giant multicolored soap bubbles to you. What about thoughts? How do you get thoughts? From the energy body?"

"Via the function of your brain that can actually visualize, i.e., make images—real images on your mind's eye."

"I hope you'll explain that some day."

"If I can.

You, Earth child by choice, rejoice in being physical while you still are. Why do you resent matter and adore mind? One is so utterly meaningless without the other. Both have equal beauty, strength, and reality. But the reciprocal action between the two, when accepted and understood, can literally raise the level of consciousness in anyone."

He knew, of course, that I did not resent matter. If there was anything I resented about it, it was the fact that I couldn't peek deeper into its mysteries. So when he asked me that despicable question, I resented it a lot. I gave him a piece of my mind and told him that he had wronged a true lover of everything physical.

His words, however, had the desired effect: I remembered that I depended almost solely on mental processes, while attaching very little weight to anything that didn't come to me through my head. Input from my physical senses was far less important to me than the constructs of my mind. This was something that I had come to dislike about myself and wanted very much to change. Which, of course, he also knew.

Learn to sense with your heart

"Learn to sense with your heart, Schwab."

"My heart? And what is my heart?"

"The home of your sensitivity, where you get sensory reality from. The definition of physical, as you know, requires both the thing (sound, light, etc.) and the instrument for reception of the thing. In other words, if you sense it, that is, if you see, hear, smell, touch, feel it, then it is real.
Well, the heart senses all simultaneously, as an undivided whole."

"Teach me about this, Orifi, you hear? You can forget about giving me the lotto numbers if you teach me this one thing. I want to learn how to be aware of my heart."

"Strange, you humans. Yes, more on this later."

O

11 Five Easy Steps

One day, Orifi presented me with an unsolicited recipe for a complete tune-up of my inner workings. I didn't appreciate it much, being more interested in juicy tidbits than in upgrading to a more efficient version of me. It was written without my presence, so I had no chance to jump in with questions and arguments.

Of course, the 'easy' in the title was said with nonphysical tongue in cheek. The notion of making all these changes in five weeks is totally absurd—and the fact that it is so only because we 'expect it to take longer' makes it all the more irritating.

Wouldn't it be something, though, if we could change that expectation?

"Schwab, for the next five weeks we will tackle five general areas of self-improvement because you need a crash course in learning how to please yourself. That's what you're here for, you know.

You are the architect of your reality, remember?

You have no say this time only because it is quicker that way. For the next project you can pick the terms, I promise.

Now you may think it presumptuous of me to believe that in just five weeks we can deal with five major life difficulties, any one of which would be a noble undertaking as an entire life's work—but I do and we shall, simply because, together, we have chosen to. It usually takes longer only because we expect it to.

In order, we will take

Happiness
Now-Awareness
Sense of Humor
Directness
Self-Control

1. Happiness

There are certain basic prerequisites to happiness:

o *Stop searching for fairness and justice.*
o *Achieve independence.*
o *Stop blaming and complaining.*
o *Know that happiness is not something you find but something you build.*
o *Love yourself, love yourself, love yourself.*

Let's begin our instant-happiness quest by clearing away a few misconceptions.

Justice and Fairness

First of all, there is no such thing as justice. It simply does not exist. It never has and it never will.

There, now we've taken a giant step toward achieving happiness in a hurry, because we can't groan about injustice any more.

To eliminate another large chunk from the unhappiness iceberg, never say, 'It isn't fair.' Saying so insists that the world be other than what it is. You needn't approve of the condition, but you do need to begin to accept it as part of reality.

Independence

Having initiated this rapid journey to total happiness by wiping away our useless search for justice and fairness, we must now achieve total independence.

First we must identify the root reason for dependence: you. With your every word or move you teach others how to treat you. If you are being dominated, you are asking for it. No person can ever dominate another without the full consent of that other. You signal others and they respond according to your signals.

Dependency is very harmful. last. Every human should take the time to write his/her own declaration of independence, clarifying exactly how he/she will function as an independent unit. It is mandatory that you free yourself of all obligatory relationships.

Begin a new habit of taking minitrips alone. Begin it now. Recognize your need for privacy and make other people respect that need. You may need to develop a tough skin of sorts about your own independence. The very people who try the hardest to keep you dependent respect you the most for being independent. Others can control you to the degree that you are dependent upon them for anything (money, security, flattery, etc.).

While you are demanding space in which to grow, be sure to leave the same for others. Allow the people you care about to make their own choices about what they want to do or be, with absolutely no insistence that they fulfill your wishes or desires. Married people, especially, need spaces. Ironically, the larger the spaces, the closer the relationship. Marriage based on the theme of dominance and submission ultimately makes the submissive partner feel trapped and the seed is sown for serious problems. The fruitful relationship we all want is one wherein each allows the other to be whatever he/she wants, with no expectations and no demands.

Create your own internal support system and you will be forever devoid of the need for support from without. You will be independent. You will be in control. You will want others in the purest sense, but you will need no one. The wanting is healthy; the needing is not. This is as true with people as with things.

The need in humans for peer approval is extravagant. The only approval you need is your own. Learn to approve of yourself. Strangely, the best way to win the approval of others is not to care if you get it, never to desire it, never to seek it, never to be consumed by a need for it.

Being entrenched in desires for outside approval is something you have carried over from childhood when, as often as not, approval was not freely given, but hinged itself upon pleasing someone and was given as a reward. [See the next chapter for my reaction to this.] Thus, you confused self-worth with approval from outside the self. Erase your childhood!

Never internalize the judgments of others. You don't need a consensus, nor do you need even a single other opinion. Nothing is as valid for you as your own opinion. Remember, it does not make one iota of difference what others think. Your self-worth is not equal to the sum of their opinions. You alone determine your worth. And do not with performance. Every person is far more than the sum total of his/her achievements.

Avoid boastful people. If you are one, then avoid yourself until you are able to rid yourself of this cumbersome habit. Remember, bragging is born of an attempt to gain the favor of others. The person who indulges in bragging is evaluating himself and determining his self-worth on the basis of other people's opinions.

Remember, if you want my opinion, that's healthy; if you need it, you're in trouble.

Blaming and Complaining

Stop blaming. It's easier to blame circumstance or another person than to make necessary changes in yourself, but blaming is always a waste of time. Whenever you blame, correct yourself out loud.

Stop wasting precious moments complaining. Don't complain to others and never allow them to complain to you. Fully-functioning beings never complain, ever.

Self-Love

LOVE YOURSELF! There can be no happiness for you unless you do. It is not essential that everybody love you, but it is essential that you love yourself.

Love yourself. Take good care of yourself. Eat well, exercise with joy, get air, maintain your weight, think, play, drink water and smile.

Do not practice self-denial. For example, always order what you want in a restaurant, regardless of price. Buy what you like, what you really love, in the grocery store. Indulge—as long as it isn't at the expense of others. As the commercial says, 'You're worth it!'

Consider jealousy. Self-love cannot live where jealousy lives for it is a putdown of yourself, i.e., it signifies that you consider another person to be worth more than you. And jealousy has another negative side: it also demands that someone love you in a certain way, exclusive of loving all others.

You have no responsibility to make others happy. They must make themselves happy. If you believe it is your mission to make them happy, then you are a dependent who will be blown to and fro by the winds of fate. When others are down, you will go down; you can't go up unless others go up. Always remember that you are responsible for your own emotions, and so is every other person. Herein you must take responsibility for your circumstances.

Still a further way to make your own happiness is to choose to be intelligent. How intelligent you are is determined, in part, by how you face trying times and whether you control yourself and are therefore completely capable of handling any situation successfully. And remember, you can't measure happiness by a lack of problems, only by how you choose to handle them.

Happiness is easy as soon as you realize that it is your choice. Choose happiness over depression, choose happiness over boredom, over tiredness, over etc. etc.

Never wait for happiness. Make your own. People who succeed in this world look for positive circumstances. If they can't find them, they never complain, they make their own.

Be happy. Create your own melody of joy in any way you will—oblivious to what 'they' say is supposed to be. Just sing.

Love yourself now

2. Now-Awareness

It is imperative that you develop your own now-awareness. If you need a gauge as to the quality of the minutes you are spending, ask yourself what you would be doing right this minute if you knew you had one month to live. To the extent that you would have to adjust your life because of this fact, you need now to adjust the way you spend your time, one second at a time.

We have spoken of those wasted spaces between your seconds. I say now that the moments between events are just as livable as those taken up by the events themselves. This is important. You need so desperately to see and understand this before we go on from here.

Now is all there is, all there ever was, all there ever will be. Don't postpone. There is no wondrous moment in the future when everything will fall into place and happiness will be yours. Don't procrastinate on living your life. To get to the heart of effective living, you need to realize your Now and live in it. It is easy to begin if you make a decision to live—first, fifteen minutes at a time, then ten, then five, then one, then one second at a time.

From this word on I decree that the only responsibility you ever need to fulfill for the rest of your life is taking care of your own present moments, i.e., determining the quality of every second you live. 'Now' living. 'Now' thinking.

As you live your present moments, make your rules apply only for that short time. Don't look for universal rules.

Remember these two crucial aspects of Now-ness effectiveness: it disallows guilt, and it disallows worry.

Guilt and Worry

Guilt and worry are essentially the same concept with opposite focuses. Guilt consumes your present moments with thoughts of the past; worry consumes your present moments with thoughts of the future.

Compile a guilt record. List the bad things you think you have done. Measure them on a scale from one to ten according to severity. Now seriously consider whether there is any real difference, in this present moment, whether you score one hundred or one thousand, or whatever. Regardless of the quantity or quality of guilt, it is a useless endeavor because no amount of guilt can ever change any aspect of the past—but it can ruin the present moment.

Of course, don't confuse guilt with learning from your past. If you are learning from your past and trying to avoid repetition of negative actions, you are not dealing in guilt. Learning from your mistakes is healthy. It is an automatic by-product of growth.

It is possible to use guilt to transfer responsibility for your behavior to some other person, and so it can be used to avoid working on yourself in the present moment. Guilt is not merely a looking back, but the inability to take a present action because of a past event.

Guilt can be used to victimize any person who teaches others (the exploiters) that he is vulnerable to control by guilt. In this way, any person can manipulate another's Now-ness with references to the past. If you are a victim of guilt, you need to learn how to defuse this reaction. Remember, guilt is not a natural human behavior but a socially-learned emotional response and as such can be unlearned. Learn not to be manipulated by it. You have taught others that they can manipulate you, now teach them that you have taken control of yourself.

Begin to see yourself as someone who can do anything that fits into his personal value system. If you do something and then don't like it, or yourself, afterwards, then simply eliminate that behavior. Also, do not confuse worrying with planning for the future. One is detrimental, the other essential.

Guilt and worry are the most futile emotions. In one moment in time, eliminate them both. I say, and this is a near quote, that it is rarely the experiencing of today that drives men mad, but the remorse over yesterday and the dread of tomorrow. Whether you look backward or forward, the result is the same, since these are simply different sides of the same coin: with either choice you throw away the present moment.

Don't opt for guilt over freedom. You can learn to savor pleasure with no sense of guilt.

3. Sense of Humor

You need so desperately to develop your sense of humor. Since it is not possible to laugh and be angry at the same time, use humor to lighten your burden and to short-circuit anger.

It's quite true that it is healthier to express anger than to store it up, but from another view, not allowing yourself to choose anger is the healthiest choice of all.

Since anger is a result of thinking, you need to change your thinking, to learn to think in new ways that are not anger-provoking. How exactly can you dissipate your anger? By learning to postpone it one minute at a time until you postpone it right out of existence.

It is helpful to know that anger is not just a habit, but a choice as well. Since you have the choice, make it.

> *The single most outstanding trait of the healthy person is a sense of humor.*

Much anger stems from wishing the world were different. Accept the world for what it is and relax. Relax.

Don't burden yourself with inflexible rules. Resist meaningless policies. Blind adherence to rules, yours or others, may be more destructive than blatant violation. Lincoln says he never had a policy that he could apply generally, so he just tried to do whatever made the greatest sense at any given moment.

Don't be so serious about everything. Enjoy the multitude of blessings that surround you. Take a lighter view of everything. Nothing is as important as it seems. Laugh again. At key points where your life is punctuated with stress, laugh at the foolishness of the situation instead of losing your temper. Be flexible. Forgive yourself. Laugh and let laugh, for laughter needs no reason for its existence, it simply is.

Remember, the single most outstanding trait of the healthy person is a sense of humor.

4. Directness

Be direct with yourself and others. Remember, you alone determine what rules of behavior you can honestly live by. Do not lie or distort the truth to keep others from being upset with you. Simply say what you mean. Be honest to yourself as well. Don't delude yourself into thinking that you are any more or less developed than the next person.

The doing of all things is only important to the doer. If you maintain unimportant actions to impress others, i.e., for some external unseen audience, then it is essential that you turn your focus inward and find out what things are most important to you. In the end, you know, all of your experiences will be judged worthy or otherwise by you.

> Be the actor, not the critic.

Stop expecting and anticipating a revolutionary change in your behavior. Realize that there is, in fact, no such thing as revolution. All things evolve, but when any given evolutionary change has a dramatic ending it is called revolutionary. If there is no drama, the evolution is not marked in any way. It simply continues.

Be a doer. Do anything. You are less what you say than what you do. Be the actor, not the critic. Be one who lives by acting, not by thinking about acting, nor by thinking about what he will think when he has finished acting.

All acts are of equal importance. This the wise man knows. He also works the ordinary work of the ordinary man, except that the folly of his life is under control. He chooses any act of any kind and acts it out as if it mattered, which it does, and yet at the same time he knows it really does not—the paradox of the actor acting out his life. Whether his acts were good or bad, whether it worked or not, is in no way his concern. He works while he works and then he is done with it. He is left in peace.

Do something. Do anything. You might say you are in Earth training to learn that it doesn't matter what you do, it only matters that you do.

Still, you must keep balance and remember that not all doing requires 'action.'

5. Self-Control

To what degree is self-control possible? Do you have total control, no control, or something in between?

It is completely possible for you to have total control over what enters your head as a thought. Consequently, you can control all of your emotional (e/motion) reactions because you cannot have a feeling without first having experienced a thought! A feeling is a physical reaction to a thought. So, you see, an emotion is not a condition but a choice, and you are fully capable of feeling whatever you choose. When you see this and really understand it, you begin to have a firm grasp on your quest for personal freedom.

To feel whatever you choose to feel and not be cast on the turbulent, unpredictable winds of fate! Such a new beginning. To never feel victimized again!

Again, you control your feelings indirectly by working on the thoughts that come before them, with the full realization that you can learn to think differently about anything. Thus, by taking control of your mind, you can challenge yourself to alter your behavior, to change your personality. You can decide never to be tired, bored, lonely!

You don't ever need to look outside yourself once you have assumed all responsibility for your thoughts and feelings. Remember, you are responding externally if you shift the responsibility for your emotional state to someone else. It is never what other people do that bothers you, but your own reaction to it.

You'll need to practice new responses. You get good at what you practice. A thought cannot become a belief unless you work on it repeatedly. Once you learn new mental habits, you will never again renounce your freedom of choice by allowing someone or something external to yourself to control you.

Tell yourself exactly when you'll wake up each morning. So much oversleeping is psychological. Once you take the controls, you will trust yourself enough to forget the clock. Try it, you'll love the illusion of power it gives you once you have succeeded.

Tell yourself never to tire, never to be bored, never to be sick, never to be anything but what you choose to be. Being tired, for example, is nothing more complicated than a bad mental habit. Change it.

Boredom is very unhealthy. All people need a little spicy uncertainty to keep their lives interesting. But where will this spice come from? It is up to each person to seek it, to find it, and to add it to his/her life. Never forget that boredom is a choice. Don't choose it any more.

You'll know this is specifically for you as soon as you read this. You are guilty of responding externally when you assign the responsibility for your 'standing still' to anything or anyone outside yourself. Why is standing still so terrible (not 'being still,' that is totally different)? Because the only evidence of life is growth, and the only barometer of growth is change itself.

Now you need to analyze this: Are you motivated by your potential for growth or by your need to repair discrepancies?

Loneliness

Conquering loneliness can be a delicate procedure. First, you must define loneliness as a feeling of separateness, of not feeling connected to anyone or anything. Second, you must remember that you control your thoughts and they create your feelings, so to feel differently you have to change your thoughts. So take hold of yourself and gradually exchange all 'lonely' thoughts for 'alone' thoughts. Being alone and being lonely are never the same, even though they often occur simultaneously. Because they happen together so often, people confuse the two or attempt to interchange them. There is a quiet desperation to loneliness, wherein the person is consumed by a feeling of helplessness. Aloneness, on the other hand, can be a positive time of inspiration, rejuvenation, and growth.

Once you realize that every individual really is both separated from humanity and connected to it, you can enjoy both realities fully.

Choices

Understand the say you have in your own destiny. Fatalists may credit luck, but in fact successful, growing people usually make their own luck. But don't feel overwhelmed. Being effective does not mean eliminating your problems. It means handling them creatively and efficiently.

Stop waiting for others to change. Stop waiting for the world to change. Don't fall into the trap of believing that you can't change human nature—there is, in fact, no such thing as human nature. You are a result of your choices. If you make positive choices, your life will change for the better; if you make negative choices, you will stumble and fall. The more successful your life, the happier you'll be and, as a fringe benefit, the happier you are, the more intelligent you will become. And since you're in the driver's seat, you can decide how bright you would like to be and steer yourself in that direction. Sounds unbelievable? Think about it. It is totally possible, and very probable.

Procrastination

All growth, especially consciously directed growth, requires one thing from all people, and it requires it absolutely: you need to eliminate procrastination.

Can you? Of course you can. You just need to be systematic while you're learning new habits that do not require strength, only perseverance.

Procrastinators constantly talk about how much they have to do, but they rarely do anything. Multitudes of projects, ongoing at all times—but only in their minds, never coming to fruition. Being busy is no excuse. Busy people get things done. Unfortunately, 'putting it off' as a life style is a way by which one can avoid doing indefinitely. To put it off is to avoid the doing of it, any doing of any it. The anti-doer only watches, analyzes, and philosophizes about what others are doing. Doing requires risk and change. Do you often comment on the performance of others? Do you ever perform yourself?

Procrastination can be a convenient escape from Now. Beware, even boredom can be a spinoff of procrastination. If you constantly put off the action, boredom fills the void.

Truly, people who love themselves don't hurt themselves by creating anxiety through procrastination. I quote again: Is putting off living any way to live?

A first step is to designate fifteen minutes per day to devote exclusively to some job that you have been putting off. Work toward setting aside an hour. Very shortly you may actually find yourself looking forward to this time.

Review

1. *To achieve happiness, do these five things:*

   Stop searching for justice and fairness.
   Work to achieve psychological and physical independence.
   Stop blaming and complaining.
   Love yourself; show that love by eliminating self-defeating behavior.
   Realize that you must make your own happiness in this life, as in any other.

2. *To develop now-awareness, be a doer, and defeat guilt and worry by existing only in the Now.*

3. *Develop your sense of humor. Learn to laugh at yourself, at your situation, at your whole world. Use laughter to short-circuit anger.*

4. *Always be direct in all you say and do.*

5. *Learn self-control. Then you can rid yourself of such things as boredom, tiredness, sickness, failure, and even procrastination.*

Some final words

Becoming a totally healthy and free person requires only that you learn to think differently.

It's easier to say 'I'm sloppy' than to clean up the mess. Likewise, it's easier to say 'I'm very emotional' than to choose the hard work and risk involved in changing your thinking regarding how much say you have over your own emotional life.

If you can't use it, lose it! Especially if the 'it' you speak of is your own value system. If the rules and principles you fall back on don't accurately reflect your present reality, it's time you break away and formulate concrete new rules to live by. So what if you do this over and over for the rest of your life. Changing is far more realistic than the stagnation you would otherwise be forced to endure. Your rules must be based on what actually works for you, not on what you hope or wish would work.

Turn off your fear of failure forever. Failure, in fact, does not exist. Only action exists. Remember, failure is only someone else's opinion of how something should be. It just does not necessarily have any direct connection with what is. Action is, and that's it. No special requirements need be met.

Trust yourself. The only true security anyone ever actually has is a result of self-trust, a trust that makes you know that you can handle absolutely anything life presents to you.

When all is said and done, it is less whether you can take the controls, and more whether you ever really will.

Well, had I been there, I would have expressed some strong opinions and asked for dozens of clarifications—and I would not have had an uninterrupted and unfragmented recipe.

Over time, this little cookbook became a welcome source of advice and an effective agent for change. Often, after having thoroughly exhausted myself wrestling with some problem, I would consult the cookbook and compare my actions or reactions to the appropriate recipe. Being shown a better way after the fact, I found, can sometimes cause more anger and frustration than not being shown a better way at all. But just being reminded again and again how easy it could be to change negative responses that I considered to be an integral part of me, was soothing and comforting—even if I did the same silly thing a dozen more times.

O

12 Patterns Made Long Ago

I don't remember much about my childhood, and I am not one to dwell on it looking for reasons for this and explanations for that. What little I do remember is mostly pleasant, although the circumstances might not seem that way from today's perspective.

I was born into a German community in 1940 in what was then Romania but is now the Ukraine, just north of the Romanian border. I spent the last two years of WW2 on the road, so to speak, part of the flood of millions of Germans fleeing from Eastern Europe. What was left of my large extended family finally stopped running in a little village in Northern Germany that later wound up in the Russian zone, where we somehow managed to get through the first tough years after the war.

I don't really know how the adults did it, I only remember helping to collect food for lots of rabbits in cages, and chickens and turkeys running around, and tending cows on large flat meadows with deep little ponds where we caught sunfish, and picking berries and mushrooms—nice warm images.

Little boys had lots of free time. We played Cowboys and Indians in the woods, and went on expeditions to find leftover stacks of munitions—I'm serious, picture a bunch of little Teutonic warriors dressed up as Apaches (they were our favorites because of some book, I think), with war paint and feathers and bows made from hazelnut bushes, the whole bit. Sometimes we would find a German or Russian helmet with holes in it—a great place for a war chief's feathers! When we found treasures like mortar shells or even bigger stuff, we would pour out the powder and make piles, then throw lit matches at them from behind trees while yelling our heads off in Apache war whoops. With German accents, of course. Can you picture it? Delicious memories.

I guess there must be unpleasant things buried in my mind somewhere, but I don't remember any. I probably accepted conditions and events of those times as normal and therefore didn't make a big deal out of them. In any case, I have never felt traumatized in any way by those days, as far as I know.

Except for one situation, and it is this memory that was awakened in me by Orifi's words and filled me with discomfort and anger and at least some recognition that my life was indeed being influenced by what was planted in my sponge brain at that early age.

There were very few men around in '45 and '46. Most were either dead or not yet back from POW camps, and so when one of my aunts took in a former soldier who had lost a leg in Russia, he assumed the role of the traditional male head of the family for this flock of women and kids. He was a bitter man and I didn't like him, but he was a powerful presence for me—and this was his favorite way of recognizing my existence: At dinner, with all of us gathered around a long table, he would ask me to make faces. Yes, funny faces. The weirder, the better. And he would reward me then with an outburst of roaring laughter.

I hated it. I was mortified by it. And yet, I swear, I was also proud of myself! It was I, little Freddie, who was making the Big Man laugh so hard! It was, of course, the only way I could get him to notice me at all, the only way I could get his approval. With all the women working hard to feed everybody, with my parents dead, this s.o.b. somehow made me dependent on his approval for my emotional food, and I am convinced that whatever fragile self-esteem I had was blown away by the humiliating behavior I engaged in to get that approval. Ohhhh, if I could get my hands on that miserable ... Orifi, can you find him up there and strangle him for me?

And now I was being told, 'Erase your childhood!' Just like that. Remarkable.

O

13 On Learning

Classroom dreams continued. The settings differed but the theme was always the same: I'm late for a class, worried about getting embarrassed or reprimanded, worried that I might flunk a test because I had missed a lot. I settle into a seat and begin listening. Nobody pays attention to me. Everybody is intent on learning. And always, on awakening, there is not even a hint as to the subject matter.

Orifi, meanwhile, seemed eager to teach me about learning itself. I was certainly interested—in a get-smart-quick scheme, that is, not in a gradual process. Since that wasn't happening, I found more satisfaction in daydreaming about lights in the sky and lotto numbers than in thinking about learning. He, however, persisted.

"You must begin to understand the learning process and how exactly the old mental set is, by evolution or revolution, replaced by a new one. Don't be impatient. Change is always slow in the beginning."

"Not just slow, but damn near imperceptible."

"You know what you want and you know what you need, but you know not how to get either. So you refuse offers to get you what you want—because you do not recognize these offers as a means of getting you what you want, which of course is what you need, amen."

"What offer have I ever refused? I would jump on an offer instantly if I recognized it. You could give advice on how to do that."

"Only you can recognize. I can only put offers before you. Learning to trust your own judgment is to invite comfort with the fact that you can function and accomplish in spite of the unknowns."

"I have a better idea: Tell me tomorrow's stock prices so I can make easy money! Hmm? Then I could stop spending so much time and energy working and commuting, you know. Why don't you? What's the reason? Sometimes I get completely distracted, to the point of pulling out my hair, when I think that you could change my financial situation by doing me such a tiny favor!"

"What you think of as drudgery, that is, your job, is an avenue for great spiritual advancement. It is not taking time away from learning. It is a tremendous opportunity for learning, if only you could stop resenting it and start using it.

Knowing human nature as you do, please picture for me, if you will, what would happen if I were to begin to help you make money, on the stock market or otherwise. How much luck do you think I would have in holding your attention to other, less worldly, pursuits? How much enthusiasm do you think you would have for such work as ours if your other choice was to make millions of dollars a day? Of course it isn't impossible, but it is most improbable that I will ever join you in an endeavor such as this. The end."

"Not fair. You haven't tried me. I would pay ten times more attention to you than I do now."

"No comment."

Finally!

The truth is that I did quite a bit of nagging in those days about this marvelous idea of predicting events for the very practical purpose of making money. One day I was especially annoyed at his steadfast refusal to cooperate and so I suggested, somewhat sarcastically, that he just do one innocent little thing for me: pick the winners in the weekly NFL office pool. Very little money involved, mostly bragging rights, so what would be the harm?

"Let's do it, sounds like fun," was the answer (by phone). I was in shock. I couldn't believe it. My hand was shaking as I recorded the picks. I was convinced that this was the beginning of something grand. My imagination ran amok.

Sunday took years getting there. I was in some state. As the afternoon unfolded, I experienced emotional gyrations that I can only describe as rare. My poor ego—it tasted levels of embarrassment and humiliation that were truly magnificent. I just knew that the entire universe of invisible jokers was having a great time at my expense.

So how did I do? 0-11-1. No wins, eleven losses, one tie. Mathematically, of course, just as impressive an accomplishment as 11-0-1 would have been. So while the point was made about what's possible, it was also a clear 'not gonna do this, Freddie.' Ouch!

Learn to fish

"Very good, oh Powerful One. You are magnificent. What can a poor little earthling do but acknowledge your magnificence?"

"I do feel something akin to guilt because of my serious efforts to drown you in your own soup. You persist with this money business for three reasons: First, you are standing on the brink of demanding immediate proof from me; second, your ego, human as it is, still seeks to impress others; and third, any form of gain, most

especially something as tangible as money, would give you a real sense of accomplishment as well as one good thrill. I'm not judging your motives, simply stating them.

I spoke to you of learning. Now I must speak again of motivation. If I give you race results of any sort, you are dependent on me—and yes, dependence in any form really does breed contempt, ultimately. If, however, I teach you to get your own results, you will be at once self-motivated and independent and eternally grateful to me. Once your motivation is internalized, you will feel limitless in your power.

You have a saying that puts it very well: If you give a man a fish, you feed him for a day, but if you teach a man to fish, you feed him for a lifetime."

"Yes, true, but I don't think it applies. In order for me to be motivated to learn to 'get my own results,' I have to first believe that I actually have some prospect of succeeding, and I don't know if I believe that. Seems so improbable. You haven't shown me how to pick winners in advance, and, besides, there are limits to what a human can learn, no? Don't tell me there aren't, it just makes me nuts.

I guess I'm just afraid I'll never learn to do anything very differently from the way I've always done it. Maybe I'm afraid you're dangling carrots in front of my face as part of some devious training method of yours."

"A quiet, unassuming little word lurks in the English language. It seems harmless enough in the writing, but in the living—this one word devastates, cripples, even paralyzes man. The word is f-e-a-r. It is a reality he rarely admits to. 'Hidden' fear is at the root of most downfalls in the history of civilizations."

"Yes, well, it is definitely part of my reality, as when I think of 'getting my own results'—and know that I can't."

"You're like your comrade Carlos. (He's referring to Castaneda, whose books I was reading.) You often take imitation grape sugar water when you could have fine wine. You are in a position of

unlimited possibilities, and yet you look at your situation from an insideout point of view, always annoyed by its shortcomings, rarely even aware of its potential possibilities."

Pick one thing

"Exactly, rarely even aware. And what can I do about it? I don't choose to be 'rarely even aware.' At least not that I'm aware of! I want to learn a million things, but I also feel that it's silly to want that, and I'm afraid that asking you all these questions makes me feel like I'm begging for cookies from Mother Orifi."

"External reassurances are an important part of learning and do have something to do with testing ideas in the real world."

"But the world is so big, O, and there is so much mystery. It just seems foolish to try to understand anything."

"If the world seems too big to comprehend at times, remember you can 'see the universe in a grain of sand.' Apply this principle. Choose one thing, any one thing, and delve so completely into it as to lose yourself. Become so completely immersed in it that you see how all things work in relationship to it."

"I don't think I know how to do that. Choose anything?"

"Anything can teach you everything, yes, about psychology, sociology, religion, even medicine, etc.
It is not silly to try to understand everything. It is simply best to attempt to do so by focusing on just one thing. If you try to understand everything, without this focus, you will understand nothing. The field is too broad to isolate truths if you scan the horizon at random. Pick one thing.
Growth leads ever onward and inward and outward, as does progress. Remember, you will make progress at times in spite of yourself. It is the way of all things, animate or inanimate."

"Well, that's good to know. But I have to tell you that because of your thoughts on subjectivity etc., I don't know how valid any understanding is any more. So what if I pick one thing and understand that thing fully—will that understanding still be valid tomorrow? Tell me, is there any possibility of some kind of external 'truth' at all?"

"This is another big question. The answer is simple: absolutely yes and absolutely no, in equal proportions.

Where you are now (i.e., in time) there is a peculiar blend of subjective 'truth' mixed with objective reality. The scale moves in degrees from most nearly objective (math) to most completely subjective (poetry or dance). Most humans tend toward subjectivity. Generally speaking, those whose dominance is in the rational (linguistic) lobe seek more objective expressions of their energies, while those who function more readily from the intuitive lobe tend toward subjective expressions. Obviously, to compare these opposite types, or to compare their exterior truths, would give us conflicting information about the exact nature of reality. Still, there is genius at both extremes.

How subjectivity and objectivity function is a result of the physical experience. Outside of the time-locked physical experience they have no meaning."

"In other words, there is ultimately no such thing as an objective reality, as you've said before. The notion of 'objective' is merely a tool to make the physical experience possible, yes? Fine. Then what about my 'inner' truth? You've talked about having trust in one's own inner truth. What does that mean?"

"Trust grows out of experience. If your inner truths never let you down, you grow to have faith in them. With faith comes trust that they will serve you in the future. In time, if you haven't come to trust your truths, you must examine them and determine whether they are indeed true.

There is nothing wrong with this process. Not every hypothesis becomes a law. Time and experience will tell."

Desire for extraordinary experience

"I don't know what my inner truths are. Isn't that peculiar? I have to learn how to recognize my own truths?

Now tell me this: If I have a strong desire for some extraordinary experience (and I do, as you know), is that somehow a denial of personal inner truth?"

"Only if your personal inner truth tells you that you are connected to no thing and no one greater than yourself. I can tell you that you are an integral part of a vast network in which all things, including energy, seek to achieve balance through action and reaction. A desire for extraordinary experience is simply a healthy expression of your need to see just exactly how you fit into the greater scheme of things.

Inner truth can actually be expressed to you through extraordinary experiences. The denial would come should you fail to open up to such experiences out of fear that this could necessitate a change in the basic structure of your inner truth system. If your inner truth tells you that you are nothing more than what you experience yourself to be, then your inner truth is false.

Remember, you are eternal. You are not your body, you are not your mind, you are not your opinion of yourself, you are not the opinions others hold of you, you are not your id, you are not your ego—you simply are, here and now and forever you are. I know you know this."

"You are speaking to the 'total' me again. This is new to the conscious me. And unfathomable."

"There is nothing new under the sun, Schwab, only things that reach your consciousness for the first time—so they seem new to you.

Remember how you puffed up with pride, as early as seventh grade, to find that almost every significant question you had ever asked yourself had already been asked, eons ago, by the great philosophers? Why were you so surprised? You are all human. The great philosophers had no secret knowledge that is unavailable to you. They lived on the same planet, saw the same things, had the same aspirations, the same fears, the same desires, the same motivations—in short, all the same raw materials with which to build their world view. That you landed at thirteen where they ended their lives should not be surprising either. That's progress for you!"

"So. I'm glad to see that exaggeration is not an exclusively human specialty. I did no such landing at thirteen, not in my conscious awareness. I sat on a hill at night with my friends and hotly debated where the end of the universe might be, and, if it did have an end, what would be beyond it—but that's about it, you know?"

Do your work now

"No, that's not it.

For awhile now, you must hand the reins over to me. From your point of view, time is of the essence.

Relax. It will be great fun for us all, especially as we gain some momentum and things finally begin to fall into place. I know many of your questions, over a long period of time, have been left hanging. Soon you will see why."

"I think that even with your intimate knowledge of my mind, you really don't know how much I want 'things to fall into place.'"

"You need to organize your thoughts and use your experiments as springboards for new ideas, as well as a guiding force of sorts that will bring focus to your work if you let it, and speed certain necessary realizations. I repeat, don't diminish the importance of these exercises just because they are far from lofty. From the most simple experiences spring great inspirations and resultant enlightenment.

While you integrate information, sometimes from diverse areas, start to investigate the functions of the two sides of the brain and the two aspects of the mind. The information must be separated, dissected, studied vehemently, then reintegrated into a system that makes sense on both the rational and intuitive elements therein."

"Sometimes I wonder about your work assignments."

"What you now consider to be rather useless information may in time be invaluable. So do not discard anything. Please realize that you are really in no position as yet to distinguish between important and unimportant. This is not a reprimand but rather solid advice that will help us all. We are learning together, remember?

Why don't you begin by attempting not to label anything as a priority over anything else."

"Fine, but I repeat my earlier remark: Not only is everything subjective and therefore totally befuddling, but everything seems absurd, unreal. Nothing is real any more, not even my own thoughts, not my existence, nothing. That's the state you have brought me to."

A mental enema

"This isn't resignation creeping across your face? Let's hope not! What exactly is the problem? Are you bored, exasperated, frustrated, discouraged, lonely, spent, or worse: defeated, depressed, immobile, stagnant, quite simply uninspired?"

"You bet your skinless bottom I am, yes, all of the above. Can you think of a few more adjectives, maybe?"

> *You are the architect of your reality, remember?*

"You are constipated, yes, all clogged up.
The very cells of your brain are clogged with your own backed-up waste. You need a few sessions of diarrhea of the mouth to clean out your pipes (I know you don't use it this way, but I do!).

The key to your personal freedom is the enactment of your personal free will. You must be the impetus, or at least the catalyst, for this enactment.
Don't sit, don't stare, do something."

"Like what, pray tell?"

"Do this: make a list of:

The ten people that are most important to you
Your ten most important positions
Your ten most important possessions
Your ten most important ideas
Your ten most important things to do

Put the list aside for six months, then write out a new list without referring to the old, then compare the two.
I want you to do this, it is important."

"Positions?"

"Those extremes where you make a commitment, take a stand.
Let's forget questions and proceed with the work you say you're so eager to do. Choose one hour per day to be absolutely alone and try during that hour not to think at all. You really need to do this.
As I said, you are a bit clogged right now, with entrenched old ideas mixing themselves with half-formulated new ones. Give yourself that well-deserved and much-needed mental enema."

"Do you have any prune juice for the mind? But you're right. My mind is stuffed with your ideas. Saturated. Basta."

"I'm thrilled to hear this. Now maybe you'll venture out and try testing a few new ideas to see how they hold up in the world of action and reaction.

Much of your problem stems from boredom and lack of stimulation. You need to do some sorting out. I can't do that for you, no one can. It's time to spend some serious time with yourself."

"I'm not sure I want to. Talking to you is more exciting. Spend more time with myself? Hmm."

"You are a warrior, too, you know! A warrior never needs an audience. (Referring to Castaneda's writings again.) His consciousness is his audience, and his judgment alone determines what he will learn and how he will learn it.

Don't be so afraid to compare yourself to the best there is. Don't wait for the ball to come to you, go for it. The minutes of the warrior's life are eternity. They are his greatest asset. He knows this. Mimic his motions. Imitate his life.

You will never move far from where you are until you surrender completely, and you don't seem about to do anything of the sort . . . soooo, you tell me."

"And what does 'surrender completely' mean?"

"It means stop being afraid to try on a few altered states of consciousness to add to your thus far limited experience. Why are you so afraid? You tell me."

"I'm not aware of any great fears. What are they and where do they come from? I don't remember putting them into my mind."

"Your life put them there, as all lives do. Your job is to recognize them, then get rid of them, mentally or verbally, in any way you can. Rationalizing will not dissolve them. Sincere meditation will. Try some. Fasting will, too. It's real."

"I'm not good at meditation. And fasting? For a diabetic? Anyway, so fears keep me from replacing old mental sets? But I don't even know how to recognize them, for heaven's sake, much less how to get rid of them. What a mess!"

"Yes, you are the builder of walls. Fears are your bricks. Still, since you are the bricklayer, you can take the walls back down. How? One brick at a time, just the way you built them. If you continue to build walls and never tear any down, you will eventually wall yourself in, and fears can then surround you. But you can tear the walls down."

Yes, start before you're perfect

"I don't feel surrounded by fears. I feel like my mind is stuck in molasses, in some thick cloudy stuff that allows my thoughts very little movement. I actually worry about this strange question: How can I work on unclouding my awareness when my awareness is still so clouded?"

"Indeed why not? It is perfectionism to the negative extreme to say that one cannot learn about love when one is unloved, cannot learn about morality unless one is perfectly moral. Likewise, it is a contradiction to say that one cannot experiment to uncloud one's awareness as long as one's awareness is clouded. It's like not being able to get a job without experience, but how can you get experience if you can't get a job?"

"Good point. But, you know, I am now convinced that learning takes place on inner levels where my fears, whatever they are, don't have the power of blocking. All these classroom dreams, for instance. I think that what I learn there will eventually trickle into my conscious thoughts, bypassing my deep fears. So why worry about removing them?

Talk to me about this interesting dream I had recently that also seems to deal with learning.

I became aware of myself lying on my back reading a large heavy book that was propped up on my chest. I read and understood, even though the script was not one I knew. Then I started wondering about why I understood it, and promptly stopped understanding. Then the rune-like characters disappeared and I was staring at blank paper, increasingly disappointed and annoyed with myself. Then I woke up.

What was that about? Did you see this dream or was it just me?"

"Yes, and no, it wasn't local. Others have had it, many times. Eventually you will all read and understand this writing, though doubtfully on a conscious level, since the script is ancient. Still, the information it will provide will be invaluable in bringing new insights to your work and thought in general. It just does not matter whether you know or remember what you read, it matters only that you see and absorb the contents on some level of consciousness.

Yes, learning is not just a conscious process."

"I hope that whatever I'm learning there gets to me here soon. Why is it such a slow process? Such a frustrating system. Anyway, how does the book get to us, and what language is that? This is so exciting to me."

"I can see you would be interested. It does not get to you, rather you travel to it when you need to know what is written therein. The language is Celtic, and an ancient variety thereof. Strange you should suppose that it came to you."

"Don't you know? I am the center of the universe and everything comes to me.

It's so intriguing to think of learning something in my dream world, and then have it pop into my conscious mind some fine day! How I wish I could access that world at will, to rummage around in dusty piles of ancient books, learning and learning and learning, and then merging it all with my conscious data files! Like the MERGE command on my computer at work. Now that would be a fun kind of learning, in contrast to the laborious, sweaty way I learn consciously."

"Indeed. Relax.

Rarely have I ever given you news of me. I move along, too, you know. I am like a balloon ready to burst in my anticipation of the newness to come.

Learning comes to me in stages, as to you. First the exhilaration of newness, and the infatuation with it! Then the deep quiet of information assimilation. Then another surge of newness, further assimilation . . . and so on and so on. And, ultimately, love. Yes, love. The beauty of the love stage is its foreverness.

> *Love is one of the best building materials you can have on any plane.*

Forgive this outburst, but now I find that sharing is somewhat as exhilarating as the news that is shared, especially among comrades such as we."

"Outburst? You're a beauty. Isn't 'outburst' a physical, emotional affair? So how can you experience one, oh unfortunate one without a belly? I know, these words are for my benefit. Same with comrades and sharing. But I love the sentiment, as you knew I would."

Go steady like the eternal sound.
Flow steady like the eternal light.
Grow steady like the eternal thought.
First go, then flow, then grow.
This is not poetry, this is process.

Light is a good crossroads.
It can take you up to thought
and back down to sound.
Likewise, sound can take you up to
light and back down to self.
Likewise, thought can take you down
to light and up to ultimate self.

To go is not linear.
To flow is not linear.
To grow is not linear.
A line is time.
A circle is timeless.

To go, feel sound.
To flow, see light.
To grow, invite thought.

O

14 Just Begin!

This was a time of much introspection for me. Memories of past behavior, attitudes, experiences, and feelings paraded through my mind, to be scrutinized and judged according to the advice in the cookbook, that Five Easy Steps recipe. As I saw more and more clearly just how much redesigning I should be doing, and how slow the learning process was, I became deeply frustrated.

In any case, the recipe giver wasn't overly impressed by what I was doing with his advice—which was: I thought about it a lot—and was ever ready to prod me along.

It's time you tire of old habits

"Try very hard to stop acting in the same old circular way that only brings you back to where you started, never ahead. It's time you tire of old habits, break out of yourself and learn some new reactions. It's not just time, it's overdue. A new point of view will show you a dazzling world that you never knew existed. It will lift the veil and introduce you to unlimited new possibilities.

Schwab, I have nothing to gain from your spiritual advancement, one way or the other. Therefore, I have no ulterior motives here. I simply need to drive home to you the necessity of not always relying on the same old methods. Same thinking over a period of time digs a deep rut. Eventually you will have to climb back out.

Smile at yourself in the mirror. Take a deep breath and start over again.
Don't just read this, do it. And relax."

"Easy for you to say. I agree with the need for a new point of view, but wanting one doesn't automatically give me one. I do sense changes in my thoughts lately, but I can't say exactly what I mean by that."

"Yes, on changes I say that many new insights come to you these days in a strange fashion, like memories. Many seem like fragments of some long forgotten dream. New perceptions though they may be, they come not to you in that form. Any strange familiarity you feel with new knowledge is as it should be for now.
Unconsciously, you know exactly where you are heading."

"Why only unconsciously? Why does my unconscious keep secrets from my conscious? I'm tired of this arrangement."

"Remember, there is no coincidence. It does not exist. It, too, is simply a figment of language used to describe physically what is not confined to the physical plane."

"Yes, well, that's still a tough one. Very tough."

A Feather

I don't know about new insights, but I did keep trying to incorporate this 'there is no coincidence' statement into my everyday thinking. As one part of my brain became convinced that the assertion is true, another part remained extremely reluctant to accept it. So I practiced by simply repeating this notion to myself again and again, in every kind of situation, trying to make it sink deeper and deeper into my awareness, trying to apply it whenever the situation called for the usual 'oh, that's just an accident.' I was even proud of my progress at times.

I found it difficult to sustain this effort for long, however. It exhausted me mentally, and so I often avoided it altogether for long periods of time. You wonder why? Next time you squish a squirrel under your tires, or get a speeding ticket, or double an investment in one month, say to yourself immediately, 'That was not a coincidence. That was not a coincidence.' And then, of course, try to picture for yourself what kind of reality might be implied if, indeed, it was not.

I was reading Illusions by Richard Bach. There's a little story in it about a feather appearing under mysterious, illogical circumstances. One of those synchronicity tales, like Jung's scarab beetle incident. I love those stories. I have always feasted on any kind of hint that things are not altogether what they seem to be.

Anyway, I took the book to work one day and read the feather tale. I enjoyed going over it in my mind on the way home. As I walked into the dining room and was about to put my briefcase on a chair, I froze and felt an urge to jump out of my skin. I remember walking around, mumbling and hitting myself on the forehead. Because there, on the dining room table, all by itself for added impact, was a big feather. I'm not kidding. A stupid feather, lying there on my table.

Now consider this: I have never in my life come home to find a feather on my table, never—only on that particular day when I had been reading the feather story. What might the probability be that this was a coincidence? Yes, I asked myself that. I love talking about probabilities and such, makes me feel so scientific. But forget even considering any such explanation in this case, it's just too ridiculous. It occurred to me then that it was actually more logical to think that an invisible gang arranged it all! And that thought, so help me, was still really tough to deal with. For my logic center, that is. Another part of me was, by now, chortling with delight at such 'winks.'

This particular wink administered a bigger-than-usual jolt to my mind, because I was in one of those complacent and smug periods when I would spend a lot of energy discussing all this wonderful stuff I now thought I knew—as long as it was just words and had little to do with me. But they never let me hide under my rock for long, those skinless jokers.

Why was the feather there in the first place? That's easy: my son Mike was involved in some Boy Scout project. Nothing mysterious, all perfectly normal.

Every mind builds its own universe

"It is extremely important for anyone seeking new planes of reality to come to an understanding of the subjectivity of all reality. This understanding does, in a very real sense, put you in the pilot's seat and at the controls.

Truly, in the realm of mind your selective objectivity builds the world in which you exist. Therefore, it is important that you be selective and choose only the positive point of view, because you are now gathering the materials with which you will build your new universe. Yes, every mind does in fact build its own universe. This is, however, far less evident in the lowvibratory region, that is, the physical plane. Since mind is the only reality in the next plane, you will have access to all that you have gathered in this physical world.

Remember, you are only capable of building a Godcentered universe for yourself if you allow your mind to function as a tool of your highest spirit. Once this relationship has been established, you will experience only positive, thus amassing a vast storehouse of materials for building your own greater reality.

This is not a futuristic thing but is ongoing here and now."

"I don't know what all that means, and it makes me uneasy. Statements like 'building a God-centered universe . . . '—isn't he already the center of every universe, even if I haven't made him the center in my thoughts? What difference does it make whether I do or not? Old resentments block new thoughts in this area. This whole God business is very difficult for me."

"Yes, I know. Eventually, you must understand more about this 'business.'

As I said, you are on the flat side of the upward spiral, or in the gathering stage. What you gather now will determine where you end up in the next leap."

"Orifi, I'm not aware of much constructive gathering, you know."

"You spend more energy worrying about this random gathering. Try to become aware of as many possibilities as you can. Now is the time for the nonlinear approach because you will need every possible avenue opened to you. Later we will need focused attention on the goal, but this is not necessary yet."

"Nonlinear approach?"

"Expansion in the manner of a balloon—in all directions at once."

"Sure wish I had some tangible sign that something is expanding."

How you long for proof

"Yes, you know you cannot deny your deeprooted desire for proof. How you still long for that physical, visible sign to show that superior knowledge and power of yours. So important is this transient knowledge to you that you desire it more than wisdom. Knowledge of rational and intuitive lobes is interesting, as is knowledge of rightmindedness, leftmindedness, language, art, music, math, etc.—but transient, as all knowledge, and only a temporal tool to gain temporal knowledge whose only real function for you is to promote eternal wisdom. Yes, wisdom that you will keep with you through all eternity.
Ego grows. It seeks selfaggrandizement, humanistic focus, glory. It is fed by the things and events of the material world. It functions out of selfpride, never humility. Spirit grows out of the unthing—the unseen, invisible, intangible world. In the material

world you can truly make things happen. In the spirit world, you need to learn how to let things happen. Again and again I say this to you.

Man displays his human nature by his unquenchable desire for proof. Proof is of this world. Belief without proof is faith. Faith is of that invisible world."

"I like being human. So quench my desire."

"What aspect of intuitive functioning do you see most clearly acted out in your existence? Your scribe writes. You sing. So use your material tools for spiritual motives: sing—until you feel yourself let go, until you feel the surge and the ecstasy when music comes through you, not from you. Be swept away! You need to feel this surge so you can truly 'know.' That will be your proof. Then, once you understand the process, it will begin to slip into, or splash into, other areas of your life.

Listen to the athletes of the Olympics. It is no coincidence that they speak of 'the surge,' 'letting it happen'—and yes, yes, their unanimous goal is to relax, before and during performance. Afterwards, to let the joy show! Yes, relaxed anticipation. Relax."

"That's all very exciting. But I feel like a groper in the dark, vaguely sensing possibilities, aching to experience what I sense. I'd love to throw myself into this surge of yours, head first. Why would anyone not want to? Why can't I?"

"You will as you must—when you can—because you should—because you must. Seriously, think about that."

"What I'm thinking is that you're lucky to be without a neck."

"Relax. Come just as you are—with your worries, your doubts, your conflicts, your fears, without and within. Dare to submit, to be swept away by that surge. You will never be lost in losing yourself. This is an eternal truth. Being part of the total flow does diminish your ego, but never your individual selfhood.

111

No path to heights can be effortless. You must be willing to function like a snake in the springtime, willing to shed the old skin to prepare for new growth. Remember, no matter how beautiful and strong and perfectly symmetrical the design of the old skin, you have always liked the new one better once you adjusted to the loss of the old."

"It's true. But it always seems to be such a troubling time, often painful and unsettling. Why?"

"Because growth needs understanding of all levels of human conditions."

"All levels? Forget it. A scary idea! I can think of a lot of conditions I don't care to know more about.

Just a veil

And, by the way, wouldn't it be a hell of a lot more efficient if you spoke to me directly? I've been meaning to bring that up again. Now that would be a new beginning! What blocks that avenue?"

"Our transmission is received. Why do you speak of blocks? There are no blocks."

"But there is something. Come on, what is it?"

"Only the veil of an illusion for the protection of the status quo."

"Who needs it?"

"You think you do."

"I do not."

"No comment."

"One of these days . . . Anyway, what is this veil of an illusion?"

"It is, as it implies, simply a veil—not even a material reality, but more perhaps a psychic protection that will rise of itself like mist does when the heat of the sun's light hits it."

"When? When will it rise? I don't want to wait. I want to see you and talk to you mano a mano until the wee hours. You hear me? Such a dumb thing, to spend time waiting."

"You want to die? Each breath you take is one breath closer on your side to being on our side."

"Who said anything about dying?"

"You inferred that some change is necessary for you to see me. I suggested dying if you want just that."

"You know, seriously, sometimes it's tempting. What harm would there be? In this soup of 'infinite intermeshed continuums,' where death is an illusion and we are all connected etc., what harm could it cause? I'm serious. And you know that something is necessary for me to be able to see you."

"Yes, but it isn't death. And you're right, no harm would be done—if you don't mind disobeying your creator and shooting water holes in a beautiful scheme."

"Orifi, come on, what kind of foolish statement is that. I know, it's another one of your devious methods to get me to think about one thing while another thing is being carted into my brain through a back door. Not nice."

Infinite choices

"Relax. Continue until the path changes direction instead of considering changing paths. You know that much of your so-called free choice actually performs on a subconscious level anyhow."

"You don't have to convince me of that. But what's a path? And why do you say don't change it when decisions about choices are made at other levels? I feel like a dummy."

"You know what a path is. The word is of your language, not mine. Of course you can change a path. What you can't change is where you will end up, regardless of the path. In any case, there are paths of different quality, and it is up to you to choose one."

"It is hard to see what you mean by choice. To have a choice implies that I have alternatives to choose from, and that I am aware of these! Blindly taking a road when I can't see any others, or can't see where it leads, is not 'choosing.'"

"Choices are based, as choices must be, on any catalog of facts that is available. 'Letting it happen' applies to choices just as it does to circumstances. No, don't ask, just think about it for a while.

You just don't seem to realize your own infinite choices. Choices, as it turns out, are the most difficult aspect of freedom. With them comes the inherent responsibility to choose.

You needn't limit the scope of your choices to just those things that you consider to be your talents or gifts. You might really surprise yourself if you stepped outside your own selfimposed limits to try something new. New patterns are always a healthy alternative. Remember, your mind rejoices in the opportunity to try new things. The more new ground that is broken, the more new space is opened up for exploration. It's fun. It can be a new hobby for you to delve into. Seek nonverbal things like 'picturing' things in your mind's eye, or hearing music that isn't there, or even remembering a certain touch or a certain smell. You can use your senses as the gateway to a new universe—and learn to enjoy, not fear, soaring.

Try to picture what your motives would be had you no senses at all. Very difficult to imagine, but it can be done."

"Impossible. But these are exciting ideas. I'll try them.

By the way, I have been meaning to tell you that I feel good lately, full of life and energy, despite my grumbling. If you could only see me, Skinless One, you would be jealous—tall and handsome, mmmm. Where is that buddy of yours you once mentioned, the one you called my 'guide?' I want to tell him these things, and make him wish he were me, in the flesh."

"Indeed, he is not in your muscles, nor in your stature, nor in your sight of yourself, but in your mind's eye as a reflection of your spirit."

"Not in my body? Too bad. It wouldn't be a bad place for him. Anyway, how is anyone a reflection of my spirit?"

"How else but by accurate mirroring in the mind's eye, where true reality rests."

"You know that I have no idea what that means, and I don't think any further words would help much. I'll come visit you, then I won't have to burden my head with 'mind's eye' and such any more, agreed?"

"Come on over so I can look at you."

"Here I come . . ."

Sure. But how I loved that invitation! 'Come on over so I can look at you'—what a wretched, and yet wonderful, thing to say. I had butterflies in my belly when I allowed myself to consider it a real possibility, even if only for a second.

Exercise: Mirror

"You never did one very, very important exercise from long ago. It's very simple, but not very easy to do. It's even spooky in a way.

Look yourself in the eye in a mirror! Time yourself for one minute. Let your mind run where it will. Look away for a minute. Then stare for another full minute, repeating, 'Who am I, who am I.' Never let your mind drift away from the idea 'who am I!' Now stare for a third uncontrolled minute. Afterwards, try to recount your thoughts during that last minute, then compare them with the thoughts of the first minute.

Surely you will find these minutes to be very long ones. This is natural, as it should be.

This is an exercise you should repeat again and again over the course of a month or so. It will help you to separate ego from self in a very real way. And if it doesn't scare you at times, you're not concentrating.

This is one of those 'trick' exercises that demands performance on the physical level but is actually having the most impact on a far deeper level of your existence. Don't discount it as frivolous, silly or meaningless this time! I have a better point of view from which to judge the importance of any given exercise, trust me."

I listened this time, and did this little exercise every now and then. I've tried repeatedly to put some words together to describe my feelings and impressions, but when I'm done my effort invariably feels incomplete and somehow inappropriate. Try it.

Try a new point of view

"You are still trying desperately to gather up knowledge. Stop it. Anyone can do this. With the mass accessibility of computers anyone can gather vast knowledge at the touch of a finger. You need to learn to see that knowledge in a new way, to try a different point of view, a new perspective. You don't need hundreds of notebooks and hundreds of books. And it is not enough that you

understand and agree or disagree with an author. You need to use the blend of his/her ideas and your own as a jumpingoff point. As in thesis, antithesis and new thesis; idea, opposite idea, new idea. From the knowledge that passes your consciousness, pick and choose those elements that will act as an impetus to new ways of seeing and thinking about yourself and your world.

Remember, there is nothing new under the sun, only new ways of looking at old things, new ways of dealing with old problems. Herein the ordinary becomes extraordinary! Boredom ceases to exist. The mental process begins to invite inspiration.

You can't change your world, but you can change your role in it. You can make dynamic new analogies between common things and thoughts. Better yet, begin to practice howtodo's. Only through handson, practical experience can the creative impulse begin to reign free, can you see your ideas grow into practical realities. The translation therein, in and of itself, can truly inspire you, can lift you to a new view of your world, can teach you what works and what doesn't."

"You know what? You make me ache with impatience. Your words get me so worked up, so eager, I feel like a runner in the starting blocks. And there I stay. The gun never sounds. I don't get the information I need, or whatever, to jump off. You know?"

"The information is everywhere, free for the taking. Relax.

Dip your fingers into the pool of life. Do as much as you think about doing and you will feel truly uplifted. The only true joy on your planet comes from creative living. That joy surges through your very blood stream when a creative impulse grows into a physical reality."

"Yes, that's what I want! There have been small tastes of this joy, and that's what I really want. Point me in the right direction, O, and I'll never ask you for anything again."

"Remember I told you to get clay and mold it? You didn't. But you should! So many of the seemingly useless pieces of information I have given you are not.

Stop contemplating beginning. Just begin! You are over-prepared as it is!

Loosen up and live. We are not to enter a phase of mystical deprivation here. We are simply to redirect our tremendous energies toward goals loftier than mere exercises in logic, which we have amused ourselves with so far."

O

15 A Knock

I was in the basement garage to get wood for the fire in our fieldstone fireplace. Some of the pieces seemed too big to me, so I got the axe to make them smaller. I love splitting wood. Especially when somebody is watching. Take a huge piece of hardwood that seems too big for any human, bring the axe up high overhead, then down in a sweeping arc accompanied by a manly grunt, and thwack!, right through to the block . . . what satisfaction. (Some claim that hardwood splits as easily as a piece of ice, but what do they know.)

I am good with toys like axes and chain saws and table saws, etc. Somehow, I'm always aware of what they're doing and which way they might jump, and in all the years of rebuilding houses and reshaping the land around them I have never as much as nicked myself. It's true. You need to know this to appreciate the strangeness of my behavior this night: Without preparation or thought I raised the axe and brought it down on a piece of wood that was lying across another piece, like a seesaw. As the axe hit one end of it, I went into one of those time warps where seconds become minutes and I saw, in slow motion, the jagged end of the wood coming straight towards my eyes. Time, however, was stretched only for my vision. My body did not react at all and the wood slammed into my skull right between the eyes. I was stunned. Then the pain arrived and a string of fine words left my mouth totally of their own initiative. And then I said to myself (I often do this, really) that there is no coincidence, none—and I started laughing.

I was still laughing when I opened the door to the living room with an armful of wood. My wife Linda and Mike and John, who were on the couch together watching TV, turned toward me, stared, then jumped up yelling and pointing at my head.

I must have been some sight: Standing there cackling to myself, totally ignorant of the blood flowing down on both sides of my nose, with a big red spot right where the Hindus paint that marriage dot. You know, where the third eye is supposed to be.

I knew that I was thickheaded, but could I really be *that* dense? What a crude way of trying to knock sense into a guy! It was embarrassing. I pictured the sweet gang up there concluding that I needed this kind of shock to get me to pay attention, or whatever their devious purpose might be. The image made me cringe.

Stop being stubborn

"I should probably thank you, beloved sheepdog. Some day, when I understand more, I'll thank you. And listen, since you perceive my physical world through my senses, does that mean that you feel my physical pain, too? I hope so. No, you probably 'read' my pain, right? Not fair."

"I must ask this question: Why do you incessantly ask, but never listen?

Ask me no questions that you have asked before. No more rehash. I simply will not answer. You're just being lazy if you can't even formulate a new question. No more daydreaming and empty wishful thinking. You haven't even begun to scratch the surface of the volume of information you have received in these past months. It is important information, and quite elaborately designed so as to stimulate you without overwhelming you. Stop being stubborn.

I must elaborate on those experiments again, as they are very necessary right now to keep your mind occupied with some productive and positive and pertinent ideas. If you can't or won't focus, I can and will focus for you. I need to lead for now.

And remember that backtracking is essential in all scientifically conducted investigations. If you refuse to think or look back, you will never proceed beyond a given limit in space and time."

"What are you talking about?"

"You are childlike in all the wrong areas. You always want just one more tidbit, and then you will buckle down and get serious—but it's one more thing after another, after another, after another."

"Yes, master."

"Get your mind out of old ruts and start to make some new grooves in your ever-willing, ever-waiting brain."

"I rush to obey, master."

Lighten up!

"You have a problem: you want a change. More specifically, you need a change. You seek that change with every fiber. You want answers, not more questions—yet the questions continue to pile up and up and up . . ."

"What questions? I haven't asked many lately. I've been a good boy."

"You fool no one. I see many. Here are some of them:
Should you be passive and wait for a change to be born of its own? In other words, should you wait and wait and show great patience or should you be the aggressor and actively seek change? Even be the impetus? Should you ignore problems or analyze them? Should you try to learn from each one or simply let them roll off you like water off a duck's back? Should you advance or retreat, jump in or jump out, go with the flow or buck the system? Watch or participate, move forward or move back, or possibly

just do nothing? Is it possible that you should watch (but one step removed) and participate? Advance and retreat at the appropriate times? Ah, but when is each indicated?

What should you do? How should you do it? Should you listen or speak? Or listen while speaking? Or speak while listening? What? How? When?

You're confused. You're stressed. You're just plain tired. You're tired of hassling yourself. You're tired of thinking and overthinking. Right now you're just plain tired of everything. So enough gobbledygook. Help is what you need and I'm here to give it to you. Seriously."

"Have mercy. I hope you're not setting me up for something. But I'll listen."

"How do babies learn language? By imitation. How do animals 'learn' survival? By instinct. How do scholars gain knowledge? By studying. How do scientists learn? By trial and error! You are more a scientist than a scholar, so you should rely on the method that is most appropriate to your natural inclinations, i.e., trial and error.

Try things. Do things. Find out what works for you and what doesn't. Do anything. Try anything. Experiment with your world. See things, touch things, smell things, hear things, taste things—in short, sense the world you live in. Involve yourself directly by doing. 'Busy hands make quiet minds,' and we both know your mind could use a rest. Give it a break, will you please?

Experiment until you get back to that place where you still knew what your gut instincts were, then use them.

Play around, have fun, and for God's sake (and your own) lighten up! My summer assignment for you is to have fun learning, so do it! Try it, you'll like it! I know I enjoy it.

Here are a few ideas:

A summer assignment

o *Repeat any common word ten, twenty or so times until its sound seems absurd, until you feel yourself about to laugh out loud, then go ahead and laugh.*

o *Play puppy—crawl around and bark, slurp water out of a bowl, feel how it feels to be unable to open a door, hold a fork, zip a zipper, etc. Castaneda's dog of light, remember?*

o *Count your material attachments, then drop one a week for a month, later more.*

o *Write a profile of yourself, an honest account; physically cross out what you hope to cancel.*

o *Stare at a white light until you can make light shadows around anything at will.*

o *Play touch therapy with a friend; be honest.*

o *Make new patterns from old ones; the patterns in a curtain, in shadows, in clouds . . .*

o *You know you never did this exercise: Look at yourself in the mirror, shifting eyes, for five minutes a day; five minutes a day is worth a lifetime of other study.*

o *Walk briskly; increase distance.*

You never try any of these things. Why do you ask if you don't intend to do? You amaze me. How many exercises have you ever actually physically done?"

"You exaggerate. I have done some things. Not enough, I agree. And why is that? I will be more disciplined. Yes, I will play puppy. That sounds like a lot more fun than getting beaten up by you."

O

16 One Hundred Questions

Not long after the knocking, sweet O promised me a 'real' reward, a reward in my physical world, as soon as I would answer every one of a hundred questions he had prepared for me. A big stick between the eyes one day, a carrot the next. What a hard task it must be, it occurred to me, to coax a human (and a Taurus to boot) into changing his ways—and I confess that I felt a quiet sense of satisfaction at the thought that the invisible gang might be sweating from the effort.

Anyway, I laughed at the promise, being familiar by then with his method of keeping me busy with some assignment while something else is going on. But when I saw the questions, I was hooked, and made sincere efforts to answer them. I have gone back to this list again and again over the years, fiddling with one answer, changing another completely, or adding thoughts where there had been only blanks.

Yes, I've found it necessary to change answers from time to time. This used to surprise and even dismay me. I suppose when you are truly sure of some opinion and identify with it, and then, maybe five years later, find that opinion to be outdated, or irrelevant, or even wrong—it does make you wonder how valid your present opinions will be five years hence.

I've found this 'exercise of the hundred questions' to be an effective tool for crystallizing vague opinions, and for proving to me that my beliefs were changing.

Here they are:

1. *Who are you?*
2. *What are you?*
3. *What does physical pain feel like?*
4. *What does physical hunger feel like?*
5. *What does physical thirst feel like?*
6. *Describe how water tastes, looks, feels, smells, sounds.*
7. *Describe red, yellow, blue.*
8. *Do you have a goal in life?*
9. *Do you have a plan for that goal?*
10. *What is your favorite color, song, food, sport, book, movie, hobby, form of relaxation, era in history, time of day, time of night, season, holiday, type of humor, state, country, planet, star, and person?*
11. *Why do you procrastinate the most with important, even urgent things, while you race like a fool to meet meaningless deadlines?*
12. *What has poignant meaning for you?*
13. *What kind of people do you like best? Least? Indifferent?*
14. *What is your favorite quiet pastime? Your most exciting and stimulating?*
15. *Why do you think you need physical proof for things?*
16. *Should you die tonight, what would you call your greatest accomplishment in life?*
17. *Is there any issue, or any person, that you truly believe you would die for?*
18. *Are you more angry with God or with the religions that cloud Him?*
19. *Do you even believe in God?*
20. *Why do you resent Jesus? Is it possibly because he was the God-man you would like to be?*
21. *Do you think there's anything innately wrong with loving, or wanting, or having beautiful things?*
22. *What does the word 'supernatural' mean to you?*
23. *Why do you consider only your waking life as real? Do you think it's possible that the sleeping life is, in fact, more important?*
24. *What do you think is the spiritual reason for sleep?*

25. Describe what you think it would be like were the Earth to meet an abrupt end. Then do the same were it to die of old age.
26. Why do you create your own guilt?
27. What was your mother's name? Your father's? Any siblings?
28. If you were God, what would you do differently? Be honest.
29. What most threatens you? Scares you? Intimidates you? Irritates you? Stimulates you? Agonizes you? Overwhelms you? Entices you? Bores you? Thrills you?
30. What, on Earth, do you cherish most?
31. Describe for me the physical sensation of crying. Of laughing.
32. What does addiction mean? How is it different from a simple bad habit? What are your bad habits? What are your addictions? Are there any you like and enjoy?
33. What do you like most in yourself? In others?
34. Is there any one thing you feel you could do forever with ease? (not sleep!)
35. What is your favorite animal? Why?
36. Give six adjectives that most clearly describe these aspects of your life—a. physical b. mental c. spiritual
37. If you could only change one thing in the world, what would it be?
38. What legacy would you like to leave your children?
39. Do you know how to pray?
40. Is there any period of your life that you would like to live over? That you would never want to live over?
41. Do you sincerely believe in inspiration? How do you describe it?
42. What does 'why' mean? 'How?'
43. Do you understand the relativity of time?
44. How are words and money alike?
45. In general, what smells good to you?
46. What animal would you be if you had to pick one?
47. What is your favorite fruit? Vegetable? Meat? Fish? Drink?

48. Can you feel the tremendous effect light has on your physical system, or is it too subtle?
49. If you could choose one person out of all who ever lived to converse with, who would it be?
50. Do you think all illness is psychosomatic?
51. How does sunlight feel on your face?
52. How many of your verbalizations are self-protective? Ego-protective?
53. What other invisible force, like electricity or magnetism, can man harness and control to his benefit?
54. Describe the implosion of an idea.
55. What do you use to pace your energy?
56. What makes you cry?
57. What is the most nostalgic thing you can think of?
58. Why do you think evil exists in the world?
59. Does the moon affect you directly?
60. What do you think is the best thing you can do for your children?
61. To what better purpose do you think TV could be put?
62. Are you able to relate in any real way to world hunger?
63. What do you think is the function of fantasy in life?
64. Do you hold any deep secret?
65. What brings you anxiety?
66. Who do you know who has the IQ of a potato chip?
67. What do you think about symmetry in nature?
68. Describe an itch.
69. Does dissonance irritate your ear?
70. What does 'futile' mean?
71. Do you prefer symmetry or asymmetry in art?
72. What does 'intimate' mean?
73. What is the most obvious experience of inspiration that you have ever had?
74. What does 'connotation' mean?
75. What is the greatest thing words have ever accomplished?
76. Describe physical motion.
77. What does 'apparent truth' mean?
78. What masks do you most often wear?
79. What role do you most enjoy?

80. What do you think is the most dynamic force in the universe? Most powerful? Most negative?
81. Is lust ever positive?
82. What is arrogance?
83. What is confidence?
84. Describe soaring.
85. What does it mean to view your pain through a magnifying glass? Your virtues? Your downfalls?
86. What is your feeling about the sun?
87. Describe infinity.
88. Describe a candle burning.
89. What does 'sense of urgency' mean?
90. How would you describe peace?
91. If you had unlimited talents and resources, what would you most like to do?
92. Describe the physical sensation of a burn.
93. Again, what does 'why' mean?
94. Describe yourself when pregnant with anticipation.
95. What is the only part of the human body (besides hair and nails) that continues to grow throughout life?
96. When is jealousy good?
97. If you could live forever, what would you do with infinite time?
98. How are you most like a watermelon?
99. Do you think the human consciousness of self is a blessing or a curse?
100. Describe impatience.

O

17 On Destiny, Free Will, and Time

"Orifi, I've been brooding lately about this business of fate and destiny and mission and free will, and who decides what and when and where—and it's all impossible to understand from my time-based perspective, you know? For instance, how can fate and free will exist together? What meaning does it have to speak of choices if there is such a thing as destiny? Oh, so we choose our destinies, too? Not on this level. Not with this will."

"To consider fate (destiny) and will, let us assume for now that destiny takes care of the spiritual realm, and that man's will deals directly with the mental realm. It is in this arena that he can and should exert his will.

As you think, so you are

As a man thinks rationally in his mind and intuitively in his heart (actually, the other side of his mind), so he is. He literally is what he thinks, his character being the sum of his thoughts. Just as the plant springs from, and could not be without, the seed, so every act of man springs from the hidden seeds of thought and could not have appeared without them! In this very real sense, man is made or unmade by himself, by his choices.

Every thoughtseed, whether sown consciously or allowed to fall into the mind, will take root there and produce its own fruit when opportunity and/or circumstance allow. It is a simple truth that good fruits grow from good thoughts."

"I like that! Every act springs from a thought-seed—so if I adjust a thought, I change an act, and all the events that are spawned by it. Bonsai thoughts! A little pruning here, a little binding there, and before you know it, my reality reflects my wishes! But can this really be true? Consciously?"

"Yes. So learn to observe your thoughts. Then learn to alter them, and eventually to control them. For instance, if some inappropriate ones slip past you, you can negate them, neutralize them, after the fact, by simply explaining to yourself that they are 'not of your choosing.'

I urge you to trace the effects of your thoughts upon yourself and others, upon life circumstances. Then learn to link cause and effect by patient practice and investigation. Utilize every experience, even the most trivial. It's fun. But also remember that your job, ultimately, is to weed out 'bad' (unproductive) thoughts.

You will only feel helplessly lost if you consider all things to be controlled from outside the self.

That man is at least master of his own thoughts is reassuring, and that he is the molder of his character, even if only in part, is ultimately to his benefit. He does not make his total environment, but he can shape the conditions that surround him by his thoughts (attitude). You hold the key to every situation within yourself. Such is the master of man: his conscious mind itself."

"Hard to believe. Really, really hard to believe."

"Man can find every mental truth connected with his own being if he will only persist and dig deeply enough into that being. The resulting selfknowledge is regenerative, even transforming.

Please think again about the percentage of brain power man actually employs. Fortunately, no one is limited to that. There are easy, obvious ways to expand the amount you are using, either gradually or suddenly, via an evolutionary change or a revolutionary one. Both are equally possible.

Consider that your brain, used at full capacity, could 'outrun' every existing computer—could, in fact, run the whole world alone! But don't get power hungry. Just realize what you're dealing with when you delve into your own mind."

"Not to worry. In fact, as I do a little delving right now, I feel more silly than empowered. And a little worried. Everything swirling around in my head takes root and grows fruit? Some fairly inconsequential things are going on in there, Big One. With a brain that 'could outrun every existing computer,' this is what I plant in it? But, on the other hand, they are fun, my little thoughts. I'm confusing myself more and more. I'm getting this really absurd feeling of being in awe of my own mind. Who, for God's sake, is experiencing this feeling? Isn't it produced in that very same mind? Mind standing in awe of itself? One small piece marveling at its own total self? Help . . ."

You attract what you are

"Relax. Confused is good. Forget it for now.

> *Man does not attract what he wants, but what he is.*

Remember, circumstance does not make the man, it reveals him to himself. Man does not attract what he wants, but what he is; not what he wishes or prays for, but what he justly earns. His wishes and/or prayers are only gratified or answered when they harmonize with his thoughts and actions. To fight circumstance is to continually fight the effect (the symptom) without changing the cause, which is in his heart (the other side of his brain).

When sick, for example, most people are willing to spend large amounts of money to 'cure' symptoms, but refuse to expend one ounce of effort on changing the real cause of their illness: poor thinking, translated into poor action. Thus the individual, out of harmony with himself, causes suffering.

Order (law), not chaos, is the dominant principle of the universe. Good always produces good. A negative attitude never attracts positive possibilities to itself. Anger hardens the world. Positive thoughts soften it.

Kept in the proper 'frame of mind,' man will find that unlimited opportunity actually pursues him!

Time

Any discussion of fate must, of course, include a discussion of time. Examine, if you will, the relative quality of time. Let me say again that you must gain first-hand knowledge of relativity and probability as they appear through physical form. Remember that in physics the theory of relativity describes the character of matter, velocity, and space in relative, never absolute, terms. And matter, time and space can only be described by their interdependence on and relativity to one another.

You must know this, too—you all must understand it—that time condenses (collapses, compresses). In other words, it speeds up. This is true of any action or event, no matter how simple. It is much simpler to conceive of in physics than in psychology, but is equally true for both.

And simplistic as it might be, it is important to recognize your own role in the process of expanding and/or contracting time. Learn this concept and apply it to your everyday life. The new control gained can make you feel exhilarated by the simplest of tasks. There is such joy in 'newness', and you can find it in every situation. Find it and revel in it."

"These are such exciting ideas. Say more."

"Yes. You have grappled with but have yet to grasp the nature of time. Relax—time will reveal itself to everyone eventually. You need only wait, as this process is automatic.

The Now

This discussion of time, of course, also deals directly with the concept of Now-ness. Allow your mental concept of Now to remain in a state of flux until direct experience gives you some foundation in physics upon which to create a realistic picture of Now—the eternal present we all hear so much about and understand so little of. No one and no thing exists outside of Now. The past can only be remembered, never relived, while the future can only be conjectured about. And if you insist upon looking to the future, you can never capture reality as it rests in the Now. You should have the quick, sharp realization that the eternal Now is all there is. You can go through levels and changes, etc., only to realize that it is all right now.

You must understand, as I said before, that we can only discuss Now in terms of time and space as these react with one another, and that outside of the reality of human perception, past, present and future are not relative to one another because they are not, in fact, separated from one another.

From your ponderings on that place where opposites meet in sameness, you do have some grasp of Now-ness. Now is more a container than an event, more a description than a thing."

"I don't have a 'mental concept' of this Now at all, so there is no way to keep it in flux. It is a complete mystery to me. I have built all kinds of pictures to try to deal with it, but they keep falling apart. So why bother any more?"

"I would say it would be most fruitful for a human to learn everything he can about time for as long as he is contained within it, but he should keep in mind that the knowledge he gains in this reality cannot necessarily be applied to other realities as he encounters them.

Live right here and now to the fullest and you can't be anyplace else mentally. When you find the real meaning of Now and practice living with it, you will thank the creator for what you already have and will never again think of having more. You can't have more love, only more time. When we all function from outside time—and you will—you won't need time. You will be able to deal with situations not in the past, present and future, but in the Now. And functioning from outside time is not a distance change but an attitude change."

"An attitude change? You mean a perception change? Anyway, so I'll simply spend time waiting in time, and then, one fine day, I'll be outside of it?"

"The more you live in the Now, the more control you gain over time itself! There's such fun awaiting you. Start now!"

"I don't know how, as I told you. You know the books I've studied. You know how I've tried to grasp the ideas of Tarthang Tulku about time (Time, Space, and Knowledge; Knowledge of Time and Space), tried to experience them through his exercises, without much success.

By the way, how can this Tibetan come out of his mountains and teach physics courses on time and space? What's the story? What is this thing with Tibet?"

"There is nothing you haven't already heard over and over, said in a thousand different ways. By its nature, truth presents itself in multitudinous ways until it has made itself glaringly obvious to everyone."

"Truth 'presents itself?' It keeps chasing us, popping up in front of us while we frantically look somewhere else? A funny picture.

Anyway, time, to me, is a linear process, always going from one 'point in time' to the next. My brain works that way. I just can't imagine an event—and isn't everything in this universe an event?—that does not have duration! No matter how short or how long, or relative to what, or objective or subjective, it must have duration! It lasts. It starts and it ends, whether you squeeze it or stretch it. Yes, I can play with the idea of shrinking a time segment to zero or stretching it to infinity mathematically. But that's playing. It is not real to me. I don't know of any way to get my brain to jump out of its linear mode of operation.

This notion of your Now—I can only speculate and wonder. I wonder what you see living outside of time, in this Now. What can it mean? How far back can you see when you exist in this eternal Now? But there is no 'back', and no 'far,' right? Big One, how much do you see?"

"I know everyone who ever was or ever will be, in your dimension and all others. It is my reality to have such knowledge."

"I think you're pulling my leg now."

"Just another classroom, Freddie. I can also experiment with physics, as you can."

"Ah yes, how could I forget, this is just one of many classrooms. No big deal. Tell me, can I walk out of my present classroom?"

"Of course. You wrote the script, you're the producer, director, and actor."

"I see. And I can keep on making new choices as I go along? I can choose or not choose to experience, let's say, the appearance of aliens into the particular society I'm in? Because such an event is just another classroom?"

"Well, it is not really quite that simple. You can't experience them if they are, in fact, not there. You can hallucinate them, but you can't see them. You see, you don't run "the" universe, you only run yours. You can choose among many different things, but you can never make black into white in any mind but your own."

"Yes, but I can choose not to experience them even though they are here.

Nevermind. Forget aliens and Nows and let me go back to that very personal question that really bothers me: why did I give myself diabetes? It infuriates me. It dominates my thoughts and drains me of energy. I realize it may be the perfect classroom for me, expertly designed for my growth requirements, much like plant foods designed for specific plants. Maybe I'll see the beauty of it some day, but for now, I hate it. Even as I suspect that in my rage and refusal to accept may lie its ultimate lesson, I still hate it. It is a stupid choice. And it could be a severe physical handicap later. Which, of course, could contain another dose of growth material! Oh boy."

"No. Your consciousness will most definitely be struck with the emphatic realization that the transitory (physical) state can be overcome with the use of that higher axis I spoke of."

"You mean this damn disease can be overcome? Orifi, I don't think I want to hear this, because I really really want to believe it, yet the evidence, well, I don't have any yet that I recognize, so this is something I'll just not think about."

"Please consider seriously the very real fact that what you perceive is happening is what is happening. Consider it."

"Explain it again. I do occasionally consider it, but it just seems so far-fetched."

"Your thoughts, and what you perceive as true, do in fact create your own separate reality.
Yes, I know that this question of designing your own reality is a confusing one. The further question of shared illusions is even more so. To understand shared illusion, you have to gain some practical experience with ESP, since it is always easier to grasp a new concept once one has a bank of experience to draw from. I can lead you to the ESP experiences you will need."

"I hope you mean that. But tell me this: Where do my thoughts originate? They seem to just appear somehow. If you, for example, put some seed thought into my head when we meet during sleep, as you have said you can do, then it is you who starts that particular thought sequence, no? And aren't you thereby affecting the reality I'm creating for myself? And I merely pick up the ball and run with it? Where is my free will? This is really baffling."

"It all happens as a chain reaction, going in either direction. Confusion is fine, as I said before. Eventually, you will get it.

Consider that your spirit has its own spark of creativity, that it can, in fact, create an idea from a unique conglomeration of thoughts.

You must participate

When you disclaim free will and make yourself the victim, a mere pawn of fate, you give up responsibility for your own transformation, because this attitude implies that the people and things around you, your circumstances, determine your actualization. To actualize the possible, you must participate intimately. You are responsible for directing your 'human' life.

Now, the life of the spirit needs, seeks and usually finds divine direction. The actions and thoughts of your life weave together this divine direction with your human direction to create a pattern of infinite variety and possibility. Your direct involvement in no way inhibits the spontaneity or vitality of living in the moment—in reality, it is only your direct (emotional plus rational) involvement that makes your life yours.

And remember that this exchange between us is not some static collection of provable answers. The critical, rational approach alone can never answer your deepest questions about human existence. Any approach that fails to account for the intuitive nature of man can never be fully adequate. Reason, for example, can describe light, but only intuition can understand it.

The question you really want answered about fate is: Did I choose this physical existence I now call 'myself' or did some higher power choose it? In other words, was it choice or was it fate? This varies with individuals. It is not consistent, as you had hoped it would be."

"I did. I'm always hoping for some consistency from you."

"The answer is: This particular choice was not written or fated but was optional, and you chose it for specific reasons that you are now beginning to remember consciously."

"I am? You are speaking to my total self again, the one that must have decided that I should experience diabetes. And so I should be happy about it? Because this choice is perfect for me in every way? When I meet this 'real' self, I will punch him in the nose for some of the choices he stuck me with."

"Marvel at what you are and at how multitudinous your positive choices really are.
Your job is not so much to build your identity, as to reveal it (a sculptor might say: Find the man inside the marble). In this exploration you have many guides, human and otherwise."

O

18 There Is a Purpose

"Why don't we know ourselves? Why do I have to 'find' myself? How and why did I lose knowledge of my true identity? I say again, this is a strange arrangement. Anyway, this particular life plan of mine includes some specific goals? Let's talk about this now. The exercises you gave me are designed to help build a bridge, you said, between my conscious mind and my total mind?"

"Yes, exactly, and more: A bridge between physics and psychology, between religion and science, between rational and intuitive, between black and white, young and old, good and bad, big and small, etc."

"I like the first three pairs, but after that it gets a little murky.

This is such an exciting idea for me, to have a goal. But the fact that you know this makes me very nervous—because you may be feeding my ego to inflate so much that it will explode with a bang heard throughout all kinds of 'intermeshed continuums,' all the way to where you are. Merciless One, it is so tough to take this idea seriously. And yet you also know, of course, how much I would love to take it seriously.

This goal . . . Orifi, can we talk about a more modest one? I just want to learn more about myself, and then pick the lotto numbers."

"Relax. Now that you have finally gone back to review *rightmindedness and leftmindedness, you should correlate as much of the information as you can to this real physiological process (building the bridge). It has much to do with the creative process and tapping the mainsprings of inspirational thought at will.*

You could read more of Jung soon to save yourself the need for human verification. Try Symbols."

"Jung? So, you know how much I liked Memories, Dreams, Reflections. How I would love to dive into this collective unconscious of his, and maybe tap some mainsprings there!"

"*You want too much too soon, which is apparently quite human. But you have little conception of the true vastness of the thing you are now irrevocably taken up by.*"

"How could I? I don't have the advantage of your bird's eye view."

"*Stop worrying about the grand plan, the overview, the way of things, and begin to use the minutes of your existence to learn very specific and concrete things about yourself and your world, that is, what works and what doesn't work in the realm of practical physics and psychology. These things you can only learn while here. There is all of eternity to philosophize and wonder and ponder, or just guess, but there is only right now to master your own unique reality. And I repeat myself—just do it.*

I feel that if you would stop feeling guilty about random thinking and learn to let it occasionally take you, you would approach your goal with more zest.

The goal: a symbolic language

Our (yes, our) goal is not only to formulate a language by which your subconscious can translate unconscious material to you, but also a system in which you can relate to the supraconscious via symbolic language."

"And what is the supraconscious? We now have 'supras' and 'supers' and 'subs' and 'uns.'"

"Nothing ever makes sense when some puzzle pieces are missing. Just be a sponge and soak it all up. We'll wring it out of you when we need it."

"That's funny. You'll wring it out of me? I like that. Doesn't make me feel much like a participant, but I like it."

"I will find some way to bypass your intense anticipation and then we will truly begin to find our way. If I can keep you busy enough, you won't notice much of the translation process. You will wake up one day and say, "Now I see it," and feel the flush and rush of inspiration in that moment, even though it has taken many years to bring you to that point. You will experience it, complete in a single moment in time."

"When? Why can't it happen tomorrow morning? Make it happen."

"Continue your experiments now, and record everything. It is important. Why have you stopped doing them? And your urge to write is a good impulse. Do it! You are not less inspired just because you are unaware of the inspiration, you know. Relax.

Let insight find you

Don't let others tease you into examining and analyzing every little experience. Rather, still a portion of your busy mind so that insight might find an easier avenue into you, through you, and back out of you. Insight is only a living element when it is in motion. You can't hold it for yourself to make yourself seem more important to yourself. No you can't. It's like water returning always to the ocean, in an endless cycle.

Don't try to earn the right to be a spiritual seeker. It is a gift. Just open it up and say thank you."

"Spiritual seeker? I'm not aware that I'm trying to earn the right to be one. A strange statement."

Don't flee; meet yourself

"*Turn around and meet yourself rather than fleeing in fear. Surrender to yourself, to the light inside of you. People (you included) hate the word surrender because they take it to mean 'give up.' More accurately, it means 'stop fighting!' These are not the same. People also fear a lack of selfcontrol. They will eventually happily realize that when they surrender, a higher control automatically takes over, to the benefit of everyone.*"

"And I still don't know what that means. I'm not fighting, and I have no idea what you want me to surrender to."

"*Try to relax away from your relentless pursuit, to allow truth to catch up with you. Leave a quiet little corner in your mind where 'the reality' can take root in you. Leave another quiet little spot where you can realize its presence. If you can accomplish this, you will not corrupt or distort your moments of spiritual insight.*"

"Any insight brave enough to come to me has to swim through my soup of beliefs to get to my conscious awareness. Poor thing probably doesn't recognize itself after it gets through."

"*All have blinders, whether they see them or not. Such is the nature of selective receptivity.*"

"We are digressing from the discussion of goals, no?"

"*No, I am describing methodology. Relax.*

It is, as you now realize, not a coincidence that you constantly receive printed verification of your own innermost knowledge."

"Yes, and it drives me nuts. Can't you stop it for a while and just let me enjoy my reading?

I've been running into articles about projection, as you know. I'm very excited about it lately, for some reason, and you have mentioned it as a key to growth and practical application."

Projection

"Yes, astral projection (I prefer simply 'flying') holds many keys that will be needed to unlock that door to the other universe that awaits mankind's experience."

"Say more."

"Your work has found a focus without real effort on your part."

"I don't know that I am focused on it. I don't know how to 'work' on it. I am just dying to experience it!"

"As I said, without real effort on your part."

"Thanks. Your praise for my efforts always lifts me up.
Seriously, I have no idea how to begin. None. When I read Monroe's adventures (Robert A. Monroe, Journeys Out of the Body) and similar accounts by others, I get frantic with envy. And now I see hints of it everywhere—in ancient writings, in religious texts, in poetry both old and new . . . Orifi, am I seeing it even where it isn't? They're going on flying expeditions everywhere! Everyone but me! How I would love to pack my bags, take a couple dozen notebooks, maybe some fruit and energy bars, and go!
Do you have any advice regarding method?"

"Yes, indeed. Realize that when you project you are in fact simultaneously leaving and not leaving. That is, you are not projecting to a place where you are not, you are simply shifting your focus of consciousness to the other place where you are right now. Consider it.
Let me give you my list of specific suggestions before we go further:

- o *Remove all expectations from your mind.*
- o *Don't concentrate; instead, unconcentrate.*
- o *Focus on your limitations, i.e., analyze all of the mental sets you carry to the other reality with you.*

    ○   *Try not to carry information with you; do try to carry information back."*

"Super. Rarely have you given such concrete information. Let me think about this before asking more questions. God, how I wish I knew how to unconcentrate."

"What you need most to do now is to simply stop trying. Whenever something is new, it moves through stages. Projection is not new, only your involvement and interest in it is. You have done enough gathering. To try to do anything at this point would be counterproductive. Know that all the information is there. You'll do many unconscious practices before you awake to conscious experience. This is necessary.

You have been so busy caring for the material aspects of your life that you have had little energy, if time, left to devote to the real job of living. Remember that far more important than forced performance is relaxed reception. In many pressure instances, it turns out that the job at hand is actually more to remain relaxed than to attempt forced output. So relax.

Relativity, too

Why don't you correlate your studies of astral projection with a study of relativity, since you are so mentally involved with both things lately. [I was reading books on both subjects.] It is very appropriate that you view these two in combination, since each will complement your knowledge of the other. I am ready to assist you, and can do that much more effectively now that you have come to the place in your mind where you cannot separate your comprehension of one from your comprehension of the other."

"You are surely seeing places in my mind where I don't walk around with my eyes open. Can you explain?"

"Yes. To fly with conscious knowledge of both its objective and subjective reality will give you a totally new perspective, with

which you can then indeed elaborate, or rather expand, upon the existing conception of relativity. Einstein took manmind to the height of relativity understanding on the conscious level, leaving you no place to go but into the realm of superconsciousness. You know this emphatically, but still tend not to trust your own deepest knowledge."

"What I know emphatically, what my deepest knowledge tells me, is that you are really full of yourself today. I am aware that your goal is to find those really tender spots in my ego and attack them with your honey-covered tongue. I am aware that you know my most treasured daydreams and delusions, and that you are intent on forcing me to look at them. That's why you mention Einstein and Jung. You're doing a great job. You're terrific."

"Schwab, discard your old prejudices and you will find everyday life adding to your storehouse of knowledge tenfold. Remember, experience is study to the same degree that thought is study, provided you experience consciously. Brushing your teeth, for example, if done consciously as a learning experience, will take you just as far as studying pure math. You can take anything and in that one thing learn the secrets of the cosmos.

Study while you fly, and eventually you can fly just by studying.

You are near realizing that even subjective and objective have a meeting place where they are indeed one and the same."

"Yes, that seems to be logical now. I'll wait for that realization.

Bilocation

Say more. You once used the term demonstration, and I didn't want to know more about it then. But now, why not. I see now that while my goal is to hear more thrilling tidbits, your purpose, dear sheepdog, has something to do with my inner growth, yes? Fine. So what is this demonstration I am supposedly going to perform?"

"You will demonstrate bilocation."

"I will what? Have mercy. Yes, that's another one of my secret daydreams, for sure—to stand in front of a group of physicists and do something really outrageous. What do you mean by bilocation?"

"Bilocation means being in two places at the same time. I mean physically, as well as in your mind. Projection is a good way to learn the mechanics of pulling your four other bodies elsewhere, but it's your fifth, or actually your first, or physical, body that must go, too. Physics shows the mechanics here."

"Physics? Present-day physics?"

"Of course. Read what your theoretical physicists are saying these days, and you will be amazed.
But remember, you need only let your mind be the tool of your spirit and you can in fact move mountains. So what's so difficult about bilocation of little old you?"

"Nothing. It's easy.
What an idea, though—bilocation . . . mmm, yum.
Why do you imply that I know how to let my mind be the tool of my spirit? You are not speaking to this conscious me, again, but to one of those supras or supers or totals. Speak to *this* me."

"You are your own worst enemy. You must overcome doubts of all sorts if you hope to advance. You limit your experiences with your doubts. It is all here now, yes it is, you need only to stop to realize it.
Yes, your ego is in the way still. This is why you cannot distinguish between fact and fantasy, between inspiration and imagination. However, feel assured that the five bodies are indeed a reality that exists and can be experienced.
I would hope that you could find enough discipline to work at projection until you can meet, whether at chance or at will, with minds from other realms. If you can project above the astral to the

causal plane, you will know when you will take the physical ride in
the physical ship."

"You really are a beauty! You do know how to make me drool.
How can I not devote every minute of my days to the study of
projection now? You have no shame."

"I never said there wouldn't be rewards."

"I wish I could hear you chuckle. I mean, really hear you, not
just see words to that effect.
Now to another aspect of the job discussion: Words like
job, vehicle, channel, service and mission cause considerable
discomfort, unease, cringing, anxiety, angst, and a whole bag
full of similar joys—even as I am simultaneously thrilled by the
idea."

*"Maybe niche, not service. Niche, reason, purpose, real goal,
meaning, even; the area in which you are most equipped to serve,
to help; to deny one part of self to enhance another; the groove
into which your life most easily fits; the talent of yours that is most
needed; the gift of yours that most needs to be given. Better?"*

"You're making it worse. I have a gift to give?"

*"Accentuate your positives. Play down your weaknesses. Better
yet, don't play them at all."*

"Fine, I'll try. But these words about our goals do drive me
crazy. I love picturing myself doing these things—and then I
look at my four-toed foot and my insulin vials and it all seems
like some outlandish daydream. This is not a nice state you have
brought me to, Sage."

*"Why do you still feel that, in some very real sense, you have
betrayed yourself, have somehow fallen short of your goals, not
quite made the grade?"*

"Why? Because I don't see the growth that you hint at, that's why."

The growth test

"Because you can't see the gradual unfolding of a flower bud, do you insist there are only buds and no flowers? So why do you believe that you are not blooming simply because the pace is at a speed that you can't notice? I wish I could timelapse your development so you could see it happening, so you could believe it's real. I can't do that, but by a simple form of introspection you can.

Pick any adjective that accurately describes you, say, impatient (wonder why I choose this example?). Trace back through past experiences that deal with that adjective. There's no real way to be objective in this process, so assume right up front that your analysis will be subjective. Picture experiences where you were most impatient. Then compare these with similar, more recent experiences. Surely you will not be able to deny that some real change has come about in you, quite without effort, simply by your growing in experience.

Do this exercise while stuck in traffic, stuck in a line, even stuck on the toilet. You don't need to set aside any 'special' time for this process. Like praying, it's meant to happen all the time, not in some arbitrary separate slot.

If nothing else, this 'growth test,' even if experimented with rarely, will always encourage you, never discourage you. Eventually you will see that growth happens at different rates, and slow speed doesn't mean it's not happening, even right now."

"If you say so. In fact, yes, that Hundred Questions exercise has shown me repeatedly that something is growing. But it's a quantum leap from a gradual changing of attitudes to bilocation, don't you think?

Anyway, just out of curiosity: How am I going to function once the bud has become a sweet little flower?"

"You will be a vehicle for power and a vessel of power, each in its own good time and proper place in your growth."

"Oh boy, power, yes, gimme power . . . Orifi, I am neither a vehicle nor some kind of vase. And because I have no idea what you mean, these words make me uncomfortable—largely because my ego likes such grandiose notions, as I said before. Some sections in my psyche are now sort of awake, and they don't like it when you feed my ego."

"You have begun to sense that this is not an overnight wonder but more a high life's work. You might be interested to know that each plane is nearing the same upward leap that your plane stands ready to receive. Relax.

We're not trapped here in an alien, unfriendly, hostile universe, you know. Our existence is a free gift from the 'all and all,' and it does reveal its meaning and purpose. There is a plan and direction for you, as for everyone. If you try to help it, however, you will surely hinder it.

"Great. I feel so useful."

"It is more actively positive to be than to analyze the act of being.

And remember, statements that are factually true can be quite unimportant, whereas certain seemingly illogical ones can be imbued with pure truth. It always depends upon which ears you hear them with or which eyes you see them with—it depends on your perspective."

A little trip

I had worked hard this particular Saturday, physically exhausting myself by moving millions of wheelbarrows of soil to improve my land, my personal patch of the universe. Loved doing that. Eighteen dump trucks of earth, all spread by shovel and wheelbarrow. Not all in one day, of course. Took weeks. So much sweat, so delicious.

Mike and John were with friends, so the house was quiet this afternoon. My wife was taking advantage of this rare opportunity by taking a nap in the bedroom, and I decided to grab a little rest before the evening's activities, too, and lay down on the living room couch. It was so peaceful, so wonderfully quiet, and I was so pooped. I closed my eyes to rest them for just a little bit, and was instantly asleep.

It seemed only minutes later that I found myself sitting up on the edge of the couch, a little groggy, wondering how long I'd been out. I was about to get up when I looked to my side and slightly behind me—and there, peacefully asleep, was I!

There was my body, lying on the couch, and here I was, sitting right next to it!

Was I dreaming? No, because I was thinking as I normally think, and what I'd learned from Big O and books about astral projection flooded into my mind. Don't be afraid, I told myself, don't waste this opportunity, this is it! You are projecting, Schwab!

But how could I move? And with that thought, I started moving! I floated away from the couch in the same sitting position, my feet a few inches above the floor. I felt clumsy, unsure, and thought I would bang into the wall. As the wish not to hit the wall appeared in my head, I stopped—and realized that I was like a remote-control car, with my thoughts being the control unit.

Excited, bubbly, I wondered what to do. Then this thought came: Find something in the house that is not always the same, something other than furniture or pictures on the walls, so you can check it out later. My sleeping wife! I wished myself around the couch, up the five steps, and down the hallway to the bedroom door. I felt a power growing in me, something that needed to be controlled and guided. I issued a mental whoa! as I approached the door a little too fast, and slowed down instantly. Such power. A great feeling. And my thoughts were exactly as they would have been 'in the flesh.'

I floated, still in that sitting position, to the side of the bed, and there she was, fast asleep. I noted the position of her head and how much upper body was not covered by the blanket. I was so thrilled. Then I found myself floating back through the hallway, down the few steps (a split-level house), around the couch, saw my body lying there, and then there was a sharp jolt and I felt myself sitting up with a start.

I looked around, and there was no body lying there. I touched one knee, then slapped a thigh, and then realized that I really was awake this time, physically awake. I got goose bumps thinking about what had just happened. I got up and stretched and stomped on the floor to feel the solidity, then ran up to the bedroom to check on what I had seen, and there she was, just as I had committed to memory . . .

I was so pleased and encouraged by this little trip. This was real, not just words, not just promises or daydreams. I knew I would never doubt the possibility of flying again.

O

19 Flaring Nostrils

I was convinced now that I had grown enough to jump into mystery. I was ready to fly and explore and be a completely new me. I was chipping away at that block of marble, ready to find the real me at any moment.

And then events conspired to show me my advanced state of flowerhood.

In full control

I was a soccer coach in the local youth program. I'd been coaching, organizing, lining fields, re-erecting goal posts, and dealing with parents and refs and opposing coaches for many years. Most parents are wonderfully supportive, refs work hard but can be a pain in the butt, but opposing coaches . . . ! It's unbelievable how unevenly the human race evolves. Not like the surface of a balloon, but more like the edges of an amoeba. Some segments look like they haven't moved for eons, and that's where opposing coaches exist.

My splendid Under-12s played a game against an arch enemy one hot, muggy Sunday afternoon. Son Mike on left wing, faster than a speeding bullet, son John the impenetrable fullback on defense—a father's chest could burst.

Both teams played their hearts out. Faces red, sweat-soaked shirts clinging to small bodies, eyes determined, happy. Parents losing their voices, referee about to faint. Great day to be alive.

And then there was the other coach. He was pacing along the sidelines like a man gone berserk, screaming "take him down, goddammit," or "trip him, trip him," and finally, "break his legs!" The guy was well known for his outrageous behavior but everyone was used to it, so neither his players nor mine, nor anyone else, paid much attention, as unlikely as that may seem.

Except for me. By the time the game approached the final whistle, tied 1:1, not one but two adult wannabe role models had been transformed into berserkers. Into this teeming scenario my sweet invisible sheep dogs then inserted a most wretched event: One of my forwards had just missed a shot on their goal by maybe two feet (groan groan pain), and now they were attacking our goal when their center forward (the coach's son, naturally) suddenly went airborne and then hit the ground in a heap of arms and legs. The ref blew the whistle and yelled, "penalty kick," my players stood there stunned, and I found myself in that place outside of time where we seem to be able to see many thoughts all at once. In one instant I knew these facts: No one had tripped the guy, it was all an act, it was done on instructions from you-know-who, the ref fell for it, there was no justice in the universe (O was right)—and I was obligated by universal laws to maul the s.o.b. right then and there.

The penalty kick never happened. After cooler heads had separated us, I took my team off the field, accepted the forfeit, and we all went home.

Days later, during practice, some little guy teased me with, "You know, coach, he might have missed that kick and they wouldn't be in first place now."

For weeks, no, months, I lay awake at night trying to make the memory of my behavior go away. I was convinced then that all my efforts at learning and growing and evolving had been in vain and would continue to be, forever. I tried to imagine forgiving myself and liking myself. Ha. No way. Impossible. The image of me out there on that field—oh God. And more: The suspicion that this coach was unknowingly serving as a very effective 'human guide' and that I should be appreciative—what a wretched situation.

Weak knees

I had always wanted to take the famous donkey ride down into the Grand Canyon. When we parked our car at Desert View for our first look at this wonder, something happened to me. My nervous system collapsed. I'm serious. I knew I had acrophobia, but I thought it would be manageable. I was wrong. One look at that immensity, and something in the most ancient region of my brain stem, probably the reptilian part, went bonkers. Some survival mechanism was tripped, shrieking warnings and overwhelming my autonomous system. It was pitiful. I couldn't walk on the famous Rim Path. I couldn't even watch other people walk there. The only time I managed to get a peek at the Colorado was when I found a scraggly pine growing between the path and the abyss. I nearly crawled to that tree, my legs were so wobbly. Holding on to the closest branch, I managed to peer through and catch a glimpse of the silver ribbon a million miles below. A couple of my fingernails are still embedded in that pine.

I went to the pharmacy and asked for a magic pill. They made sympathetic noises and shook their heads. I spent most of the night trying to force myself to that rim in my mind, again and again visualizing myself taking one step at a time, telling myself that my thoughts create my reality (I really did)—but every attempt ended in failure and increased the stress on my system. Totally uncontrollable panic. Horrible feeling of helplessness. Relaxing was useless. Breathing exercises were useless. I tried to trick the frightened thing inside me by skipping that impossible last step to the rim and picturing myself on a donkey, well down the trail already—and remembered a story from dinner that the wonderful donkeys walk on the outside part of the narrow trail, which means that one of your legs is dangling over the . . . It was hopeless. The only way I'll ever see the bottom of that canyon is from a rubber raft.

The stresses caused by such experiences made me at times shy away from any communication. You may not believe this, but in a state like that, the last thing I looked for were more words about human potential and such. So I did not seek comments from Orifi—but, as he once said, "Ask not, you shall receive anyway."

What's the matter, Schwab?

"Are you struggling with discouragement?
Facing the grim antagonist?
Sinking to despair?
Living in the depths?
Feeling the impending collapse of a beautiful dream?
Do you feel inadequate?
Is your zest for living diminishing with age?
Have your selfrespect and 'joie de vivre' been damaged in the long fight to survive?
Do probing questions seem shallow?
Do you miss their depths?
Do you strive to recapture them?
Do they seem just a haunting memory?"
"The answer is yes, dammit, all of the above."
"Attacking yourself mentally for not moving out of the bog will never help. Just add one small change per day. At least at the end of 365 days you can say you made 365 adjustments to your thinking!

Do you feel like you're wandering around aimlessly? Going around in circles? Making mediocre progress? Don't ever try to follow someone else. Don't even follow yourself. Follow the silent voice of that spirit that guides you. Trust that spirit with your life. It has infinitely more information to draw on than you do. It doesn't promise that you'll never be confused or perplexed again, but if you are willing to trust this inner/outer guide, you will find your way. Have you spent years wandering in the wilderness only to wake up and find yourself in the same place? For God's sake, ask for help. Everyone needs help, you know! Help is available on demand. Take advantage of this straightforward offer.

The rut, the humdrum, the usual, the expected, the ordinary, old hat, boring, uninspired, totally without surprise . . . truly, your methods need revision. Awaken them. Lure them up to another level. Don't lull yourself to sleep along with them.

Every day, write and sing. You need the intuitive outlet each offers. If you need to go into the isolation of the woods to sing with abandon—do it. If you can't write at home, do it elsewhere. It doesn't matter what you write or sing, only that you do both.

When a troubled mind overwhelms you like one towering wave after another, when they crash into your life incessantly and try to wear you away by friction—take heart, you can challenge your own depression and summon it to give account of itself. Question your low moods. It's all in how you look at it (replacement thinking). It is never what happens to you that brings you down. It is always by your reaction (rational and emotional) to those events that you are brought low."

"Well, that's not exactly a revelation. But my reactions seem to be triggered at levels of my self that I don't consciously control. This is true, as you must know. So what can I do about it? Nothing. I can fume and protest, as I am doing now."

The smell of fear

I must relate another story to illustrate this dilemma. I was asked to be the project manager for a new piece of system software being designed for my development division by the sages at IBM Research. That is, while they supplied the brains, I was to make sure they didn't get too exotic with their design. Because of my role, I had to perform one of those deeply ingrained rites of corporate culture: I had to present the status of the project to upper management at regular intervals.

Now this was usually not a big deal and I had done it often enough, but the first status report for this project turned into an absolutely harrowing experience.

Because I was not yet familiar with the complex design, I was nervous about revealing this lack of knowledge to my professional colleagues. While waiting for my turn I got so nervous, in fact, that I broke out in a strange oily sweat that made me smell bad!

I'm serious, I stank of fear. And the thought that others might catch a whiff of it frightened me into even more sweat. My whole skin seemed to be covered with it. It was horrible. I can't recall any other occasion when I was so drenched by irrational fear.

The actual event, when the time came for me to get up and do my song and dance, bore no resemblance to the anticipation. It went just fine, no big deal.

Some physical factors probably helped create my state, such as high blood sugar and lack of sleep from burning the midnight oil getting ready, but I was convinced that there was more to it—like the sprinkling of some fear dust by the Invisible Horde.

Whatever the factors, it was such a gross example of how little control I had over my thoughts and emotions that I was crushed and enraged once again. What a stupid, ignorant, helpless way of being.

"Stop persecuting yourself. Open up every pore in your skin and drink up! Yes, drink, drink water, no other fluid but water. Doesn't sound relevant, but trust me, it is! Relax, relax . . .

Being preoccupied and aggravated with yourself will change nothing. A change in perspective is needed. Show patience. Then, quite unaccountably, a new heart will spring up in you. Quite mysteriously, quite wonderfully, the spirit of heaviness will be lifted, either by evolution (over time), or by revolution (quite suddenly). You will realize that you are exactly where you should be. You are already there, you simply have not realized it yet. That thought alone should help to revive you. Proceed expectantly. Anticipate the best.

Understand that anger by far surpasses apathy. Positively directed anger is a legitimate tool for change in any arena.

However—fury and resentment, bristling hostility, blazing eyes, fiery flare-ups, bitter thoughts, vengeful plans, shortfused, out of control, raging, temper tantrums, physical or mental destruction, pure emotional reactions unguarded by the rational function, flaring nostrils, a pounding heart—all of these are destructive anger. What you need to express is constructive anger, that form of righteous indignation that results in positive change—physical, mental, spiritual, whatever."

"Eyes blazing? Nostrils flaring? Don't be enjoying my state too much, OK? Tell me about constructive anger."

"Suggestions for constructive use of anger: Don't camouflage your healthy anger, express it; don't hold on to it, don't nurse it along until the chill hardens into malice. Strike a balance between healthy expression and healthy control.

Funny that you believe you're more apathetic than angry. You're wrong, you're not. Much of your previously seething anger is now buried anger. Don't bottle it up and then act surprised if it explodes in an exaggerated form, so out of proportion to the problem at hand. Keep each storm from becoming a hurricane.

You spend such energy trying to keep the lid on your anger! This is a formidable task. You must be exhausted."

"Not too exhausted to visit you tonight and snip a few feathers off your wings."

"An invigorating freedom and sense of intense energy comes with letting go of anger in any appropriate manner. Unload your dreary burden. If no one is handy, give it to God. He's available to anyone, anyplace, at any time—now that's availability!"

I didn't remember until the next day at work that 'availability' was one of our latest buzzwords for our software. I burst out laughing when I saw the word on the first foil of a presentation. What else is there to be done? Laughing is the most logical reaction.

"And, yes, I know your health is a major reason for your rage.

Physical and spiritual health both need to be considered, but you must always be sure to start at the root of the problem. Considered on a firstthingsfirst basis, you are likely to approach health upside down, or ass backward, as the case may be. People so often think and say that as soon as they get their body straightened out, they will deal with their spirit. Not possible. Focusing on the body first, they'll never get straightened out!

Start new patterns of thinking and doing immediately. Don't be afraid of trial and error. Many astounding discoveries in the history of science were made in just that way.

You fluctuate dramatically between weakness and defiance, feeling defiance to be the stronger reaction to life, if only because it is active. Passive weakness annoys you, especially in yourself."

"Oh yes indeed, especially when I know I missed out on fun because of it. I have a bag full of examples from my life that always help me get annoyed all over again whenever I need to.

Were you there, so many years ago, when I was a fine young airman in the Navy, stationed near Pensacola, and I had a date with that magnificent redhead and we were driving by the local marina and she pointed to her father's cabin cruiser and asked me to read its name, WHY NOT, with that mischievous look in her green eyes—and I did nothing? Nothing! Godalmighty.

That's one of the examples in my bag, and I've used it repeatedly over the years to beat myself over the head with. Isn't that amazing? Years—so stupid."

"Your flood of negative thoughts is a useless exercise. This experience is not now, it is then. You should be here now.

You don't need me to direct you and tell you what to do next. You only need a strong enough sense of humor to allow you to venture out into the unknown, alone and in the spirit of fun. Remember, most people only proceed as long as there is fun within the discipline. Relax, relax, and make your own fun for awhile."

"All right. Here's something that might distract me from this 'flood:' When I go to your plane and meet with you during sleep, as you say I do, and you give me advice that later pops into my consciousness as if it were my own thoughts—couldn't we have some fun playing with that?"

"In fact, before you fall asleep, you might designate a time when you will consciously recall any advice (input) received. Yes, that is fun! You should try it."

"What do you mean by 'designate a time?'"

"Mentally choose a time, for example 2 p.m. the following day, when you will set aside other mental considerations and await the arrival of input."

"It's that simple? Let's do it. And I will recognize your stuff? Do you mind telling me how to wake up while we're meeting so I can be aware of what's going on?"

"Don't bother to try to wake up in your dreams. I'll wake you up when I need you. Seriously, I will."

"Great. What about when I need you?"

O

20 This Stupid Illness

He was, of course, right about the underlying reason for much of my rage: my diabetes. I could complain bitterly about lack of progress in getting closer to his vision of what a human can be, about disillusionment and disappointment and other dis-things, but these were not the real cause for my troubled state. The real cause was my illness. It robbed me of energy, sapped my strength, often deadened any enthusiasm—not good. My resentment fed on itself, reaching deep into my heart and soul.

"I no longer like myself this way, Orifi. I know I have mismanaged my disease, and I hate myself for it.

What a release it must be to die. I see myself there, on your side, glowing with energy and health, ahhh, so delicious—no illness, not a trace of fear or anxiety. No, I don't want to die, but I *am* so tired of struggling with this crap. And what makes it worse is that it seems so stupid, such a stupid waste of time.

Hey, how about starting over again? I want a body like Arnold's in *Conan the Barbarian*."

Act as if

"Your focus is so damn near 100% on your illness that you can't see the forest through your own trees, the ones you planted! You automatically translate every new bodily reaction as health related, or actually ill-health related.

Schwab, don't put a magnifying glass (i.e., your mind's focus) on your illness. Why add fuel, in the form of your attention and energy, to a fire that is already burning out of control, at least at times? Turn your mind around the other way. Distract your mental energies away from yourself and on to something bigger than yourself. Do this as soon as possible. Distraction can be a tremendous healing tool.

Illness causes increased self-centeredness, which is necessary to keep the ill person alive. Distraction removes self-centeredness. Practice it. You'll see nearly immediate results!

You need to pretend. Act as if you are healthy and ultimately you will be. I swear it's that easy! Your imagination is stronger, more potent, than your illness, I swear again. It's like faith—sometimes you have to pretend you have it and act accordingly if you actually are to have that faith.

Flatly refuse to dwell on your illness. Do what you must to appease it, then forget about it. If it scares you, it will gain a stronger hold on you. Anything you focus your attention on will cause trouble if it's bad, joy if it's good. And who wants to exaggerate the bad? The more of your energy you spend building up (using) your strengths, the less of it you will have available to brood about your weaknesses. Do what you must to maintain your health, but do not dwell on it."

"That is extremely difficult to do. I am physical, and this broken aspect of my system makes me feel imperfect, inferior, and endangered. How can I not dwell on it? It stares me in the face every minute of every day."

"Maybe you are staring in its face? I repeat, simply move your focus to something else.

If you had a choice between witnessing the unfolding of a rose or glancing into an open septic system, which do you think you would choose to spend your life's precious time on?

Let us consider your toe or, better, your lack of one. It is amazing that it stands (or doesn't stand) as a silent testimony that proclaims, 'He lives,' and, simultaneously, 'He doesn't live well!'"

One less toe

I pitched batting practice to my Minor League team (that's before they get anointed into Little League) one beautiful afternoon. For about three hours I ruled on the mound, trying to look like Sandy Koufax by raising my left knee to the sky while pivoting on the right foot, then firing a 15 mph fastball to some two-foot high batter. They laughed and giggled and relaxed, and I loved being the center of their attention.

This time I had done a little too much pivoting and clowning, it seems. When I took my shoes off later and saw the blood-soaked right sock, I was shocked, but when I saw that the cause was only a big blister under the big toe, I calmed down. A blister, big deal. Being a warrior, I ripped off the pieces of loose skin, put a band-aid on the raw flesh, and ignored it.

Three weeks later, the staph infection was endangering my leg, and all that the IV-fed drugs could do was drive the mess back into the toe and contain it there. The surgeon urged me to let him do an 'exploratory' to see what was going on in there. When I woke up I found myself staring at a distinctly shorter foot, all bandaged up. Just then my manager called to see what was what, and I, still groggy and nauseous from the anesthesia, yelled into the phone, 'They cut the damn thing off!' and passed out again. She thought I meant the foot, and by the time I woke up again I was surrounded by my entire department.

When they realized that I had only lost a toe, sympathy waned somewhat, but to me, it wasn't *only* a toe. I was stunned. I felt violated. They had cut off a part of me. To lose a tonsil or even an appendix is one thing, you can't see them. This, however, was a piece of my visible temple, and now it was no longer complete, no longer perfect. I was marred. I felt a vague sense of shame. Isn't that odd? One toe less, and I felt I was no longer the same me.

But mostly I felt rage—at my illness, at my disregard for my body, at my inability to cure my physical self, at everything, even at my invisible Know-It-All for not intervening. I was doing fine managing lots of things: An IBM department, a Minor League team, a soccer team—I was even president of my town's Youth

Soccer League at the time—and I couldn't even begin to manage myself. What a cruel reality check. A bunch of mindless little bone-eating bastards had chewed up my toe, and all I could do was curse.

"Yes, exactly. He doesn't live well. This is not something I didn't know."

Spirit is the foundation

"To some extent your illness will always control you, but the extent to which you can actually control it is way beyond anything you have even imagined as yet. You will see.

And I remind you again that spirit is the foundation of this world and every other. Many circumstances would appear to indicate otherwise because people tend to invert spirit and material, and therefore they see only what they already believe, that is, material, then spiritual.

Dealing with health in this inverted fashion—the attempt to take care of biology before psychology—runs the risk of forever treating the physical symptoms and never reaching the spiritual causes. The physicalistic school sees chemistry affecting thought and emotion. The spiritualistic school sees thought and emotion affecting chemistry. Now there is a kind of reciprocal action involved here, where each affects the other to some extent.

Those who see mainly the effect of chemistry on behavior, for example (as in psychiatric drug therapy), will have one drug for one surface problem, another drug for another surface problem, and no idea how to get at the root cause. Those who see the problem as mainly a spiritual one, however, will attempt to study and dig and delve into the roots of the problem. In so doing, those roots can eventually be killed and the 'true problem' along with them.

Ultimately, how you think has more to do with your health than what drugs you take. Drugs can do a beautiful job of camouflaging problems, but they do nothing toward promoting a reality based on truth. In certain cases, drugs are necessary to make a person stable enough to realize this situation, i.e., serious physical imbalances must be controlled first if the person is ever to have the freedom to seek spiritual answers. But once he is stable enough, he can work on his spirit until fewer drugs, or none at all, are required for health.

As you involve yourself with these realities, remember these two points:

There is no coincidence. Your disease was chosen by you, for you, for many very good reasons that you don't need to deal with right now.

You must treat yourself simultaneously from the outside in and, more importantly, from the inside out.

Also remember that all disease is the result of long-developing processes that finally saturate the body with toxins. These toxins, when localized in a joint, cause arthritis; in the liver, hepatitis; in the kidney, nephritis; in the skin, dermatitis; in the pancreas, diabetes; in the brain, mental illness.

Improper eating, living, and thinking habits are the prime cause of such degeneration. If you can change your thinking, you can change your health, absolutely."

"My thoughts directly determine the chemistry of every cell in my body? That drives me crazy. And why is it a mystery to us that this is so? It doesn't seem rational. But then, of course, since there is no coincidence, this illogical situation is just what the doctor ordered? I am going to redesign this crazy system.

And another thought: if I do learn to change my thinking and thereby my health, what would that do to those "very good reasons" why I chose this illness? Or maybe one reason was to give me a strong enough incentive to learn to control my thoughts?"

"Relax, Schwab."

No control

I crossed the Kingston-Rhinecliff bridge every day on my way to work. The Hudson is very wide there, and so this is an immense bridge, very long and very high. It's not a suspension type, so there are no structures above the roadbed. I love that bridge. The view of the Catskills when driving west in the morning is a feast for the eyes. Sometimes fog hides the water deep down under the span, making the bridge seem suspended in space. So many different variations to that scene, depending on the weather and the seasons. A great way to start a day. So many different moods. And surprises: Once I was startled out of my daydreams when huge white birds suddenly rose up over the guard rail to my immediate left, crossed over my car so low that I could have grabbed a leg, then sank down below the level of the bridge again once they had passed the right-hand railing. They were swans, flying in perfect single file, beak to tail feathers. I was enchanted.

Dream: The Bridge

I became aware that I was floating high above the bridge. I was enjoying the feeling of flying, as I always do. Such a thrill to be weightless, such a feeling of freedom, even of power. My invisible buddy was right behind me, of course. Wouldn't dream of going solo. I think he suggested that I land on the bridge, I'm not sure. In any case, I did, and the moment my feet touched the concrete, I was in a more 'normal' consciousness, and that was bad. Because as I stood there feeling my heaviness, the side barriers of the bridge were suddenly gone. Vertigo flooded through my nervous system. That bridge is exceptionally high, and I hate it when there is no barrier between me and any edge. Even a low rock wall helps, but when there is nothing . . . I was terrified. I wanted to flee, but stood frozen. Then I heard a voice and remembered that I had just been flying and felt myself relax and then, to my delight, I floated up a little and the vertigo was gone. But only for a second. Then I dropped down to the surface again and stood there with wobbly knees, feeling heavy and afraid. This now repeated itself several times—float and feel relief, plop down and feel dread, while moving in and out of the corresponding level of awareness. Until I moved completely out of the 'you can fly' state and finally just stood there, scared stiff.

Then it got horrible: Most of the bridge surface crumbled and disappeared, leaving only a strip of road about four feet wide with ragged edges! I was totally paralyzed with dread, unable to move, trying to avoid looking down but aware of the height in every cell of my body. Then I looked ahead and saw how terribly far it was to that end, knowing that going back was just as far. Desperation gripped me. There was no thought of flying any more, as if that possibility had never existed. It was simply unthinkable for me to walk upright on this narrow band, and the realization sank in that there was no way for me to get off this damn bridge, no way to overcome the vertigo to keep from swaying and falling. I was doomed. The thought occurred to me that I could just stay in one spot, close my eyes, and wait until I starved to death. Anything was preferable to facing that long narrow ribbon so high above the water. Then I realized that I was still standing upright, making the situation worse than it needed to be. I forced myself to bend my knees, slowly, almost fainting from the effort, until I closed my eyes and sat down abruptly. I pressed my shaking hands against the road surface for support, then opened my eyes and saw that the strip was now so narrow that my feet were sticking out over the sides.

I was ill. After sitting like that for a while, trying to collect myself a little, I had this idea: By supporting myself on my hands, I could lift my butt up off the surface and in this way shimmy forward a little bit at a time. I knew that this would take forever, and I probably wouldn't make it, but I had to do something. Again I looked up to estimate the distance, and that almost did me in.

That's when I woke up, trembling and very upset.

O

21 Deep Wounds

Marriages, I think, are like the American bittersweet vines that grow all over my bushes and trees. Some shoots curl around each other and form a tight spiral all the way up. Some start off side by side and stay close together as they wind their way upwards. Still others choose different branches altogether and eventually find themselves out of shouting distance of each other. There is no way to tell what a pair of shoots will ultimately do what when they're just tender, sweet little sprouts.

After seventeen years, it had become clear that my marriage had taken the third path. My wife and I had grown apart. We had been aware of this for several years but had decided to hold the marriage together for the boys' sake. But now it had become too difficult. Our attitude toward each other was unhealthy not only for us but more so for them, and when we fully realized that, the decision had to be made to separate.

Not until I drove around the sharp turn in the road that obscured the house from view did I break down. I tried to see the road through the flood of tears. No use, had to pull over into an apple orchard. There I sat for a long time, face contorted until my jaw muscles hurt (it's so very hard for me to let go and give in, to *any* feeling).

My sons had been sleeping when I left, so I had quietly kissed their heads—Mike's rather sparse brown hair, John's thick black mane, and Andrew's forehead. I knew I would see them regularly, and that knowledge helped. I wouldn't be there when they left for school, I wouldn't sit at the supper table with them every night—but I would see them often. And they would be safe and comfy in the house they grew up in.

But I no longer had a home. The land and the hundreds of bushes and trees I had planted were no longer mine. As I walked to my car, the sense of loss was like a physical force twisting my innards into knots. I touched one young blue spruce, caressing its needles. I wanted to kiss it, too, so attached was I to that first house and land. They were part of my image of myself.

I had built an in-ground pool for my family, and I so treasured that "successful provider" feeling when my sons and their friends splashed around in it for endless happy hours, and when we had those nice big parties for my whole department when I was a manager. In my head I knew it was just a piece of land, but in my gut I felt otherwise.

And now I was moving to a dinky little apartment.

Many months passed before I said hello to Orifi again. I didn't want to hear any advice, especially from one who has no physical and emotional pain to deal with. I knew that my pride, and various other shortcomings, had much to do with the dissolving of our family unit, and I wanted to be 'alone' with the feelings churning inside me. These were so unsettling that I often hid them under a veneer of cynicism, which showed when we did talk again.

"Isn't everything so absurd, O? So much silliness. How can you stand it? Why don't you go play golf on Venus or something?"

"I see this 'churning' you speak of, Schwab. It roils your psyche as a lake bottom is roiled by a storm. I see guilt and fear and anger and self-pity. I see bitterness at wrongs you think were done to you, and vast resentment at circumstances, especially your illness. You blame it for many of the regrets you carry."

"You bet. And isn't all this emotional stuff useless? Who needs it? I feel so helpless."

"I see your pain. I wish I could show you the powerful currents of change that are set in motion by these circumstances. I wish I

could show you what a magnificent opportunity for growth your human emotions, springing out of the physical reality you resent right now, really are."

"Great. You can have them."

"Try not to feel uninspired, as the very thought itself keeps inspiration closed out. Stop, consider, ponder . . . And remember, 'You will never be alone, no, never!'"

"Yes, well . . . But I miss being a part of my sons' daily lives, I really do. Weekend soccer games are not enough. I know I am not alone, but I feel alone when I drop them off Sunday night and wave an outwardly cheerful goodbye. I feel guilty at such moments, too. I don't know exactly why, but I do. I feel so many regrets then, and my heart is so damn heavy."

"Remember faith, Schwab. Faith is that in man that enables him to do the seemingly impossible, that makes him greater than his circumstances, mightier than the challenges in his life. We need it now, as we'll have to venture from here to a number of very important shared assumptions. If faith is to work for you, you must not set limits. To strengthen your faith, practice using it."

"Faith in what? That these emotional gyrations serve some deep, mysterious function? That this is all more than stupid human weakness?"

"Schwab, the world is vast and wonderful. Visible and invisible so intermeshed in the dance of life, so complementary.
And did you enjoy skimming the surface of the water with your bare feet in your latest dream?"

I did remember flying very low, in a sitting position, across alternating stretches of water and tall, wind-swept grass. It was a joyful and exciting dream, but this is all I could recall.

"So, you're reminding me that there is stuff going on in my inner world? Who else is having fun participating in my dreams? I still don't see even one of those 'infinitely many helpers.' I could use one or two right now."

"They're there, you just haven't realized their presence. It's up to you to identify them. They will never open up to you first."

"Sounds like that despicable old wisdom, 'When the student is ready, the teacher appears.' I hate that saying."

"Accept it. It is true."

"Wake me up in my dreams, will you?"

"Learn to call me in your dreams."

"I'll yell my head off. I'll wake up your whole neighborhood."

Your mind: your arena for control

"Listen to me now. Whenever your mind attempts to dwell on a negative aspect of you, distract it immediately to a positive aspect. Love yourself when you do this. Sounds trite, but this is in fact the only way to truly forgive yourself, and is one of the most difficult lessons in life."

"Sounds like rationalizing to me."

"You will not be rationalizing, you will be growing. Relax. Calmness of mind is the jewel of wisdom. Only the wise man who understands his part, who realizes that the arena of his control is his own mind—only he can tame the winds of his thoughts and the storms of his emotions. He understands where man's will can effect change. In that arena he grows and learns. Ultimately, he soars.

If you hope to be more than a mere pawn of fate, tossed about mercilessly by your life's circumstances, you must control your thoughts and feelings, as I have told you before. If you allow them to control you, you will be the slave of each passing event of the present moment."

"But I am not a wise man, Orifi, nor can I see myself in that role for as far as my eyes can see."

"Stop huffing and puffing. It's a waste of time. Relax and go with the flow.

Until thought is linked with purpose, there is no intelligent accomplishment. Focus on a purpose, a need, a reason. Goaloriented action is the road to selfcontrol—and, as always, practice makes perfect. Eliminate procrastination, doubt, and fear.

And remember, you need not render beautiful music or translate lovely ideas into paint on canvas in order to make a contribution to your world. There is the subtle, unseen realm of positive mental support also."

"I'll leave the subtle and unseen to you and your kin. I'd rather look at a stone wall that I've built and pat myself on the back."

"Good idea! Turn your attention away from the things you can't do and focus instead on the things you love and do well. Replenish yourself by doing them often."

"It's a deal. I'll go build more walls."

"Education and psychiatry aside, man's weaknesses and strengths are his own and can never be altered by anyone but himself. Remember, all achievement is the direct result of positively-directed thought.

Formulate mini-goals. Success brings confidence, confidence breeds further action, and so on.

In any case, find that focus and go. Do not use this difficult change in your circumstances as an excuse to postpone your good resolutions and allow your faults to rule your life. This will take you no place, and that noplace is called hell."

"This is real advice, yes. But not easy to do."

"Just do it.

Be especially on guard against guilt, Schwab. Guilt is, as I have said before, a human, not a godly creation. It is the child of self-judgment and as such functions in a shadow dimension out of the light of elated existence. Guilt is a harsh, unproductive form of self-recrimination that reeks of anti-life sentiment. Unlike fear, which has a universal function as a safety valve, guilt serves no positive role and only drains energy which might better be directed into positive, creative action.

When you endeavor to work on yourself, be sure to take mental mini-vacations of, say, three to five minutes. These mental breaks will refresh you, relax you, renew you, restore you, rejuvenate you, revitalize you—literally change your life. And live and laugh along the way."

"I really don't feel like working on myself now, you know? I want to jump out of this skin and run somewhere. Escape. Wisdom is not on my wish list. I am not ready for wisdom."

"I know. And when all is said and done, no one can make wisdom happen. One can only clear one's mind to let it happen. But even clearing the mind needs to be approached as a nonprocess, never as a process. Relax!"

"I don't know what a nonprocess is. Right now I need a lot of 'refresh, relax, renew, restore, rejuvenate, revitalize,' and if wisdom wants to attach herself to these and come to me that way, she is welcome."

Dream: That bear again

I was taking part in some kind of mission to bring essential supplies to a remote place. To get there it was necessary to travel on foot through big forests and over mountains, a long trek lasting days. About a dozen of us spent the night in a spacious log house. We set off at first light, dragging with us a bulky, heavy sled loaded with stuff. There was no snow, so pulling all that weight on runners was an absurdly difficult task.

After nearly a day of good progress we came to a fork in the path—and there he was, the bear, in all his threatening glory, about a hundred yards ahead on the right fork. He was ripping out trees and bushes by the roots, flinging them madly all over—huge, wild, immensely powerful, a mindless force like a tornado or lightning. A magnificent sight. We stared, terrified, for what seemed like a long time. Somebody finally suggested that we sneak by on the left fork and take a chance that he wouldn't see us through the thin strip of trees separating the two roads at that point. But the thought of getting that close drove us into panic and everybody started running back the way we had come.

Everyone but me. For some reason I decided that I couldn't leave the sled behind! So I wrapped the ropes around my shoulders and midriff and started pulling. The sled was very heavy and my progress was agonizingly slow. I was acutely aware that if the bear saw me and decided to charge, I wouldn't stand a chance. Unless I let go of the sled, of course. But no, not me. I refused to look back and I refused to let go. On and on I trudged, pulling the sled with all my might, fear making my belly sick.

I think some of the guys finally came back to help me. We all made it back to the log house. I remember somebody saying that we would try again the next day.

What perfect symbology. Fear blocked my path, stopped me from going where I wanted to go; I retreated, but not without dragging my heavy load with me against all reason and common sense; in fact, I willfully risked my life to hold on to that baggage, so determined was I not to run free of it. I would gladly have awarded a ribbon to the clever dream maker, if only he showed himself—but I would much rather that he had shown me how to get rid of my baggage instead of showcasing my dilemma. Or, better yet, cut the damn ropes for me.

Ah yes . . . The divorce made me more aware than ever of the size and complexity of the emotional load piled on my sled. As in the dream, my energy was totally committed to dragging it along instead of taking stuff off and lightening the load.

O

22 On Prayer

"You never pray, Schwab. You never talk to the spirit. You never even let on that it exists. You would feel less mentally alone if you would."

"Yes, I know. I stopped praying a long time ago. And who exactly is this spirit you think I should talk to?"

"The spirit that I speak of is the allcohesive source of reality, the undifferentiated unifying force of all that is. It is not gentle or passive. Its mighty wind will blow into your life and compel you toward positive action. This process is transforming, pulsating—the vibrant power of the creator expressing himself in human life. Ultimately you, too, will be in a constant state of surrender to that spirit. This experience of submission to the creator makes you truly alive, a vital force in your world. If you must be addicted, even possessed, be addicted to using that power within you. Draw upon it always and in all things, great or small."

"You better teach me how to pray, then, because the images that come to mind when I think of prayer are not very inspiring—please, God, do this for me; please, God, do that for me; make me healthy, make me wealthy, etc.

I know, I shouldn't judge. But I can't help it. The word prayer evokes these images in my head, and because of that I shy away from it.

And yet, as you know, I yearn so very much to get into a place in my mind where I might feel comfortable enough to say 'hi' to that spirit. Not to beg for something, but just to sense its presence and to feel close to it. How I long for that.

Teach me about prayer, Orifi. I mean it. I'll listen."

"Yes, Freddie. When I speak of prayer, I am not talking of ritual, which too soon becomes meaningless habit. I am talking of existing within mystery, or, better, of looking directly into your own heart without flinching, without judgment."

"Will you help me get started? Don't explain it to me, just help me get started."

"Start with this: 'I am my spirit. My spirit always was and always will be.' This is a verbal representation. The prayer is the feeling therein.

Prayer is a bridge between the seen and the unseen, between the creator and man, his creation. Talk to your creator, will you? He always hears you. How could he not? You and he are not separate, remember? Use the thoughts I give you now to talk to him, or use your own.

Orifi's prayer samples

Invite me with your bold tenderness.

Remove my fear of quiet, and teach me to recreate your soothing silences.

Lure me to gentle receptiveness.

Let me hear your faintest whisper.

Prompt me with loving urgency.

Slow me to unhurried serenity.

Teach me wordless prayer.

Help me to discover the continuously renewed immediacy of each minute of my life.

Let me know eternity knit into the fabric of time and thought.

Overcome me with your tender power.

Urge me to develop a secret habit of being perpetually bowed.

Drench me in joyful abandon that gives way to quiet, glad surrender.

Dissolve my will.

Submerge me in sweet rapture.

Enlighten me to the great joy of discipline, the benefits of listening, the joys of learning, and the thrill of action.

Leave me alone in my amazement and wonder.

Let me astonish myself with profound rediscovery.

Allow me to dream, to imagine, to fathom my own unfolding.

Lead me toward a balance between the introspection of theory and reflection and the action of worship and commitment.

Reveal to me, as often as need be, that absolute commitment is not an event but a process.

Alleviate my fear of commitment by showing me its joys.

Lead me to be in, but not of, this world.

Show me how to blend my outer and inner experiences.

Fulfill my wistful longings.

Envelop me until I glow intense.

Rip away the veneer of goodness that I carry and replace it with true pureness of soul.

Enlarge my heart.

Help me to find the amazing sanctuary of my soul, and to carry its frame of mind out into the world.

Touch my life with your terrible tenderness and carry me away in your allenfolding love . . ."

Come inside now

"My belly is filled with warm molasses. Such rich and beautiful thoughts. I will feast on them and swim in them and bask in them. And use them."

(But . . . "Rip away the veneer.?" Ouch.)

"Come inside where eternal warmth glows, and when you come, add your fuel to the existing warmth to keep it perpetuated. Know

that every soul gets the opportunity to add energy to the total spirit. If you could not or would not offer warmth, this universe and all others would be cold and lifeless."

"I don't know what that means, Sweet Guide, but lead me inside. Show me the way to your blue tepee."

"Come on over and let me look at you."

"You know that I want to. And you will like what you see, I guarantee it."

"So come."

"Better change the subject, or I'll scream."

"It is so pleasant to glow with you more than for you. Your positive emanations reverberate as all of that nature do—infinitely so. I bask in them just as you do.

Sometimes one goes within just to look around and get a feel for the landscape. In this relaxed state, this exploring mood, this nonchalant state of being, one might unearth a treasure beyond one's wildest expectations. One might actually find oneself.

And then you will remember that love is the most complex, yet the most simple, all-inclusive vibration that exists, and its strength is your strength, as it is mine."

O

23 Moving Along

After a time, new partnerships were formed. The day came when my ex and I and our new partners sat down to Christmas dinner with our offspring, presents were exchanged, and all was fine.

Vikki and I bought a big old farmhouse with lots of acres, several barns, a big pool, a small pine forest, huge trees, and much wild stuff. A lovely place, good for my self-esteem—and so much work, inside and outside, offering endless opportunities to bond with my sons again. Their muscles, energy, and enthusiasm helped sustain my stubborn determination to complete the many projects. We cut a mile of paths through the thickets. We ripped out walls, ceilings, floors, doors, windows, and staircases.

John helped me put up a cathedral ceiling and regaled me with his sharp tongue and perfect impersonations. Mike helped me install a hot tub and lay with me in the sawdust as we studied blueprints and giggled at our mistakes.

I wish this could have lasted forever. We shared so many happy hours of sweating, grunting, and cursing, and devoured mountains of the superb Italian hero sandwiches from the little country deli down the road.

Then Mike graduated from the Culinary Institute and found a great job in Florida. John and his girlfriend transferred to the University of Oregon at Eugene because he wanted to see the mountains and open spaces of the West. Andrew and I helped him pack his old VW bus and hugged him goodbye, and I choked back tears as he disappeared around a turn.

Meanwhile, I was playing in my second season in our local IBM soccer league. It was a wonderful experience to actually participate after so many years of watching and coaching and flapping my lips on the side lines. I was in much better shape physically since taking more responsibility for my health by doing regular workouts and eating better. Emboldened by my progress, feeling healthier and stronger, I was out there on the grass running and sweating to my heart's delight. It was dawning on me that my health was actually improving.

Couldn't keep up with those thirtysomething speedsters, of course, but so what. Not yet, I said.

Must've opened a blister on the next-to-pinky toe of my right foot. In the heat of battle I hadn't noticed anything (nerves in the feet are somewhat shot). When I felt a slight discomfort later, I ascribed it to the pounding the foot took during play, and so didn't take a closer look. A few days later the infection was so bad that the toe had to come off to save the foot.

I crashed again. I raged and fumed and cursed and begged Orifi to stick all his fancy words up his nonphysical derriere.

"Lay down your sword, Schwab, and defend your body and soul barehanded. Strip defense mechanisms away to see how little you actually needed them in the first place!"

"Sounds great. What does it mean? What the hell does that mean? Never mind, don't bother answering."

"As a man thinketh, so he is, remember? The connection between your physical being and your psychic self is at once simplistic and, yes, bizarre. Isn't it ever so glorious to begin to understand this connection? Remember, what you can realize on any given level will automatically happen on every other level. Example: As strong as you know your body can be, is as strong as your mind will let it be."

"I don't know anything about this connection that I can put to practical use. Really, I'm not whining, this is a very clear-headed observation."

"You are really so much more flexible. Relax. Enjoy. Growth will be automatic (except for your toe)."

"Your compassion warms my heart."

*"Please, stop now to pinpoint exactly what it is that you love and plan your life around doing as much of that as you can.
You want to get off this train sometimes, don't you."*

"Yes."

"Dream on. You didn't decide to get on it and you will have little if any say in getting off. Why not relax and enjoy it? It can be fun if you just go with the flow, even be fluid yourself. Such joy! Not confusion."

"If I hear this 'go with the flow' pap one more time . . . Orifi, help me dive into all this strangeness and tell me how to bring back just one tiny morsel that I can examine and chew on, will you?"

Listen to your body

*"Tonight, stay awake through your falling asleep process. This will scare you, but do it anyhow. As you drift off to sleep, allow your body to sink back, but hold your consciousness so that you feel exactly what sleep is to the body—so you can hear the blood rush, the heart beat, the brain hum electrically; so you can sense the very intricacies of each system's chemical activity; so you can hear the breathing change in depth and character, in rhythm from one nostril to the other—so you can, in effect, listen in on the body's workings. What you will learn can easily be applied to your wakeful wellbeing. You can learn to control negative thoughts and emotions, and much more!
You want concrete action? Do this thing."*

"OK, I will. I will try like a warrior, like a mighty Teutonic knight. Will you be there?"

"I'm always there. And yes, you will."

A few weeks later

"Hi. I've been trying your assignment. Nothing. Damn. Sometimes I still feel that only death will free me from my boundaries.

What a crazy world. Is yours like that, too? Now that's a thought I really like.

I think I'm going to focus on concrete, material, practical things. Like making more money. That could be fun, you know. Driving a forest-green BMW would most assuredly be fun. Or, in the words of a friend:

'Don't wanna know what the universe is all about, just wanna be free to twist and shout . . . '"

"Play with color for awhile, please. Now that's really fun, and quite enlightening. A balanced color experience produces a balanced mind! You need do nothing more than expose yourself to the pure spectrum of light as it is broken down into its component colors. A simple prism works well.

Or get paint strips from the hardware store. Start with bright, contrasting colors. Try to feel the differences as you stare at them. They're dramatic, not subtle. Color has a direct impact on the endocrine system.

Spend some time with color. Not pondering color, with color!"

"You are so incredible . . . I say all these weighty things, and this is your response? A man could pull out his hair. Play with color. Amazing.

How about you study my Teutonic mind in more detail now and report your findings to me? I mean specifics, not your universal generalities. How about it? You can twiddle with any knobs you find and make adjustments. Go ahead, change the thing. Be my prism. I invite you. Enjoy yourself."

"Why would I want to analyze you again when you do such a fine job all by yourself? Introspection can become a sickness and, once it has, become contagious. Talk less, think less, do more. Relax.

This whole culture of yours could use a serious dose of action instead of all of your talk, talk, talk."

Dreams will take you . . .

"Dreams will take you where you need to go whether you want to be there or not. Go there for awhile. There's so much to learn and to unlearn."

Yes, some very lucid dreams lately. In one, I was given the important assignment to carry a ring across a rickety hanging bridge. Danger waited on the other side. I took it across, but when I opened the little pouch it was in I was surprised and a little angry, because this ring was not very precious looking at all. It looked like a piece of old dirty pitted iron. Then there was some kind of struggle and the ring got knocked against a stone and broke open like a clay mold and inside was a truly beautiful shiny golden ring with all kinds of carvings and inscriptions on it.

"Counselor, interpret this symbology for me."

"Like you with your coarse outer shell, the ring has a coarse, not so valuable, exterior also. You must trust that beneath your physical shell there is a gem of great value."

"All right, I trust. What about this prism image from another dream?"

"Yes, Alfredo. That prism image, and the reflection of its ability to separate essential components, is a universal truth. You see it because it is universally true. You might even mentally send your personality through the prism and see your own components."

"What a strange notion! How can that be done? I do wish you'd be more straightforward sometimes."

"To get to you I must go around every bend in your mind—how straightforward can I be?"

"Every bend in my mind? Very funny.

I know you're being a good sheepdog, O. A little yip here, a little yap there—gotta keep the Schwab sheep going in the right direction, yes? Sometimes I really appreciate it, sometimes I don't."

"I only give you what you need when you need it. That's all."

"Yes, I know, I remember. I think of these words a lot lately.

Let me ask you about a little word you sometimes throw into the conversation out of the clear blue: love. Can you say something about it that I can understand? Something other than 'life is love and love is God and God is life . . . ?' Something that has to do with things I am familiar with, like the feelings I have for my sons?"

"As far as earth life goes, love is the first and foremost goal of every single being. The one you lovingly call 'Big One' stated flatly that this should be what you seek to do—not to learn about—while here on this planet. You must learn very quickly to live it in everything. Can't you realize how short your time is? How quickly your life has already passed? Make learning to love your #1 priority. Don't ask questions, trial and error will suffice. See the invisible behind everything and everyone and see that at the core they are all love.

It's so simple that it's actually hard to describe. You, for one, are always drawn to it like a moth to light."

> Only in an insane world do you fear loving.

"I am, but my ego shies away from it."

"Only in an insane world do you fear loving. My God (and yours), the variety of love that is available!"

"Hmm. My head is not enlightened, but something inside seems to agree. I have to think about this."

"Then ponder this also:

> And who are you
> To question inner yearnings
> That flow to you
> And through you
> From God the source?
> Relax . . .
> And the God-ness of your self
> Will steer that ship of yours
> Upon life's waters.
> Trust in God
> And trust in Love,
> As they are one."

"Whew . . .
Sweet words. Now if I could only be consciously aware of the steering of my ship . . ."

A wall comes down

I was watching a replay on TV of those happy people demolishing the Berlin Wall. Such energy, such enthusiasm. Wish I could do the same with my inner walls. I want to take my beloved crowbars and tear them down. Then I could come visit you in your Saturn nest, and you could teach me about love. I'll bring you something from Earth, would you like that? Maybe a plant, or a piece of apple pie?"

"Apple pie to me is not physical but a delicious mental warmth. A plant I have no eyes to see nor hands to feel. To me it is its vibration only.

Oh yes, the wall—the symbol, the immediacy, the inspiration, the whole earth uplift. Yes you can, you can be free, too! And you cannot help but feel camaraderie with these people. They do physically what you long to do mentally. You will do just as you have seen them do, and that's the truth!"

"The first wall I'm going to demolish is the one that keeps me from seeing the invisible places where you romp around. You can count on it."

"There is no mystery here other than learning to see the truth below the surface in all people and all things—the invisible world from whence comes the visible world.

Just stop and begin again. Give up, surrender, quit your old ways. Disarrange your point of view. Start over. Try not to mutilate my message by reading into it support for your old way of thinking. Become like a child that is very much like a sponge, absorbing all.

But make it a serious and consciously chosen surrender, not a personal defeat.

Also, get used to being without yourself."

"Without myself? Very useful advice."

"I mean without your physical, mental, spiritual self. I mean you need to prepare to not exist for awhile."

"And how do I do that? Do you have any more impossible suggestions?"

"Surrender. Do nothing. Don't just do something, stand there . . ."

"I know you're having fun, but I'm getting a little bent out of shape trying to understand."

"You try too hard. Crawl, then walk. Walk, then fly.

You shouldn't waste your physicalness. Use it to learn, now, while you still have it. You have absolutely everything you will ever need to grow and change, and it is all right there with you now."

"Yes, yes, I do take your word for that. But I want more conscious involvement already. Where is this kin of yours who helps me land on bridges and attends classes with me? I want to meet him or her and take part in planning our nightly adventures."

"He is one of your many guides, one of my comrades."

"Fine, but where is he? I want to go there."

"You are there, you're just not remembering. You know this is so, why do you ask me??"

"Because I want to participate and not sleep through it!"

"It never ever happens without your participation, but sometimes without your awareness."

"Sometimes? There's no end to your wit today. I want to step out of this old me already and fly along!"

"Go jump off the Kingston-Rhinecliff bridge."

"You know, you're really enjoying my fix, aren't you."

"Not nearly as much as you are!! You know so much of what you ask me about, you do—why do you do this?"

"Some day we will do this thing: we will have a learning session for you! I will lecture you on what I, in this conscious head, know and what I don't know. Then there will be a test to see how well you have learned this difficult material.

Orifi, I simply don't remember what you say I participate in. Why?"

"Because you identify with body senses and thoughts. Go behind the veil of the senses, then go further, go behind your thoughts. Remove yourself from your own drama."

"Right away. Give me a minute . . . Seriously, you obviously still don't understand how difficult it is to 'go behind the veil.'"

"Time lapse makes visible what is too gradual for you to see unfolding, remember? I invite you to watch the unfolding from a different 'speed,' a different point of view."

"I'm ready. Take me to your time lapse room."

"Come, I invite you. Come and doodle with me. You want joy? You'll get joy. Consider less obvious possibilities.
I'm right here, waiting for you. I want you to approach me now, right now. Stop waiting."

"Of course, Meister Skinless, here I come. But where are you? Let me get my atlas."

"Walk with me now, tonight. Come to your woods and commune with me. Talk out loud. If you can't hear me, talk both parts."

"What a fine idea! I love that thought. I'll do it. You and I on my beloved nature paths, communing. I'm drooling. You are a wretch, turning my impatience into warm chocolate pudding. I will do this. And you better be there."

"There is a certain smell deep, deep into a summer night that you should relish, should learn to savor. When the night dew kisses the land, all things come alive in a new and wonderful way. Moonlit walks, so associated with romance, are also deeply connected to health. The moon's light helps to align you at a cellular level.

I'm finished now. I hope you have enjoyed this as much as I have. Relax."

"I kiss you, Ornery One. Remind me not to come to you for sympathy."

"Start writing the book, Schwab. Why haven't you started?"

"Where did that come from? Well, because I have a hard time coming up with a good reason for doing it. 'Everything has already been said,' and 'There is nothing new under the sun.' Remember?"

"Yes, but you can share your fears and dreams with others. You can touch so many who have been where you have been."

"I'll think about it. Let's go to the woods first."

Dream: Making a date

It was dusk, as always. I was walking alone on a dirt road. On my left was a very wide and long grassy field, on my right a thick tall pine forest. I came around a sharp turn and saw that the road ahead was straight all the way to the lights of a town maybe a mile away—and stared transfixed at an alien craft sitting astride the road halfway to the town! I was so excited, so thrilled, so absolutely delighted, it's hard to describe. There was some fear in my belly, at some deep level, but that, too, changed to pure excitement.

Then I became aware of a being standing in front of the craft, looking my way, and it was waving to me! I was rooted to the ground with amazement, and now some anxiety crept in again. A craft is one thing (so I thought in the dream), but having a guy wave to you . . . The next instant the figure was gone, vanished into thin air—only to reappear right next to me on a little grassy knoll. I almost jumped out of my skin and, I think, was ready to run into the pines behind me. But then he (seemed like a he, very human) talked to me, in my mind, something like, 'It's time to start doing some practical things, so let's go.' The implications of this statement were buzzing around in my head when I felt myself blank out. When I became aware again (don't know how else to describe it), I was walking between two guys, one tall and one short, towards that town just over a hill behind the craft. We talked, but I don't remember specifics.

We went to a shopping mall, walked around, and bought something in an electronics store that reminded me of Radio Shack. There were lots of people, and I couldn't get over the fact that here I was, walking with two aliens who had assumed temporary human form and were obviously completely familiar with our ways, and nobody knew but me! I swear I was so tickled by the whole scene I had to suppress giggles. I was dying to see what they really looked like, but they didn't show me.

Then we were back at the craft, and one of them gave me a date when they would return and wanted to know where a good place was. I told him that this spot was just fine, and he said OK, and that was that. This matter-of-fact agreement to meet again filled me with an incredibly satisfied, happy, glowing feeling. That's how the dream ended. But the feeling didn't. I can still taste it today.

One remarkable aspect of this dream was how 'normal' my thinking and reactions were. Just as if it had been the real waking-state me. And the remark about 'practical things' did a number on my composure. I loved it.

"Orifi, comment please. This was what I call fun."

"Enjoy. These dreams were always there. You just now begin to remember them. Next time you will be their guide. What will you show them first?"

"I'll take them to a soccer game, explain baseball (a good test of their IQ), a concert, maybe, to see whether they know music? Food, yes, I'll offer them some real New York cheese cake. I'm bubbling over at the prospect."

"Schwab is waking up. You see it, don't you?"

"What? What does that have to do with this? No. Maybe. Fix my foot first. It's wounded again."

"OK."

"Fix my diabetes."

"OK."

"Fix my head."

"Maybe."

O

24 Still Hanging on

Dream: Prying me loose

I became aware that I was floating above the alfalfa field just north of our house, maybe a hundred feet up, gliding towards the house being erected there (in "real" life, they had just framed the second floor, no roof yet). I felt happy to be flying. And yes, my companion was there behind my right shoulder, saying things to me, as always.

We glided down gently. When I felt my feet touch the flat roof, gravity grabbed me and I instantly lost that lightness I so enjoy. I found myself standing, heavy as lead—on concrete! I knew how absurd this was, so I walked to the edge to investigate and saw this unlikely scene: The first floor was as I knew it to be, i.e., lots of spindly-looking 2x6's and 2x4's, but sitting on top of these were two floors of solid concrete! This can't possibly last, I said to myself, and decided to get off, pronto. I grabbed the slightly raised edge of the roof, swung my legs down—and panicked! I saw how far it was to the ground, and knew that I would fall like a stone and get hurt. So I hung there by the tips of my fingers, looking around anxiously to see if my companion had noticed my predicament. The next thing I saw were his hands (that's the most I've ever seen of him!) peeling my fingers off the edge, one at a time, firmly and without so much as a single word! I stared in disbelief and growing terror, felt myself beginning to slip—and woke up in a sweat.

"Talk to me about this concrete house and your wicked kin."

A lesson in building

"Row, row, row your boat gently down the stream.
Merrily, merrily, merrily, merrily, life is but a dream.

Why are you in such a hurry to wake up? This dream continues further . . .

You float, mute, suspended between heaven and earth, not entirely sure what is a dream, not entirely sure what is true. You often think, "This is no dream," even as you know you are dreaming. Even though you feel sleep wrapping you in its deep sweetness, somehow you know it is no dream. You sense how often you are asleep while awake, and, oh yes, how often you are awake while asleep.

Neither was that building a dream. It was a lesson explaining the very foundation of existence to you. The visualizations therein were designed to pass practical information to you in a common-sense fashion, thus demanding that you use your imagination to grow in understanding.

A reciprocal exchange goes on between your conscious awake self and your sub/unconscious sleep self, but this relationship between levels of the self exists only when the dream is remembered. Of the multitudes of dreams that you have, only those few that are eventually able to break through into consciousness can teach you on the conscious level. Much valid learning is, of course, subconscious, but only that information is immediately usable that you are made aware of by direct sensory input or intuitive input from dreams.

In this case, the information is given to you more or less directly, so you can understand how to build upon a solid foundation, why you must build on such, what happens if you do not, and what happens if the builder doesn't understand the character of the materials needed for different aspects of the structure.

The lesson: You must liberate your soul before you liberate your body, each in its proper order. Don't start building from the roof downward. First build the foundation, and that is the soul! It seems that the body is the foundation, but, no, it isn't. It seems that the material world needs to be dealt with first, but, no, it doesn't. I repeat: A house isn't built from the roof down. It is built from the foundation up.

You must handle every problem in the invisible dimension first, whether it be health, money, emotions, or whatever."

"I'm not conscious in the invisible dimension. So how can I handle anything there?"

Only fear makes you hold on

"You will never sprout wings as long as you hold those fingers tightly to that wall. Fear made you hold on for dear life. Had fear not been in your dreaming heart, you would have let go automatically, and you would have been drawn straight up, the power of the wind under your wings being greater than gravity's pull on your body. Who attempted to unloosen your grip on the wall was friend, not foe. Somewhere inside you knew this, yet fear remained the ruler.

You grope in agony, trying to find a magic formula to make your freedom from fear permanent. A disquieting air wraps itself around your still aching soul. Fearing fear itself, large tears hide in your eyelashes, waiting there for permission to roll down your cheek.

Deep in your mind, at all times, you can just barely hear your own soul's wings flapping slowly and creating a gentle murmur, wishing always for the opportunity to take flight!

One's wings, though invisible, are many. And just as surely as we know that man's thoughts can take flight at any time, so, too, can his body. The body is the horse that the soul mounts in order to traverse the grassy moors. Flesh to spirit, spirit to prayer—to be scattered by the wind but to cast no shadow, to raise no dust.

You must be willing to let your soul escape your body if you wish, ultimately, to take flight. In return, the soul will stand upright, holding the body high out of the reach of the ravages of aging.

Your mind will jolt up, first leaving your body asleep on the ground below, then drawing the body up also to be devoured by the sky.

Your wings can wrap themselves around you, swaddling you like a new babe. They can exhilarate you in flight. They can comfort you in your private distress. They can be fashioned from moonlight or starlight or directly from the light of the God-source.

You will feel hot wounds on your shoulders from which unfold your own glorious wings, stark white and glistening in the moonlight. But remember, if the yearning is broken off and fear should enter there, even for the slightest instant, your wings will become chains again and you will remain downtrodden until you rid yourself of fear forever, from the inside out."

What can I say about these words. I felt that Orifi was communicating with my inner levels and that my conscious self was merely witnessing this exchange. But that fact in itself meant, I decided, that the veil must be thinning. I felt strangely satisfied and at peace with myself.

In my conscious everyday reality, I found joy and encouragement in every sign that the invisible was alive and well and that I was surrounded by it, floating in it. An example follows.

A big little wink

I was alone late one night at my desk upstairs. Dishes were done, the Mets were done, all was quiet and fine. I decided to do one of my assigned exercises for fun and relaxation before going to bed. I chose the dice, because that's my favorite 'exercise.' It's fast action, no tedious counting, about as simple-minded as anything can be, and yet capable of spawning more theories and 'systems' than the stock market. Such fun. Of course, any roll has nothing whatever to do with any other roll, and any prediction based on previous patterns is totally meaningless. Try to tell that to a craps shooter at Resorts. It would be safer to insult his ancestors.

My objective was to think about one number only, to wish for it, and after many rolls see whether there was a variation from the probability-based expectation. My favorite number was 12.

So I rolled. And rolled. And wished. And rolled. When I reached 240 rolls without having seen a single 12, I stopped and sighed. A 12 is supposed to occur once in 36 rolls, on average. This wasn't the first demonstration of my vast wishing power, and so a sigh was the extent of my complaining. It was OK, I didn't mind. I enjoyed the dice. Something about the fact that the coming-to-rest of two bouncing little cubes can determine one's financial fate always held such mystery for me.

Anyway, I decided that a hot shower would be more fun. I undressed right there by the desk and was about to walk to the bathroom when a clear thought flashed into my relaxed brain and stopped me in my tracks. A tingly feeling ran up and down my back, and I knew, absolutely knew, that if I threw the dice one more time, it would be a 12. A shiver ran through me. There I stood, naked before the invisible gang, not knowing what to do. If I rolled the dice and did not get a 12, I would be crushed with disappointment. Such a clear message and then 'no dice,' no, that would be a bummer. If, on the other hand, I did roll a 12, then I would be sure that Orifi had shot a message straight into my brain, and I had received it! Oh boy. Either outcome would cause all kinds of problems. What to do?

I don't know how long I stood there, debating, procrastinating, but, of course, there was no way I could not do this thing. So naked Schwab grabbed the two little red cubes and let them fly—I'm convinced that I saw a mischievous gleam in every one of the 12 white dots that looked up at me. I let out a yell and ran into the shower and furiously scrubbed my hair with too much shampoo and made crazy little noises.

Eventually the flow of hot water calmed me down. I relaxed and considered how exciting it was to be aware of such a small, yet so very personal, demonstration, such a wink. I felt a real nearness of invisible things, a closeness, as if I could touch 'them' by sticking out my arms. I closed my eyes and felt all around me with my hands, smiling to myself and happily listening for the 'flapping of wings' deep in my mind.

O

25 On Being Water

"I've never asked you about water. I'm sure you know that it has a calming and maybe even healing effect on me. There is something mysterious about it. Just sitting by the pool and looking at it does something for me. At the shore of a lake or ocean my thoughts wander off somewhere, replacing their familiar routines with daydreams, and I feel healthy.

I've been dreaming about water lately. In one dream, I slowly swam around in an Australian river, always under the surface, looking for someone or something, apparently not wanting to be seen by anyone on land. I was aware of both shores, "seeing" trees and bushes and grassy plains and a few houses. The water was not deep, and the bottom was smooth and clean, as in a swimming pool. I had no need for air. And yes, that kin of yours was there again, just behind me, out of sight, making comments.

In another, I was standing on the deck of a fairly large boat, staring in bewilderment as five or six people gently floated down out of the sky and landed on the deck, without any kind of device—and they were made of water! Water splashed on the deck and on those standing nearby as they landed. They looked normal, they spoke and smiled, but I knew that they consisted entirely of water.

I think that these water people represented a part of me that is very primitive, very basic—and that I now needed to get in touch with, or allow myself to feel or experience. I feel that the fact that they splashed water on me symbolized being 'touched' by that realization.

Explain this to me, Sage. What is the significance of all this water in my dreams?"

"I thought you'd never ask! Seriously, I've been waiting patiently for what seems even to me a near eternity! Realize, right up front, that a lesson on what it means to be water can be nothing short of what it means to be human, seriously again."

"You've been waiting for me to ask about water? You don't 'wait' for anything. Don't disillusion me. And since when do I have to provide the trigger for your lessons? Anyway, go on, tell me about 'being water.'"

Water, the basis for life

"Life's watery beginning is reflected throughout your body, your mind, your very spirit. In water began the long evolutionary chain of events that ultimately resulted in man, in you, in your every thought, emotion, deed, even memory. It is water that has so intimately linked you to life on this planet Earth, and to every other living thing thereon. It is water that determines your physical, mental, and spiritual health. It literally decides your actions and reactions in every situation you find yourself in. This is not an overstatement.

Your deepest human roots are sunken into water. You are literally up from the ocean. Man could survive only by taking his own enclosed portable ocean with him, inside his body. Salt in human protoplasm is .9%, exactly the concentration of salt in the sea that he left three billion years ago. The two-thirds of your body that is water is, in fact, your own mini-ocean.

Closer to your experience than the oceans of three billion years ago is your experience in the womb, where you floated in beautiful oblivion. So much of your later psychic life is an attempt to return to the comfort and security of that watery world. Mostly, you don't realize you are doing this.

Water, water—remember, ten days without water and you no longer live. It is not only man's internal world that revolves around water. Man uses water. He bends it to his needs and wants. He uses it for recreation. He harnesses its tremendous power. He transports himself across it, he studies its depths, he stands in awe at its mysteries.

Ice: your body

Ice: its density, its molecular speed, its reality, its ability to be seen and touched and tasted—ice is the physical you. Your physical body functions at a lower, slower vibration. Yes, solid matter, by its very nature, is rigid. Thus it maintains its shape regardless of its surroundings. This is the you that is your body, it is you as ice.

Water: your mind

Fluidity is the state of the human mind—its most natural state, at least. This is water. It ebbs and flows, waxes and wanes, rises and falls. Thus the mind, with its near infinite tributaries, flows ever onward to merge with the ocean of your existence. Understand the fluid nature of all of your thoughts and emotions, and you will begin to grasp the full nature of the you that is water. You will suddenly realize what it means to 'go with the flow'—to immerse yourself deeply in the fluidity of your own mind.

Tremendous misunderstandings arise when people treat the water (mind) as if it were the same as the ice (body). Though they are of the same element, they are not of the same state.

Mentally, man's thoughts and moods reflect his relationship with water. When he is anxious or confused, his mind is not just like murky water, it is murky water. Likewise, mental clarity is akin to clear water. When man is elated, he feels like he's floating. He drifts off to sleep like drifting along on a calm sea. The rhythmic sounds of ocean waves kissing the shore soothe man on a deeper level than he can understand or explain.

Water is the mental you. Your mind is not solid like ice, it is fluid. It takes the shape of its container. Your body is just one container available to it, however. Put into a container of any size or shape, it will take that shape, and yet it will not lose its identity therein. Because the mind is water, it can clean itself, heat itself, cool itself, refresh itself, wash away inappropriate twinges, rinse debris away from itself, even heal itself. It has fluidity, it can surround. It can drench its very self in any thought, any mood, anything.

Water's vibration is, quite obviously, faster than that of ice, but slower than that of vapor. This state suits your mind precisely.

Water vapor: your spirit

The state of water crosses over from being solid ice to liquid water to gaseous vapor. At the threshold on the surface of boiling water, when the molecules move fast enough to 'jump' out of the visible, physical realm and into the invisible, intangible—right at that instant a miracle is occurring.

Man comes to this same juncture in his evolution toward perfection because he is more than 'as' water, he is water. His spirit is the nonvisible water vapor! Only the spirit is totally aware of the you in the other two states. Only it crosses over that thin line to become invisible. Surely it exists just as ice and water, but access to its mysteries cannot enter you from your physical senses. This spirit is 'visible' only to your 'inner' spiritual eye, but is no less real for being invisible. In fact, from a certain point of view, it is much more real. It all depends on what point in time and space you attempt to see it from. Actually (this is a trick), you can never view it from within time and space.

Immerse yourself in the study of water

To understand something of this earth experience, you need only study water in its different states. I mean study. Immerse your whole being in this process. You need not analyze or interpret, simply watch and compare. I know you will be astonished by viewing yourself from this new point of view. You will also, ultimately, become more forgiving of yourself in so doing. Likewise, more forgiving of others, of life itself. To allow your body its solidness, your mind its liquidness, and your spirit its natural vaporousness will reduce much of the tension, stress and anxiety of everyday living. You will learn that your body functions best when your mind is floating and your spirit is soaring to ever new heights. There's a naturalness about understanding yourself as water—somehow, a feeling of coming home to the center of yourself.

No one state is, of course, in any way superior to the others. They are all the same thing in different states. That's all. It's that simple and, at once, that complex. It's wondrous, it's awesome, incredible, even inspiring. See yourself as water and at once all things will be as they should be. Glide through life as ice, float through life as water, soar through life as vapor. Rise, rise above the mountains, above the clouds, beyond, beyond, to quiet space and beyond, faster and faster and faster, exhilarating. Or lay there in your pool, understanding exactly what 'to float' means. Have a ball. Laugh at yourself, with yourself.

A mind encouraged to be wet is a mind refreshed within itself.

As water, mind does know certain bounds. But spirit, as vapor, knows no bounds at all.

So here you stand before your watery self, in some ways so limited, yet in others unlimited. Such opposites within each entity, somehow reconciling themselves to keep the soul on a straighter path toward the source of all that is.

And then there's snow

Stop now. Back up. Listen. You have been having some serious problems believing that your ice is worth as much as your other waters. Believe it.

Consider this angle: halfway between solid ice and liquid water there is snow—yes, snow, in all its glory! Snow is just as much you as the other water states. Its whimsical but glorious beauty is you. Its many faces are your many choices. Its many moods, your changes. The infinite facets of its flakes, the myriad experiences that you have had. As snow covers the earth in a quiet, peaceful, blue-white fantasy, your snow blankets you, blankets your life, in a fantasy all your own. Its coolness refreshes the planet. That same coolness wraps itself around your psyche to likewise refresh you. Its quietness can be overwhelming, yet you invite that very quietness into your world.

Love snow. Love all water. For God's sake (and your own), love yourself. Stand in awe of your own vulnerable humanness. Feel a constantly pulsating appreciation for all that is you. Harness the power of your mind like man has harnessed the power of the mightiest rivers—both water, both usable for your wants and needs.

Drink water and you take into yourself the only true 'soul food.' Yes you doooooooooo. Drink it, savor it, touch it, stare at it, gulp it down, love it, praise it, dive into it! Feel it caress your total person, feel how it holds you suspended in time and space. Feel how it surrounds you, how it is you—know what it feels like to be water. Accept yourself as water. Enjoy yourself as water. Consider joyfully your total waterness. Experiment with drinking infused water, even ionized water.

You glisten, just as water does when it dances in the sunlight. You sparkle, just as water does when it teases the moonbeams that chance to hit its surface. You lie quietly waiting, like the fog on the English moors. You begin to rise as the mist when it is first kissed by the morning's glow. With the day's heat you evaporate into seeming oblivion. When you cross that ever-so-thin line between visible and invisible, only others who have crossed over like yourself will still be able to 'view' your presence. Like the intricately beautiful pattern of frost forming on your car window, your experiences imprint themselves on your spirit, forever to be lost from memory perhaps but never from your total reality.

As water, you will fluctuate from state to state during your earth stay. On the grand scale of things you will always be heading toward matching the heat of the sun, and beyond. But, on a day-to-day basis, you will always change according to the psychic heat around you and your ability to 'go with the flow.'

Relax and enjoy

If only you could really know how much of your development is on automatic pilot, you could relax and enjoy the whole process much more. You far overestimate the control you have. At its best, your control is minuscule, in spite of the fact that, with discipline, you can control most of what is conscious.

Remember that the conscious part of the self is no more than the 'tip of the iceberg' (pun!). The rest, that vast unknown part of your humanness, is invisible even to you."

"Now I am speechless again. So much to ponder. Maybe we can stop right here so I can just feast on this material? How much of this is symbolism and how much is 'real'?

But I would like to know this: If all this material about water was sitting there ready to be released, why did you wait for my mention of the subject before letting it flow, so to speak?"

"You tell me."

"Thanks. Probably has something to do with free will and my reality, etc. I can only wonder what else is waiting there to be released. And, now, how about a few words about those dreams? Indulge me. I have to spend a few years thinking about this material."

"Practice interpreting your own dreams. They are, after all, yours. Start now.

Why does it surprise you to be meeting water people in your dreams? They weren't ice, so you're not dealing with the solid physical world. They were not the invisible water vapor of the spirit. Resting halfway between these two, they came to you as water people, symbolizing your persistent reluctance to leave the comfortable world of your mind. Truly, the watery fluidity of the mind has such tremendous lure for you that oftentimes it becomes your prison instead of your full release—as it must, of course, ultimately be.

You need to study this water writeup. Don't allow yourself to believe that just because it was fun and entertaining, it was not also extremely informative on another level."

"I will study it until my brain evaporates."

O

26 In-Between Is Perfect

More than a year after the prayer and water write-ups, after much work with both muscles and head, taking care of my busy physical life and trying to be aware of changes in my inner landscape, I reached one of those points again where I needed some gas for my tank.

"Sweet One, your student and admirer is a little bit weary. I feel like some tiny bug buried in a huge bowl of oatmeal, trying to understand the kitchen.

It would be a lot more fun now to just talk about thrilling subjects again, you know. How about telling me more about the pyramids?"

"Stop focusing your thoughts on yourself. I've given you many other more interesting and important options."

"Very funny. But I agree."

"I'm not trying to confuse and overstress you, just trying desperately to jar you, to shake you loose so you can proceed without so much excess baggage in your mind. (Can't leave that sled behind, you know!) Why do you resist me so? I have never hurt or misled you, have I? Think about it, seriously. What exactly is it that you want from me?"

"What do I want from you? I thought I made that clear a long time ago: just next week's Lotto numbers, nothing more."

"Sincerely, I have given you all I have to give, straightforwardly. Sometimes I do tease you, for sure. Unfortunately, the more I cajole you, the less sense of humor you have? Normally, it's easier to change moods than minds, easier to entertain than to instruct. But you, you're like a rock! So impenetrable at times, so like a sponge at others? Who's actually confusing whom here?"

"Could it be that I'm giving you a headache?"

There's so much help available

"You brood because at times I have told you to seek help, and at other times I have been insistent that you don't need any. I'm sorry if I have only confused you once again, but, in fact, these opposites, like most, are both true!

You always hesitate when I mention contradictory things together. Get over this, please. Contradictory is not at all what it seems to be in your verbal, linear, time-locked world. Maybe, if you relax your attitude, opposites could happen simultaneously.

"I have no idea how to do that."

"You definitely need help with help. You humans surely are a strange breed. You don't understand help, simple help. This astonishes me, even shocks me sometimes. You have such a vast array of help available to you. You have me and infinite others like me! You even have direct access to God Himself! And yet you never seem to know when you need help and when you don't. When you most need it, you seem to least seek it, and vice versa? Some instances obviously require that you stand strong and help yourself, while others need immediate outside assistance. Is it so difficult for you to distinguish between the two?"

"And what would it matter if I could? I wouldn't know how to seek help anyway. Do you know that? I don't know of a number I can dial. Where are all these helpers??? I don't see any. I need to be aware of them! Do you know how frustrating it is to actually believe that they're there and to be unable to consciously interact with them? No, you don't."

Go fill some need!

"I am not leading you down the garden path, seriously, I'm not! I just feel the need to guide you at times, away from one thing and toward another. You are, of course, in no way obligated to try any of the things I suggest. They're simply new options for you to try if you wish. Relax.

I have no secret formula to remove the confusion from your life, but you do! Why not take a few years off and focus your magnifying-glass mind on some need outside your own. You would not have time to wallow in confusion if you found a good cause to pit your intellect, your energy, and your time against.

Go fill some need!

Give, give, give, give, and give some more. Tire your whole being, body, mind and soul in pursuit of some great challenge. Any great challenge outside yourself. Maybe you could start writing? You get to choose. Do choose, because with the selfanalysis you are now putting yourself through, you're bound to run out of intellect, energy, and time, in short order!"

"I don't doubt it. But it's your fault. You've been planting all these seeds in my head, that's why I do all this analyzing in the first place. You have screwed up my poor brain to the point where I'm scrutinizing every little thing like a possessed fool. And it's getting worse, this obsession."

"So hop off this selfseeking bandwagon and find some need that you can fill. You are your gift to yourself, and yet you best meet your needs by meeting the needs of others. Sound contradictory?

Yes it does! But in fact this is as true as any word ever spoken, ever. Also, the more you give your time and energy, lovingly and joyfully, to others, the more time you will gain. Giving it all to yourself is an inverted, withering, draining process. Giving it away is an outward, growing, energizing process! The more you give away, the more you get. This is true. This is universal."

"Universal? So, then avail yourself of an excellent opportunity for growth and give me next week's stock listings. You would be so energized, you'd be the envy of your blue neighborhood."

"You know, Schwab, time, energy, and mind are all relative realities. Your personal choices determine how much of each will be allotted to you. If you don't use it (outside of yourself), you lose it. It's that simple!

So go fill some need. It matters not one iota whether the need be grandiose, important sounding, earth shaking, or drastic. It matters only that you find it and you fill it.

Be on the alert. You may find some serious need right under your nose. Need hides itself in some of the most unexpected places and people. Find it, fill it, and for God's sake, and your own, relax!"

"All right, I'll keep my eyes peeled. Why didn't you mention this before? The need I have been feeling is to find a door to that inner world we have been talking about for so long. I really want to go there."

"It is all in you, in everyone, and you only need to have the desire to know what worlds lie within to find yourself there, and that place is not there, it is here, this moment, in spite of the fact that 'moment' is in and of itself an illusion, a time coating.

And there is nothing that needs to be added to get 'there,' Schwab. I told you this once before when we spoke of

> *Impressionable is fabulous! Gullible is ridiculous! Work to save the one and lose the other.*

your analogy of the vessel. You need only to open up to what already exists right now."

"Can you be a little more helpful, perhaps?"

"Yes. You are in transition between two opposing belief systems. Things are different for you now than they have been in the past. The difference is a good one. You are far less pipe-dreamerish than before. You are more trusting, less gullible; more clearminded, less confused; more accepting, less pressured, than ever before. You are approaching the state of relaxed anticipation that we have spoken of so often in the past."

"I have to confess that your report card has some truth in it. But 'more clear-minded?' Are you sure? I feel very confused still, even if I don't resent it so much any more."

"While in transition you bounce, sweet confused earthling—sometimes back to your old ways, sometimes forward to your potential self. It is never an easy time, but still an invaluable one—a time for analysis and experimentation, for study and rest. Transition is wonderful, beautiful, and exciting in its own way. Enjoy it. It's your right after such sincere efforts.
Now you take off your rain coat and step out into the rain, and of course you feel refreshed right down into your very soul. Don't question yourself. Verification is a common human impulse. Don't ignore it, but don't be obsessed by it. Learning always involves verification of some sort, but a need for too much is unhealthy."

"But where I am in my mind now is so in-between, neither here nor there . . ."

"In-between is really a perfect place for anyone to be or to get to. It has what I call absolute clarity. I'm dead serious, tell me about your 'in-between.' What do you think boundaries are made for? You place your boundaries where you need them. I do. You're no different. Why do you think you are?"

"Why do I think I'm different from you? Where do you want me to start? Let me count the ways . . .

I am not consciously aware of placing boundaries. If my real self thinks that I need these narrow boundaries that I seem to play within, then I am embarrassed before my self. Got it? Orifi, help me get out of this sandbox, will you?"

"For God's sake, you don't need help, no you don't. Help yourself—that's what you're there for. Move from incessantly thinking about helping yourself to actually helping yourself—maybe?

Come with me, just once. I'll show you your own real glory, yes I will. You're afraid though, yes you are."

"I may still be afraid, but I am also eager to see this 'real glory.' But I need your help. I need you to help me get rid of these deep fears, O."

"No, you chuck your fears yourself. The honeymoon is over, the infatuation worn off."

Dream: Crossing a line

I was walking alone on a narrow, paved road. Only my immediate surroundings were visible, illuminated by a pale white light that seemed to have no source. I could make out the edges of the pavement and maybe twelve feet of road in front of me. This lit area moved with me as I walked.

There was no sound. I felt a little spooked by the silence and darkness. I was aware that I had never experienced such blackness in a dream before.

A white line appeared out of the gloom in front of me, a solid, fairly thick, white line, straight across the pavement. I stopped and stared at it. I don't know why, but I was immediately afraid to cross it. It seemed to me like a dare, an obvious challenge. I stood there, getting more nervous and apprehensive by the second. I looked around but saw nothing. Just that line. I listened intently, but nothing. I knew the line was something very special, but I had no idea what. I considered going back, but for some reason that was out of the question.

Gradually, a feeling of defiance and stubbornness rose up in me, a determination not to be intimidated any longer. I felt my shoulders straighten and my chin pick up a little. That did not reduce my unease, but it gave me enough of a boost to move one foot across the line. I waited. Nothing. So I moved my whole body across—and a loud male voice said, 'Hello, Schwab. It's about time.' A voice without hostility, but also without warmth. I can only describe it as neutral, like that of a disinterested observer. I think it was that aspect, more than anything else, that scared me so.

I have no idea what this voice touched inside me, what fears it awakened. Just a line and a voice, and I went bananas. There must be strange things buried in there somewhere, out of awareness, but not out of reach.

I really disliked that voice. Why couldn't it have been a friendly one? If I ever get to design my own reality in full awareness, such voices will be friendly and warm and nice.

The possibility did occur to me that maybe, just maybe, some inner Berlin wall was knocked down. I was thinking that maybe facing these fears, experiencing them in this stark manner, might be the chucking process going on inside. I didn't ask for an interpretation.

Just live

"As far as your frustration: It's only because you are aware of your desire to grow and advance that it seems so frustrating. Everyone is on a path—some consciously, some unconsciously. There is no way to say which is better or quicker. They're just different, that's all. However, those who strive consciously often tend to get in their own way, to confuse issues drastically by the multitudes of mental games they play. This is not a personal fault, only a characteristic of this method. Don't pass judgment for or against yourself. Use that energy to simply live.

Searching, Freddie, involves crawling and sweating as well as dreaming and flying. Your continuation of the pursuit, in spite of countless rebuffs and evasions, has had the excitement of the chase wrapped up with the monotony of any relentless pursuit.

Another old topic that is, however, always new: the objective and subjective aspects of time. I told you a long time ago that you could actually learn to live in the spaces between your seconds. You never even tried? Maybe now you should."

"Why? This will help expose hidden fears?"

"And much more."

I was, in fact, studying Tarthang Tulku's ideas again. He says we can slice time into ever smaller segments and, for example, experience the same number of thoughts in a fraction of a second that we normally would in a full second. Very tough. My mind simply refused to do it, except for very brief moments that were thrilling enough to keep me trying.

"You might wonder, why read one more book? I say because it will help you in so many little ways. It will help you to relax. It will help you to see some truths in a way that is not quite as safe and familiar as my way is to you now."

"And you have a reading list for me?"

"Just read what you need because you'll need what you read. You'll recognize what you need when you see it."

"There you go again. So helpful. But I believe it."

Dream: A tiger in the grass

It was dusk, as usual. I was walking in the apple orchard behind and above my first house. Other people were nearby, on the slope below. The grass between the trees was tall, unmowed, going to seed, and I enjoyed dragging my legs through it and listening to the sound. I loved strolling there in "real" life, and the feeling in the dream was the same.

When I became aware of the huge tiger lying in the grass no more than ten feet in front of me, I froze and stared in disbelief and rising dread at this improbable sight. I knew how ridiculous it was for a tiger to be there. But there he was, crouched low to the ground like they do just before pouncing, with elbows sticking up above the shoulder blades. I heard panicky voices shouting from below, urging me to run. But I was in one of those time warps where dozens of thoughts and pictures seem to come instantaneously. My mind had already informed me that my chances of escaping by running were nil, that the tiger was in total control of the situation. Yet a complete calm came over me as I thought about a course of action. I decided on something that I thought might surprise him: I got down on my knees to be more on a level with him, and then moved forward until I was only maybe two feet from that huge head, all the while keeping my eyes fixed on his yellowish cat eyes. Amazing. My thought was that if I made this a really personal affair, then maybe he wouldn't hurt me.

So far, so good. I kept staring into the eyes, wondering whether I could somehow send a message into that head. But I knew that that was wishful thinking, and then I began to wonder what I would do next. I couldn't just keep staring, and turning away was not an option. Then I found myself thinking that what I really needed to do was to make contact with his spirit, his tiger essence, or whatever tiger higher consciousness might be—and presto, I was 'there!' I was communicating with something that represented all tigers, some intelligence that was the life spark, the origin, the director of every tiger!

I was absorbed in this communion for some time, while simultaneously, as if from another me, I was marveling at it all, amazed how I had managed to make this jump into another state when faced with death.

When my thoughts eventually came back to the 'real' flesh-and-blood tiger in front of me, I knew that I was not only safe just then, but that I was forever at peace with every tiger everywhere. What a super feeling.

The big cat then got up and rubbed against me. I touched his head and mussed his hair. On a sudden wild impulse, I embraced his neck, climbed on his back, wrapped my legs around his incredible muscles, and as he started to run through the grass, I shouted and laughed and yahooed with carefree glee. Before long we were literally careening around the trees, low to the ground, grass stalks hitting my knees—God, how often since that night have I daydreamed of doing that again! I felt so great, so free, so full of life. I felt his power flowing into my body, so strong, making me senseless with joy, giddy with wonder—and so silly that I unwrapped my legs from around his belly and lifted my feet way up high so that only my butt touched his back. What a ride. We must have been some sight, that tiger and I. I remember directing him along the edge of the hill to make sure that all those speechless folks nearby could see us. Then I woke up. And found myself thinking that I was really beginning to enjoy this 'ride.'

O

27 I Urge You to Try

Dream:

I was walking through a small town perched on the side of a mountain, with narrow, cobblestoned streets (Greece? Italy?), searching for the place where I had to attend a class. My shadow was with me. After a tedious, anxious, convoluted search, we found the 'classroom.' It was outdoors and looked like the remains of an ancient amphitheater. Stone benches were carved out of a steep horseshoe slope, with tall clumps of grass growing between them, giving the scene an unkempt but very comfortable and natural feel. Down where the stage would have been, at the lowest point, stood a big blackboard. An elderly man with bushy white hair was pointing to the board with a long stick while lecturing to maybe two dozen people. Behind the man, the slope continued to drop off for quite a bit more into a far-off deep valley.

I was afraid I'd be noticed (again!) and catch hell for being late, but no one paid attention to me. So I found myself a good spot about halfway down and settled in to listen. End of dream.

Your world is a classroom

"Well, I'm still going to school, Professor. I may not have wings, but I'm attending my classes. And what a beautiful setting."

"Yes you are. Relax.

See the seemingly endless repetition in all of nature and forgive yourself for the need to repeat in order to learn and accept."

"Yes, endless repetition. You saw my thoughts yesterday when I was riding on my Deere and brushed up against the seed-laden yews? The air was saturated with yew sperm, and I was covered with it. Eyes, ears, nose, everything was filled with golden dust. Such reckless abundance, such profligate excess, I thought. Then I shook my head in wonder and laughed, because it all seemed so obviously playful. And I had the distinct feeling that something was rubbing the stuff into my nose as a means of urging me to look at it all in a new way.

So I have to practice projection a trillion times before I master it? That's not funny, Big One. I hope you're allergic to yew sperm."

"Be motivated now. Doubts dispelled, difficulties resolved, mysteries cleared away, incomprehension made comprehensible, greater illumination, firmer assurance, deeper knowledge, sounder understanding, fuller wisdom, clarified vision, no more blind alleys—how wonderful. Together we will find all the answers!"

"Yes, how wonderful. You're a wonderful guide. The best."

"Of course we won't find all the answers. There is no such thing as having all the answers. The idea is counter to progress.

Still, we might proceed as if it were possible. Certainly we cannot reduce the world to a neat formula, but we can glimpse enough of the universe to gain some clues about its ultimate meaning. Some of the most insignificantseeming things are inexhaustibly profound.

As I said before, yours is not an alien and hostile universe, but more a classroom designed for you to learn certain spiritual truths."

"Well, maybe not alien and hostile, but this physical world can sure seem cruel and even horrific sometimes. And it's all to learn spiritual truths? Who designed this system?"

"All spiritual truths are designed to be worked out in the physical realm of reaction, to see what actually works. But this learning doesn't have to be stark and stern. It can and should be overflowing with joy and gratefulness!"

> There is no spiritual truth that was not designed to be worked out in the physical realm.

"Wish that it were so. You know that it isn't."

"You are here to win, not to lose. Not to learn to win at any cost, but to learn to win the right way: by pitting yourself against all odds and striving to succeed. It is your rightful heritage. There is no space here for the timid or the hesitant.

Seriously, Schwab, would the creator send us into this complex situation called life that we might fail, and fail abundantly? No!"

"The creator's purposes are not the issue here. The issue is my struggle to get rid of the fears that keep me from flying. I don't want to hang on to that stupid roof any more. And I don't enjoy physical misery, no matter what lessons there might be in it."

"Just try things. The trial-and-error method works well, as I've said before. You needn't trust me, find out for yourself. And don't let a few blind alleys deter your quest. Your sincere efforts are not futile.

You are upset about your foot these days. (Yes I was. A hole had opened up in the right sole and was slow in healing. Eventually, it did.) Go run with it, as insane as that may sound. Circulation is the worst, not the least, of your problems. Adapt shoes to your problem and run, gently and not too far, but do it."

"In the midst of all this talk about the creator and spiritual lessons, you think about my foot? That's nice. Almost human."

"And laugh about it, Freddie. Laughter really is the best medicine. It literally changes the body, and thus the brain chemistry,

almost instantly! Do it, cause it, promote it, indulge in it, revel in it, bash yourself. It's as healthy and invigorating as sunlight."

"I often do, O. Just not always. There are times when laughter seems not to be available. Especially when I yearn for meaning and don't see any."

Move yourself out of the center

"As I said before, life is not a meaningless cycle of live-struggle-die, live-struggle-die, generation after generation. Its meaning, though invisible, is the heart and center of your visible world.

When you feel the need to give your allegiance to something greater than yourself, realize that this urge is a positive one. It insinuates that you are moving yourself out as the center of your universe. You may still have a kind of blurred image of what exactly will replace you in that center slot, but at least you're heading in the right direction. The creative impulse that is planted in you will help you realize what deocentric means, as opposed to egocentric. You do occupy a unique spot in this order of things, but, again, not its center."

"I don't know what that means, but it's good to know that something is in me that will help me."

"A sense of abandon and nonchalance is okay sometimes, but the vast responsibility of being human always looms in the background: the necessity of allowing yourself to become clay in the potter's hand.

With a little effort, human potentialities can conquer any difficulty. One need only root out those elements that encourage self as center and perpetuate the ego's dream of supremacy. If you are only as big as your conscious self, you are minuscule indeed. However, you can be as great as the spirit you allow to work through you."

"I don't enjoy being frustrated by such noble goals, O, so becoming clay is not one of my top priorities. Learning how to let go of that roof is."

"Relax. Changing one's priorities is less a matter of intensive training and more a question of opening the heart. You will react rapturously and feel silent internal joy beyond measure once you do. And remember, each human embodies all that is needed to successfully fulfill his/her earth destiny. All.

If this seems not quite exacting enough to you, remember that it only seems ambiguous to you now. Later it will make sense to you."

"I believe you. I just don't know what you mean by 'later.' Your 'laters' are not the same as mine."

"Let nothing stifle your enthusiasm. Even when my words are disquieting, knowing not the bounds of human thinking, heed them—but remember, they are not allinclusive either. I am not omnipresent or omniscient. I do not see, or know, all things, although you tend to think of me this way."

"I do heed your words, in my own way. And stifling my enthusiasm? I don't think so, in spite of the frustrations."

Lay bare the secrets of your heart

"Now view your passions and go to work accordingly.

Change does not require that you ignore your feelings or stifle your longings, but rather that you let them float to the surface of your consciousness where you can face them squarely and deal with them. Any mistaken notions you may have learned about yourself and your world can be cleared away with very little effort, once you face them.

Once the secrets of your heart are laid bare, it will not matter if you are the only one who sees them. It matters tremendously, however, that you do see them.

You may feel the sting of life, as always, but your reaction will no longer be to try to annihilate the bee population of the entire earth! What will become yours is the honest recognition of yourself as you 'really are,' all images stripped away.

No one can compel you to do these things, but I can urge you to try."

"You urge me? I like that. Makes you seem more like the colleague you say you are. Urge me more."

"Each student in life has two choices: to jump in or to jump out. Jumping in, you learn to soar. Jumping out is the coward's excuse for living.

Jump in and learn, Freddie. Take the bull by the horns and really blaze across the universe, right from your seat at work!

Laugh your silly ass off. Go ahead, rip the lid off the universe, open the flood gates, welcome the surge. Release that tremendous ball of energy you keep locked up inside you. Love life, love even death. But first and foremost, love your creator and love yourself. Enjoy your own presence. Babble on and on."

"That's my Orifi! God and love and bulls and asses, all in the same breath! Yes, this is my kind of invisible advisor!"

Spackling my soul

The contractor had finished sheet rocking the extension we had decided to add to the house. Now it was my turn—I had to tape and spackle. I had become quite proficient at this, having replaced more than half the walls and ceilings. The walls are not hard to do, but the ceilings are a real pain. And this new ceiling was large. I took three hot August days off from work and attacked the room like a true warrior. I was sweating nonstop and spackle dust mixed with the sweat and I got dizzy every so often and my arms hurt . . .

At the end of the third day, I had just about had it. I was ready to leave well enough alone, even though I knew that there were still some imperfections that might show up with the ceiling light on. But after lying in the dust on the floor for awhile to regain some strength, the idea of flaws was no longer acceptable, no, not to me, never. By God, this ceiling was going to be the most perfect one ever done. So I motivated my weary body and began a final application of "mud" wherever it seemed even remotely necessary.

As I was slowly and meticulously scraping away the excess from one little area, a clear thought appeared in my mind: this ceiling is very much like my soul, the spackling knife and sanding block are my daily experiences, and as above so below, and the inside equals the outside, and all that . . . I stood there for a long time and stared at the scene, marveling at the symbolism. When I got back on the stool I felt happy and strong. All weariness and impatience were gone as I consciously proceeded to perfect my ceiling-soul.

Every blob of spackle took on special significance as I smeared it on with exaggerated care and deep satisfaction, and a happy grin on my sweaty face. What pleasure. Every spot I attended to represented some little wound on my soul, and as I smoothed it out and made it perfect, I pictured the inner wound healing also. This felt so good that I even concocted things that might need fixing in my soul.

O

28 Warm Fuzzies

"There are eternal doors. They are within your reach now. They always have been. They always will be. I need only to direct your attention to them. These precious doors, though few, are important to your entry to other realities, to new worlds, to different dimensions.

Serious old hurts, whether comfortably buried in your psyche or still open, festering wounds, are doors. Mythological stories of man's deep past can be doors. Your love of anything good or beautiful can be a door. If you so utterly love the Earth—its beauty, its grandeur, its mystery and majesty—if any or all of these absolutely overwhelm you, this kind of love is a door. It can be love of solitude, love of crowds, love of babies, love of animals, and on and on and on—true love of almost anything.

I say 'precious' doors because they are. I say 'few' because there are so few instances of love intense enough to lift one to another place.

I hate to even begin with you about overintellectualization, but hear me: it camouflages these doors and makes it difficult or impossible to see them, even before your very (psychic) eyes! The doors I speak of were designed specifically to give the voyager in time a sure pathway to places he ultimately needs to go to to become actualized."

"Help me find one and open it, Orifi."

"I say again, you are not left without guidance during the Earth passage. The voices of such guidance are the voices of the deep psyche. They are available to everyone, but one must not expect to actually hear them. They are born out of the realm of 'the sounds of silence.' As such, they make no physical sound—but neither do physical voices remembered, and yet you hear them in your mind!"

"Do you have any idea how I long to hear those voices? How that would change my life? My world would be different."

"You think you need those voices to change your world? You do not.

And why do you never speak to that watcher who is always behind your shoulder? He is your permanent internal other. He is a mentor who will guide you if you get to know him. He lives at the edge of your world from whence he is able to look also into the next. He can only grow and thrive if you do. If you decide to go into the darkest parts of the forest, he will be your intuition. You speak of him but never to him, partly out of fear that he might answer. You act as if he's just a joke you've made up about yourself. He is real. Eventually you must, and will, know this. You always think you will (or must) leave home to pursue him but, really, he is with you now."

"But I only hear him in my dreams, and even then I never bring back to my conscious self what he said. Isn't it about time for that?"

"Longing for the unseen is your constant companion, as you have said yourself. You live with it. It saturates your daydreams and your night dreams. This is good. You follow a path that will not run out. You cannot lose your chance. Your breathing time is your chance.

To proceed forward, all you need is a vision of yourself as functioning on a different level!"

"But how can I create this vision? Out of my imagination?"

"Plug into nature on a spiritual level. She can teach you the mysteries of the universe, if only you will approach her directly and without fear. You may believe you already have. No, you haven't.

Don't spend any more time, money and energy on having; now spend all three on doing.

I think you should make it your new focus to deal with me and my kind. Speak to me of bridges, will you? You have already bridged many a gap between the seen and the unseen. Both now seem to hold equal weight in your mind. You already interweave your experiences with their spiritual roots. You're willing. You can. Yes, you are ready.

Talk from the heart. We hear your opinions translated through your intellect all the time. Now it's time you come to understand your emotional colors, instead.

Hey Schwab, come on out and playa!

There's such a beautiful, wideeyed child inside of you just aching for the invitation to be silly, to talk silly, to look silly, to act silly. How I love that child in you! When I speak most directly to you I am, in fact, speaking to him, to the pure heart of you. You have had to keep him under wraps most of the time because of the demands of your culture, your society, your very civilization.

So listen to me now. Laugh your way into surrender. You'll love it. You'll find it so much easier than 'running the show' yourself.

Can I come over to your house and play? If you won't come out to play, you'll hurt my feelings."

"You skinless beauty. Hurt your feelings! You don't have any feelings.

I would love to play with you. What would you like to play? Horse shoes? Bocci? I bet it's hide-and-seek."

"Lately, as often as you envy my world, I find myself envying yours."

"You should! Come on over and enjoy some of my joys. How about joining me when I play goalkeeper on a hot August evening? You could keep the gnats out of my face."

"It's so strange. I've never been a physical entity, and I told your scribe that I've never wanted to be one. And yet something in you that I can't explain stirs me. I feel that 'physical' might be a worthwhile trip.

Come out and play. We'll talk about it. There are so few who would listen to me, take me seriously. You do. Thank you."

"You're thanking me? Tongue in cheek?"

"No, I am stating a fact.

You have mighty wings

I speak to you now of wings again. Take the wings of the morning: wings renewed and refreshed, wings free of the weariness of yesterday or the past, wings filled with new power and new strength, wings with power of their own when your own power is seemingly spent, wings that have power to bear you upward when things of the world would seem to cast you down."

> Let your thoughts be an open door to all that your heart desires.

"Soothing words. More."

"Whoever you are, wherever you may be, you have mighty wings to bear you up amid the demands and problems of this day. When you make the inner demand and feel the inner need for wings, new wings will be there, eager and strong, ready and dependable. If today your environment is something you must rise out of, let spirit lift you out, accept divine aid and the wings of morning.

Rise up and be free. See and hear and touch and taste the freedom—now! You can be free right now, right where you are, for this freedom does not come with the immediate changing of the situation but with the changing of the thoughts and beliefs about yourself. It comes as you remember the truth about yourself—that you are first a spiritual being.

Think thoughts of health and wholeness and let your body respond with strength and energy that glows with vitality. Let your thoughts be an open door to all that your heart desires. Be open and receptive to divine inspiration and guidance. Be attuned to the allknowing flow. Use your access to the bright, shining, living, radiant ideas that are of that flow."

"Wondrous images . . . You stuff my mind with cotton candy and then you take me to other places, places of your choosing. I know you do this."

"By your very nature you grip the seed of life in a tight, resourceful fist and give it its chance to live and to grow into tomorrow's crop.

Yours is the sign of hope. You are good, solid, patient and persistent. Your sign is of the earth and your affinity with nature is your rightful inheritance."

"You can stop buttering me up now."

"If you abound in common sense and practicality, you also have a keen sensitivity to beauty and harmony. You create and appreciate with equal gusto. To strike a good balance between them is your forte."

"OK, don't stop. Whatever your purpose, you are succeeding in warming my innards. You are making me feel very fine."

"As beauty feeds your mind, so nature feeds your spirit. Surround yourself with both and you will flourish internally and externally. Make nature your therapy, beauty your nutrition. Nature will always recharge your batteries, but you must not be apart from it as a spectator, but a part of it as a participant."

"What do you mean by beauty if not nature? You seem to be making a distinction?"

"For example, a work of art. The artist who, through imagination, offers the perceiver a vision of beauty also offers the

perceiver a vision of truth. He/she is as much a channel as any medium, mystic, or faith healer. He causes the viewer to 'break through' to a new experience of even the most common everyday things by using a particular style and medium. He may use sound, sight, touch, or any other sense to present the way things are.

True art is not merely the luxury of a few sophisticated connoisseurs, nor the activity of just a few disciplined artists. Many people turn to art for the same reason others turn to religion: to create order and transcendence in a world that seems often impersonal, chaotic, even brutal. It can carry the artist and the viewer of his creative expression to a new world that lies beyond habitual and conventional awareness, to a place beyond surface selves. They both enter the harmony, the mystery, and the vividness of the sensuous experience.

True art radiates a subtle nuance that only unfolds gradually. Over time, its effect has awesome power, an undeniable 'presence' all its own. The viewer becomes the recipient of potential energy and becomes engaged in that vital process wherein potential energy is transformed into the motion of kinetic energy—in short, the viewer is moved.

It's one thing to simply look at a work of art. It's quite another to look again, and by so doing tap the roots of one's own invisible existence.

Whatever is beautiful is a perfect expression of 'what is'—not necessarily a representational depiction of something in the physical world, but a statement, no matter how abstract, that creates for both the artist and the viewer some revelation of the deepest meaning of existence.

Beauty, whether delicately or roughly expressed, has the power to transform life."

"Well, all I can say is that I probably need to 'look again.' Please continue with your sweet talk."

"Your patience, endurance and determination astound me. How you still press and pursue where others give up amazes me."

"It's called stubbornness, and probably has more to do with my Teutonic genes and the fact that I'm a Taurus than with anything noble like patience, endurance, and determination."

"Take a chance by not being too cautious to act on your own inspired ideas as they present themselves to you. Next time the acuity of your judgment and the soundness of your intuitive capacity give you an immediate impulse, act on it."

"I have these things? Still buttering me up?"

"Yes. Yes. Try not to let your sometimes domineering intellect dissuade your uncanny intuition. Don't think when you can feel your way.

Beware your tendency to preserve what is, exactly as it is, only to avoid sometimes needed change."

"Yes, I do hang on to sleds, don't I. Maybe that's my nature."

"Yes, to abhor radical change is your nature, but remember that gradual change is essential to move from past to present to future in the natural progression of history as it expresses itself in time.

And yes, I know how much you love beautiful words, and how you reread them and reread them and then read them again, until you have allowed your precious intellect to go to sleep while your intuitive side enjoys the images evoked. This is good. Allow me to lead you into that state now by drowning you in the kind of words you love (again).

Fear not the unknown . . .

Feel the texture of the universe.
Smell the sweet aroma of love.
Taste the bittersweet taste of life.
Tune in and hear the perfect harmony of nature.

See the tangible, the visible—as well as the unseen, invisible flux of matter and energy.

Sense the presence of God.

Hold on to the handle of life; drink from her cup.

Wander through the wideopen corridors of your own mind.

Bask in the stark light of inspiration.

Explore the recesses of your existence.

Revel in the glory of your own body.

Quiver with anticipation.

Tremble in awe of yourself.

Tingle with joy.

Realize your potential.

Aspire to the heights.

Descend into the quiet depths where you may restore yourself. Be still there and consider the very real isolation of your own soul; then externalize again to appreciate the sublime nuances of earth's beauty.

Invigorate your very existence with pure light and clean air!

Soothe yourself in the cool, clear waters of the human experience.

Free yourself through knowledge of this world and wisdom about the next.

Climb wisdom's tree and eat the fruit thereon.

Conquer your innermost fears and desires.

Consider your soul blanketed in its physical body.

Feel the love vibration.

Delve into the secrets of the universe; share her secrets.

Prepare for impending changes.

Approach heaven's gate with respect and awe.

Kiss the lips of the sun, feel his warmth and terrible brilliance.

See the smile on the face of a rock; understand its purpose.

Walk in the wind like the willow tree that attempts not to withstand the fury of the storm but bends with it.

Let the sweet warmth of the sun wrap its arms around you and shelter you from the cold.

Let your mind wander through the sundrenched meadows of the known, through the infinite fields of the unknown.

Fear not the unknown, for once, as a babe-in-arms, all things were unknown to you!

Seek the tranquil fluidity of Alpha.
Touch the hand of God . . . quiver under the influence of his vast
power."

"Oh my. Such beautiful words. Such lovely images. Yes yes, I want to let my mind wander through sun-drenched meadows and infinite fields. How do you come up with these thoughts, Orifi? Where do you find them?"

"There is nothing new here.

The eternal sound

Now I speak to you of something that can lift your spirits much higher than sweet words, something that is always with you and always available to you: the eternal sound.

The eternal sound is everywhere, at all times. You need only quiet yourself enough to hear it. It will soothe you and embrace you. It will gently caress your psyche and lift you to hitherto unknown heights.

The eternal sound is hidden deep within every silence that ever was and ever will be. It is always there waiting for you. You need only go in and find it.

A peace comes with being carried away by the eternal sound that surpasses human explanation or understanding. It is a peace so allencompassing that you need only be taken into it once, on that sound, and you will have a vivid memory of that sound forever after, one that is at once haunting and yet so real that its very memory creates a retreat for you, a quiet place within your own mind.

Better yet, learn the process by which you go to that place and go there as often as you need escape, refreshment, replenishment, or even inspiration."

"Teach me, Orifi . . . I yearn for that place."

"I am teaching you. Relax.

You are so vast, so neverending. I want to show you that. I plan to show you. You're ripe."

"I don't feel vast and never-ending. I'm ripe? Like an apple?

What you have done to me, Beloved Wizard! I feel like that guy in the soap commercial—floating a foot off the ground, feeling incredibly fine. I'll get you for this one day."

Dream: The deer

It was dusk, as usual. Dozens of people were gathered on a large meadow somewhere behind my house. There was excitement and anxiety in the air. We were apparently all waiting to see UFOs. There were shouts of 'Look, there they are!' and I saw a string of lights approaching, maybe 200 feet up. As they came closer they descended, flying one behind the other, until they stopped above a small pond. Now I could make out shapes—and found myself looking in utter surprise not at any kind of craft, but at a line of deer! Yes, deer. Maybe ten in all. Like Santa's reindeer. Something about them sent tingles through me and I wanted very badly for them to land so I could meet them. But instead of landing, they simply dropped down into the water and vanished.

There was much shouting and running around and I heard somebody suggesting fire trucks to drain the pond. I felt an urge to help the deer, to keep them from being found and maybe endangered by fearful people, and so I jumped into the pond, dove down to the bottom and poked around in the mud searching for them. I found nothing. Not a trace. I searched for quite some time—air didn't seem to be a concern—before it occurred to me that they must have a secret place under the mud. How else could they have vanished? So I crawled out and hid behind a bush, watching with amusement, happy with my secret knowledge, as fire engines pumped the poor pond dry. Excited voices were everywhere as the bottom appeared in the glare of search lights, and there was nothing there. They were still talking about alien craft—was I the only one who had seen deer?

Suddenly I was alone, looking dumbfounded at three or four of the deer standing casually in front of a wide, flat-roofed building. One of them started prancing slowly towards me. With every step it took I became more excited and happy, yes, so very happy that I wanted to hug the thing! But just when I was about to run forward to meet it, I found myself staring at a high chain-link fence right in front of my face, separating me from the deer. A wave of frustration and disappointment swept over me, only to be followed instantly by a feeling of relief—because what was standing in front of me was radiating such powerful feelings of intelligence and love that I actually felt safer, more at ease, with the fence between us!

I stood there, hesitant and nervous, with the deer calmly waiting for me to collect myself. Those big brown eyes looked at me with warm bemusement. What intelligence in those soft eyes, I can't describe it. Then it took another step forward, lifted up a foreleg, stuck it through the fence, and held it there for a moment while I instinctively grabbed it with my right hand. When it withdrew the foot, my entire body was glowing with warmth . . .

The real deer

About a month later I was driving home late one night, doing maybe fifty. As I came around a sharp curve I saw two deer standing in the road, one in my lane and one in the other. I jammed on the brakes and pounded on the horn button. The one in my lane jumped off to the side and I was able to breathe a millisecond of relief before the other one decided to follow, which put it right in front of my bumper. A sickening jolt sent it flying through the air.

I screeched to a stop, then backed the car up along the shoulder until I saw the deer lying in the road. It wasn't moving. I got out and grabbed its two hind legs and dragged it into the grass to get it out of the way of other cars. While I stood there staring at it, not knowing what to do, I felt a strong urge to say something, to speak to the dying animal. I knelt down and put my hand gently on its throat and felt the pulse, while looking straight into those big soft brown eyes! How strange. I mumbled some words to it at first, but then I simply waited until the pulse got weaker and weaker and finally stopped. Life was gone from the eyes, and I said good-bye.

Here's what I wrote about it at the time: The deer in the dream was a symbol for my real self, greeting me warmly in a disguise I could handle. The 'real' deer showed me, by dying, by destroying the very symbol used by my real self to present itself to me, that I no longer needed the symbology.

As I sat writing these thoughts, a huge wave of love for the dead animal surged through me, and in my heart I offered silent thanks.

O

29 Why, My Son

In May of '92, after much soul-searching and worried vacillating, I accepted IBM's buy-out offer. So there I was, without job, without title, without colleagues, without daily meeting calendar, and without income for three years. They call it a "bridge"—the span of time to the start of your pension. I seem to have a thing for bridges.

But I had my nest egg, and our big house in the country, and plans for a thousand projects, and tickets to fly to Eugene, Oregon, with Vikki in late summer to spend some glorious days with John tasting Oregon suds and exploring Northwest wonders, then on to San Diego to experience the fabled beach volleyball scenes with Mike and his latest 500 mph Kawasaki or something—yum.

John, happy to have finished his junior year at the University of Oregon, decided to come East first to spend a few weeks with his family and his old high school buddies. Such joy to meet him at Albany airport, big bear hugs. He swore he would make time to sit with papa by the pool at night, with a couple of St. Pauli Girls, and b.s. to our hearts' content about the meaning of life etc.

When we got to my house, his two brothers (Mike flew in from San Diego, Andrew just finished 8th grade) and some friends were waiting, and for the next three hours the berserkers played soccer in pouring rain, stripped to the waist—what a delicious sight. My heart was filled.

That night we gathered for a Father's Day dinner at an inn in the hills, fireplace and all. My ex and her partner, I and mine, and all three sons together for the first time in years. John was wearing one of my shirts, a soft warm blue flannel, because all of his were incredibly wrinkled. He seemed a little distant to me, dreamerish, as if his thoughts were far away. But I was only fleetingly aware of this, so filled was I with the pleasure of this gathering. What more could a father ask for?

How fragile are the thought structures on which we hang our conscious joys.

Two days later the boys took off for the hills, to their favorite camping spot near Kaaterskill Falls. The next day Mike called from his mother's house and urged me to come at once. There was something in his voice that stopped my questions, and when I got there, he came to meet me in the driveway. It was such a long fifty feet for me—when I saw his swollen eyes and his tears and his contorted face, time slowed down, and when he put his arms around me and sobbed, 'Papa, now you only have two sons,' I started yelling like a demented fool, insisting that it was impossible, that it couldn't be true, and on and on and on.

But it was true. John was dead.

He had stumbled in the blackness under the pines, fell about ten feet, knocked himself unconscious, and drowned in only two feet of water.

I put a soccer ball next to him in the casket. There he lay, my son, with his beautiful black mane, wearing my soft blue shirt, tall and strong and young, and dead.

Many came, including his high school teammates. And all we could do was stand there and shake our heads and cry. It was incomprehensible. A few days later a small group met at the top of his beloved falls and watched the wind and water carry some of his ashes away.

Weeks later, Vikki and I honored our tickets and flew to Eugene and spent time with John's girlfriend. She took us to his haunts and I took pictures. Of everything. Even of the spot where he used to park his bicycle at the school. It helped me. Then Mike showed us beautiful San Diego, and his enthusiasm and energy and zest for life helped start the healing.

He knows

I did not want to hear any words from Orifi for many months. I felt betrayed by him. I thought I had a friend on the invisible side. A friend would have warned me, prepared me, done something, anything.

Time, however, does seem to heal things. And why is that? How does the mere passage of time heal such wounds? Just let enough minutes, or years, pass by, and a hurt isn't what it used to be. Seems callous to me that time alone should be able to do that.

So eventually I came out of hiding in my grief and said hello again.

"It disturbs me a lot, Orifi, that you knew all along what was coming. All that time you were talking with me you knew what was coming—I have to tell you, my friend, that really hurts. I've wanted to quit this relationship and tell you to go to hell. You *and* your buddy God.

But you know all that. Now I'm asking you to help. I want you to help me stop the crying in my belly, so deep, I can't reach it. It just wells up and overwhelms me, and all I can do is wait it out one more time."

"Yes, dear Schwab, I know. I feel your pain very keenly. But I also hear you reminding yourself of the things you have been learning about your reality, and these truths are leading you to a deeper understanding, using your very pain to sweep away what is no longer true for you."

"I don't care about deeper truths. I'm trying all sorts of mental games to see what will help, but I don't really care about deeper understanding. I'm so weary of it all."

"I want to share what is crushing your heart. I want to experience your spiritual pain. I want to share. Yes, I hear the cry of your heart. Please listen until you hear mine."

"A surprising statement. I don't understand it, but I am moved."

"Also, Freddie, remember that I am only available to watch and comment upon, not to influence, human behavior. I can only seem to influence when my mental presence becomes enmeshed in some action that was, or will be, happening, not because of my presence, but in spite of it."

"Yes, I remember. But I need your thoughts now."

"Yes, we need to be in touch right now. And remember:

> *Whenever you need me*
> *I'll come*
> *to you*
> *with you*
> *through you*
> *I'll surround you*
> *penetrate you*
> *fill you.*

Even as you sit and brood and wonder, your son sees you, this very minute. You don't need to rely on memories or memorabilia to remember him. You have Now. Use it. Talk to him, even out loud. You will come to 'hear' him answering you. Try it."

"Talk to him? Answering me? I can talk to him? I don't know, Big O, that idea makes me uneasy. How I would love to communicate with him, share what's in my soul with him, make the hurt go away maybe, but the thought of talking to him now—I know, he's only physically dead, but I guess I'm so afraid of failing. I know I accept *you*, and so why not this? What a mess. I can see I have reached a watershed here. I think the time has come for me to do my business or get off the pot."

"You can indeed get through to him, but you need to await his invitation. He's more confused than you are right at the moment.

He isn't sure he was finished! And he feels the lack of 'meat' around his soul. Right now is a time for waiting and learning for him.

There is a finality about death that is no more than illusion. The self's center will never be terminated, only released for higher work and offered far greater options for positive functioning. Understand that death is simply a way of talking about the fact that 'life' is broken up into pieces."

"These are good words. They soothe my mind. But not my belly. Why can't I stuff such ideas into my belly to soothe it, too?"

"Do not obsess yourself with this tragedy. Live with it, but not because of it."

"Ah yes, I have already promised him that I will do certain things so that his death won't be 'for nothing.' I guess that's a sign of the onset of obsession? Oh man."

"Write out prayerful letters to him as a way of saying goodbye—or hello again."

"Write out letters? Orifi, it's so hard to think about him in precise terms, in specifics. I crumble when I do. I keep myself together by keeping my thoughts vague and mushy. I miss him so."

"He knows you all miss him. Yes, he absolutely knows."

"Can you tell him I love him? Please? I panic when I try to recall the last time I told him that."

"You have shown him, in many ways you don't even realize. Yes, he knows, absolutely."

"Ah . . . That is one of the most human things you've ever said to me. That really is.

Touch the physical while you can.

So I can really reach him? Then he could teach me what he now knows? And maybe he can participate some day in my foolish endeavors on that lovely mountain you once mentioned without further explanation? Were you talking about a real physical place, or was it one of your symbolic concoctions?"

"Yes, Freddie, physical—but oh so much more than that. You, also, will be there on more than a physical level. You go there sometimes in your dreams even now, and when you wake you never fully lose the vision.

Did you forget 'merrily merrily merrily merrily . . . life is but a dream?' This simple tune holds profound information for humanity. Think about it."

"All right. I don't know what it means, Orifi, that he will participate, but for now it is enough to just close my eyes and allow myself to believe your words—that I can be aware of him while I'm still physical. This is very fine."

Although I was too timid to try 'talking' to John at this time, the thought of doing so stayed with me, and I was sure that I would find the courage one day.

O

30 Coming Back Slowly

Time passed. My interest in talking with Orifi, and in almost anything, waned. A job would have kept me occupied, but I had none. I worked out at the gym, had occasional lunches with old IBM friends, worked on the house and land—and pretended to myself that I was normal again, that I was starting to 'get over it.' But I wasn't. I found it hard to begin new projects, or to care that my savings were draining away. I gave up coaching and sat by the pool.

Slowly, a little bit at a time, I began to look into the notebooks I had filled over the years, driven both by the need to become productive again and also by the need to find consoling words. The thought of chiseling a book out of this pile of unorganized writings began to look attractive, mainly to keep me busy, but vague notions of doing something 'meaningful,' of sharing what I had with others in similar need, also began to assert themselves. I even thought that I could make some money this way. That was a good, practical thought, a sign of a returning will to get healthy.

After more than a year, I began occasional chats with the Big O again.

"The universe celebrates its existence in the harmonious song of vibration. Even the seemingly still cries from your heart ring out in harmony. Don't stifle its voice. Don't ignore the depths of your own life."

"Strange words."

"I say again, find consolation in the knowledge, even if it is subconscious as yet, that exactly what you need has been provided, is being provided and always will be provided you. Have consciousness of the reality that you are not alone, that your will is not the ultimate decision-making factor in your existence. Some things you do and some things are done for you, according to the plan of your destiny."

"John's death is something I need? Oh man. Do you know how hard it is to think of it that way? I admit that I have considered the idea that John and I (and, of course, many others) must have agreed on this course of action for our mutual benefit, deep in the heart of our being. But I am, at the same time, repelled by these thoughts. I feel ashamed for having them. It's as if the pain has a life of its own and resents any idea that would lessen its power over me.

Orifi, what I really want is to come over to where you are. I want to escape from this level of thinking. I am tired of this."

"Over where? Pinpoint where I am, exactly, and then tell me."

"Don't be a wise guy. Not now. You are somewhere my conscious mind cannot go. You are inside and outside and near blue—and it all means nothing in my terms. Tell me, instead, what's next on the agenda. It feels as if everything has stopped, as if my inner development has come to a screeching halt. There doesn't seem to be anything inside that is growing, or is interested in growing."

"Do you really want a road map up front? Why don't you just wait and see. No preconceived notions, no grandiose expectations. Simple readiness and willingness, no other framework involved.

Genesis now. For one full day, say nothing that refers to you. No me. No I. No you at all. Talk about beginnings."

"What beginnings?"

"You tell me what beginning means. As if you didn't know. The 'clear the slate' philosophy."

"Forget beginnings. I want to get away for a while, truly get away. And if I can't get to you, then tell your gray-skinned little friends to come get me, now! I have a perfect landing spot."

"Go spend much time with your other two sons—a healing balm."

"How are they doing? I've been so wrapped up in my feelings, I've hardly even thought about theirs."

"Andrew will cope in his own way, over time. Michael will ride out the wind for now and later settle down to his real center. Relax.
Now get yourself a bonsai tree."

"What an odd suggestion. Why?"

"Because you need to understand discipline and guidance. You need to know that you can direct nature, even and especially your own.
Your bonsai tree, yes, you are its sole keeper. Whatever can happen to this tree can happen to your soul. You can hunger. You can thirst. You can be dehydrated or drowned. You need to weather many a storm. You can reach neardeath only to 'bounce back.' You can be diseased but will be healed. For you this tree is a direct connection to the lifedeathlife cycle.
You will decide where this tree's tiny branches will grow. They will not wander at random but go where you direct them. Are you God to this tree? No, you are circumstance.
You, too, are subject to miracles. Do not cringe. These are not idle words.
Find a consistent time to devote just to caring for and loving your tree. Do the same for yourself."

"An appealing idea. I will do this."

"Now saturate yourself with music. Start today. Don't analyze it, but 'live in it.' It's your best avenue to get here, where I am."

"I can get to you through music?"

"Especially music you most love to hear, to sing, to enter. You have all the tools at your command. You may, however, need an altered state of consciousness, a very different point of view, to help you with the beginning of 'being music.'"

"Yes, a very different point of view—a view from your lofty perch, to be precise."

"No. I repeat, you have everything you need right 'where' you are.
It is my considered opinion that you have moved mentally, especially lately. You seem not to realize the difference. Tell me what you think of this."

"What I think is that I want to fly with you, to explore, to see for myself. I don't want to know about subtle mental movements. I want to escape. I want to fly."

"Join the club. Everyone wants to fly, but no one wants to make the preparations to do so. Like prayer and/or meditation. How much time do you actually spend, per day, doing these? Have you made any attempt at all to have more direct experiences and to spend less time with memories of them?"

"You know that I have. But progress is extremely subtle. I hope there's a threshold or something, like a step function in math, where one suddenly finds oneself on the next level in one abrupt, totally unforeseen jump. Yes? Say yes."

"Maybe. You can arrange your activities so as to induce more directness. Not to think about it, but to allow places and spaces for it to happen 'to' you—experiencing!

If you were to use all of your experiencing energy on the perception of a particular event, you would have no memory of that event at all. The idea is to spend as much allotted energy each time as you can, while still leaving energy to remember it. Some people get so far away from direct experience that they spend almost all of the energy on the memory of events. If you could recapture some of the dynamics of your first six months on earth—i.e., absorbing everything like a sponge—you would be, as they say, born again!

So, go ahead, look askance at my suggestions. What better plan do you have? Tell me."

"I do have a plan. I will look at color and listen to music and watch rhinos mate on Discovery and walk in the snow and feed the chickadees. And if this incomprehensible thing you call God needs me for some service, It knows where to find me."

"He is always with you. You need to seek Him out!"

"I am willing. But where do I find Him, or Her? Same old problem. Why doesn't He just tap me on the shoulder? Actually, since He and I are the same, according to you, why doesn't He just tap Himself on the shoulder and thereby wake me up? What's the story? Arms too short? Anyway, the real me is available."

"The real you is hiding beneath a veneer of strength, even at times when you are a bundle of fears. You know exactly how true this is.

It's good to stop and ponder the ordinary occasionally—until you remember exactly how extraordinary it all is. Be in awe now. Allow yourself to be overwhelmed, totally swept away as it were. Be outside more often. It is so good."

"You sound like this Australian author whose extraordinary connection with nature I'm enjoying so much (Michael Roads, *Talking with Nature, Journey into Oneness*)."

I often go into the woods and fields behind our house and see and touch and smell and listen. There is so much mystery there, so many life forms living and dying and being born, like in some morphing program on the computer screen, constantly making and erasing and transmuting forms, on and on.

I like to observe some activity and dissect it into its components, and then try to reconstruct how that behavior might have evolved. You know, like in programming: one step, one instruction, at a time. If even one step is left out, or incorrect, the entire program is useless. I usually pick something that I used to take for granted, like the inconspicuous little wren that moved into one of our bird houses. It flies back and forth with nest materials, and I try to imagine how the first wren learned how to do that... Really, I do. Every bird species has a unique way of constructing a nest, and it seems a valid thing to ponder how and why and over what period of time the first of each species developed its unique method. I have no answer, of course, but such musings fill me with awe and wonder. I feel closer to something real when I do this, something bubbling with life and meaning, something that laughs back at me ... What can I say.

Recently, on TV, I watched an African bird called hammerkopf build a nest that weighed in at 200 lbs! Now why would a one-pound bird expend such energy? No one can even venture a guess. (Maybe dummkopf would be a more appropriate name?) And they build a new one for each brood! It gets more amazing: after the hammerheads move out, lines start forming at the nearest real estate office—various geese, hawks, rats, owls, smaller birds, etc., vie for this incredible home, and often several couples of different species will occupy sections of it simultaneously. That's how huge the thing is. Doesn't it seem as though this bird has a well-defined and indispensable mission? If only I knew mine.

"Orifi, say hello to my son for me."

"Done."

"And what does he say?"

"Nothing right now."

"What's he doing?"

"More like what's he being than actually doing. He is very busy being."

"I don't know what that means. But if he's busy, then I suppose he's fine.

I am keeping busy, too, you know. I've decided to see if I can really do a book from this giant heap of words you've given me over the years. I'm busy organizing and categorizing. A monumental task, but just the right thing for me at this time. I am actually grateful to see this grunt labor stretching out before me in time. I know it will take many months, and that is good.

But sometimes, dear Orifi, sometimes I fly into a rage when I look at this ocean of words and then look over at the little urn with some of his ashes. Such a terrible rage comes over me—and nothing seems worth doing. Nothing. Least of all the idea of massaging your pretty words.

Then, after the rage has run its course, I go look for solace in those very same words I cursed! What's wrong with me?

I do think about destiny and free will and 'death is merely a door' and 'out of the invisible comes the visible' and about each of us making our own reality—and I try hard to pound these words into my head because they help. They soothe me. Then I ask myself whether I really believe your stuff, deep inside, or whether I just pretend on the surface in order to hide in your lovely visions. And I know that I do believe that we are not just future ashes, and I breathe deeply and feel better. Until the next attack of rage."

"Stand high on your hill and breathe deeply of life. It is not complicated. There are not multitudes of answers. There is one and only one.

Ponder this message: Some insights are born of our griefs and carried off with our sorrows, while others take flight out of our joy and land precariously on the edge of our existence, resting there a little breathlessly."

"Ah, you do have words. They seem to engage something in me, even though their meaning is hidden from my stretching mind. But you know what? I want more than words. I want to get to that part of me you call the heart."

"Yes, we are left with linear language as the tool we use to express nonlinear thoughts and feelings. But even though it often barely mimics truth, it's the best we have, and in and of itself is actually somewhat of a miracle.

So, don't belittle the importance of the word. It links us, serves as an avenue for us. It has served us so well.

Also, do not belittle reason as if it were somehow smaller or less important than intuition. Praise each. Use each. Mix them together as you would a wellbalanced and wellmeasured breakfast drink. It's a system of checks and balances. Alone, reason can never explain the mystical. Alone, intuition can never describe your world. But together they can weave a rich and luxurious texture into your experience of earth life.

Praise your ability to reason, to draw mental pictures with words as your symbols, pictures that will link you to others like yourself, now and forever.

Why don't you use your reason and start using the language of science, which is math, to explore the geometric reality of all physical things, yes, even health. Yes?"

"The geometric reality of health!?"

"Indeed. You should understand your full physicality, which will then help you to understand your five selves.

Let me remind you again that life in this 'real world' of yours is a matter of point of view only. Life's realities are infinite.

Change your point of view, and you change your reality. But don't try so hard to change things about yourself, Schwab. Sometimes, when effort doesn't seem to work, try living around the problem for a while. You still won't like the flow, but at least it won't be draining your energy twice. Think about it. The water in the stream feels no anger for the rocks in its path, it simply flows around them. Do the best you can with what you have to work with.

Here are three simple steps, for example, that could initiate real changes:

Sleep consistently, eat well, breathe fresh air, and exercise—in short, take care of your physiology. Lots of H2O.

Expand your psychology to include a new, better, more realistic image of yourself and your true value.

Stretch your theology toward an understanding that there is, literally, a piece of your creator in your soul, and that you can 'tap' into it anywhere, anytime you need to. This awesome realization will bring about drastic changes in you, in and of itself."

Dream: On the bridge again

I landed on my familiar bridge, my shadow right behind me. I walked around for a while, stamping my feet a couple of times as if to feel and enjoy the solid surface of the roadbed. I was confident and satisfied, even elated. As I was standing by the north railing, leaning over and marveling at the height of the bridge, my compadre said something. As always, I can't recall a single word, but there's the memory of a feeling, a sense of friendly teasing, of egging me on to do something, maybe using words like, 'Have you really gotten over it? Let's see . . .'—if words were actually used. A twinge of anxiety stirred in my belly as I realized that I was about to prove to both of us that I was no longer afraid of stupid heights, but it lasted only a moment. Without further ado, without a word, I climbed on top of the railing, stood there for a moment letting my eyes take in the vast view before me, smiled a little smile to myself—and jumped!

I fell and fell and fell for what seemed like an impossibly long time, so long that I got nervous about the velocity I must be gathering and the impact I could not avoid. But when I hit the water, I felt almost nothing, just the sudden cold and then a long, long dive deep into the river, so deep that now I started to worry about having enough air. But nothing could go wrong. I floated effortlessly to the surface, popped up out of the water, looked about me happy and thrilled, splashed around a little, and started swimming toward the western shore.

O

31 Now Appreciate

"Dear Schwab—let's you and I get together soon."

"Of course. Just don't use your 'soon' on me, if you can help it."

"Really, we need to talk. Are you willing to let me into your mind yet? Seriously? You have not been in the past, regardless of your words to the contrary."

"Come."

"We must begin in your sleep, where your defenses are down. Talk to me while you're fully asleep, I will answer you in your dreams. You will remember only if you are able to program yourself to do so."

> I can come to
> you and knock
> on your door, but
> only you can let
> me in.

"I should be able to do that. Programming is my thing."

"Relax. It is not difficult.
Please come to me in thought now. Spend time alone with me—complain, share, wonder, ponder, whatever. I say I'm easier to find than a needle in a haystack, even if only slightly so. And remember, while I can come to you and knock on your door, only you can let me in. I cannot tell you how, but let me just say this: Yours need not be an action, but more the inaction of not keeping

me out. Like the chick's shell, yours is so easy to break from within, nearly impossible to break from the outside."

"I trust you are right. Wouldn't get many chicks if it were not easy to break from the inside. Wish I were like a chick. They know how to do what they need to do, no classes necessary. I'm going to get to that state one day. Then I will peck my way out without needing to be told how a thousand times, in a thousand different ways. Just peck peck peck, happily . . ."

"One day? What—why don't you just wait till you die, again, like everyone else does. Will you go to the next place only to be looking ahead to the next and next and next? When do you plan to be 'here?' I say again: you limit yourself to a ridiculous degree by your acceptance of your limitations. More accurately, by your creation of your limitations."

Limitation imprints

I have to digress here with some thoughts. This repeated mention of limitations had usually caused me to react with impatience or even anger. But by now my response was just a lot of thinking, mostly about how and why these limits are set and maintained. I no longer doubted that somehow we have something to do with setting them, but the how's and why's were unanswered.

A few days after this conversation, while relaxing in a delicious bubble bath, I let my mind wander off into musing about what might have caused my inner templates to be what they are. Curiously, my thoughts wandered back to my earliest childhood memories, back to those days after the war—and this scene appeared on my mental screen: it was Christmas 1947, and we had received the first package from my grandfather in New York! Everybody was excited. A package from America! A miracle. I saw us sitting around a long table, at least twenty of us, having finished Christmas Eve dinner, waiting for the big moment. There was a tree with real candles on it, and the scent of pine needles filled the room, and somebody was playing a piano, and everything was so fine.

That box from another universe contained numerous wonders, but I remember only these: oranges and chocolate bars. I had never seen either. The oranges were carefully peeled and divided, and everyone got two little sections. Then the bars were broken into their little squares and we kids each got one piece more than the adults, and what a wonderful thing it was.

I savored the memory until a question interrupted my daydream: so maybe I carry a memory deep in my subconscious of how limited and finite all good things are? How you get your little allotment and then there is no more? That world of my childhood was so completely ruled by the reality of limits that there must be a permanent imprint in my mind that this is how the world is. To this day I cannot leave even a trace of gravy on my dinner plate. One small piece of bread or potato always gets saved somehow to sop up those remaining atoms. I don't need to wash my dishes.

I lay there for a while wondering about this neat example of just how the etching process may have occurred when, quite on its own, another long forgotten scene from my life unfolded in my head, from a time when I was maybe fourteen or fifteen, now living quite comfortably in southern Germany. I was alone in the forest where I loved to go to pick berries or mushrooms or just explore. I was leaning against an oak because my knees were a little weak and my head was buzzing from the powerful sensations I had just experienced. What a wonderful thing for a shy young boy, to see that such forces are present somewhere in his body. I was quite happy with myself. But then I began to feel anxious and fearful, because the teachings of my priest came back to me. He had told us little altar boys that in each man there is a certain amount of seed stuff, and no more, a life's allotment, and every time you "sin against yourself" you reduce that finite supply, and if you do it often enough you may not have enough left when you get married to become a father. I remember how that worried me, and how it made me cringe to think that I would one day marry my one true love and then find out that I didn't have any stuff left in me. What a miserable thought.

Of course, such fears didn't affect the course of events on my next visit to the holy oak tree, no, Mother Nature is much too disrespectful of such nonsense, and so the cumulative impressions made on my young mind about a world of limits must have been very deep. How many other such messages from the religious, cultural, economic and other realities of that time influenced the design of my deepest beliefs? Thousands, I bet.

I was amazed at the appropriateness of these memories, and wondered whether their appearance in my conscious mind was a wink hinting that the power of the old imprints was fading.

"Don't talk to me about limitations, please, do me a favor. And I still don't really know what 'here' means."

"Yes you do—direct experience, perception without analysis, reaction without projection."

"A surprising explanation. I need to think about this."

About appreciation

"Now might be a beautiful time to reflect on the differences in your life and overall attitudes between 'before me' and 'after me.' If you ever tried to elaborate on this, in writing, even you would be amazed at the volumes.

But it is not only good to grow and learn, from birth to beyond death, it is also very good to appreciate your ability to do so—I mean really appreciate.

Let's talk about appreciation. It is very important. Taking miracles for granted just because they are ordinary robs life of much joy. People think that joy is the absence of sorrow, when it actually is the presence of appreciation—deep, sincere appreciation."

"Define appreciation."

"To appreciate means tears come to your eyes when you see the reflection of your own face. To appreciate means you are

thankful for every move your body makes, every tree your eye sees, every blade of cut grass you have ever smelled. To appreciate means being grateful for every person who has ever helped you. To appreciate means never taking food and shelter for granted, ever! Appreciation is . . . love."

"You're really something. I hope this doesn't sound too corny now, but I do appreciate you. Just so you know."

Everything is extraordinary!

"And believe it or not, everything matters when you're matter. In fact, normal, everyday things are the essence, the tiny miracles you came here to see! Pick any common thing—a foal, a mosquito—could you make one? Do you know who made them? Do you ever think about staplers and shoelaces and the feeling the "first" person to ever think of them felt?

Name one ordinary thing that is not extraordinary upon examination."

"I know this is so, but I have to keep reminding myself."

"Also, sweet earthling, you tend to forget the reciprocal relationship we have, the one wherein I get something from you also."

"And that is?"

"Emotion. I can only 'feel' emotion through you. Your emotions are like seasoning—they attach shades of meaning to your actions. I have no emotion, as I am not physical. Energy I have."

"You feel love, don't you? Isn't that an emotion?"

"Love is something very different, something universal. You interpret its effect on you as an emotion because it 'moves' you. It is much more than that. However, emotions such as fear of loss, for

example, can only happen in the physical realm where there are 'things' to lose. Through you I understand such emotions, though I have none."

"Interesting, although hard to imagine. But it gives me great satisfaction that you're experiencing this physical world through me, as I've told you before. I don't think of this very often, but when I do, it thrills me.

Satisfy my curiosity: if everything physical is energy motion, does that mean a rock has emotion? Maybe I shouldn't ask . . ."

"Rocks, of course, do not express emotion as you know it. Still, molecularly they are bursting with energy and motion. Because you see no emotion from your point of view doesn't mean it isn't happening on some level beyond your immediate perception. Say one rock is stationary, another falls off the mountain top. And so what—unless you know whether (how) they have an opinion about their separation!"

"Orifi . . ."

"Relax. Feel free to see things in a new way. Appreciate my 'other-worldly' point of view, just as it is, just as I present it to you.

About clearing the mind

Let me speak to you now of the lifetime process of clearing your mind. Imagine that you can't leave here till it's altogether empty. Empty, not stupid. Oh no, not at all the same—empty as in making vast spaces free for new stuff.

To clear, don't allow yourself to finish a single thought for just one minute . . . If you can, you can empty, you win."

"Be specific, give me a step-by-step, and I'll do it."

"Here are three simple steps:

257

- ○ *Block your mind from completing any thought.*
- ○ *Try to trace a single thought back to its origin, or at least to the point of your first realization of it.*
- ○ *Practice nonthinking, e.g. sensing, as with music. Just hear it, don't analyze it. Do photography for a while, and do not analyze it, just 'see' it. Do something with your hands. Grow mindless.*

So, Mr. 'No words,' are you afraid that if you don't talk you don't exist?"

"Nonsense. I long for that state."

"Don't long for it, step into it now. Think one thought without words, just one.
From here we go, to where we don't know. Confused, wandering souls. We all are lost to the extent that we have no idea where we are going. Join us, will you?"

"What??"

"Here→ there, without knowing the vehicle that transports, transforms, transfigures us . . .
More on this later."

Dream: Graduation

I was walking with another guy on the lovely campus of an old school. There were lots of trees and well-groomed bushes, flower beds along walkways, the works. We stopped and looked at a massive stone building, very similar to Shepard Hall at CCNY. I don't know who I was with, but we knew each other well and had spent years studying here together. We knew we'd never see this place again because we had to move on now. A nostalgic atmosphere, happiness and sadness all mixed together.

'Come, we need to go,' I said to my friend and turned around reluctantly, looking back at the building.

'No, not yet,' he answered with a note of urgency in his voice, 'I'll wait until I get my diploma. I want to take it with me.'

At the mention of diplomas, images of a festive graduation scene appeared in my mind. I was holding a gorgeous diploma laminated unto a thick piece of oak or walnut, and there were happy people all around congratulating me and others, and I felt very fine. Then I was back to where we were standing, realizing that we would miss all those pleasant activities. After some hesitation I sighed, 'Come on, they'll send it by mail.' We lingered a while longer, then walked slowly away.

Since I never recalled the subjects of all those classes I attended, I couldn't say what I graduated from, but I knew that a phase had ended and a new one was beginning. I was thrilled, ready to throw a party to make up for missing the festivities in the dream.

O

32 Are You Having Fun Yet?

I continued the attack on the mountain of words with increasing self-confidence and a growing sense of purpose. I admitted to myself that I had always secretly cherished the idea of writing a book about it all, and now I openly set myself this goal—and was happy about it.

After six more months of labor, the builder of that mountain checked up on me.

It knows it will happen

"So, Freddie, when's the book gonna be done?"

"Don't you know? Just look at what is, and you'll know. Anyway, with you providing some connecting glue, it might just turn out okay."

"You don't need me to glue things together. They will begin to fall together—with a little help from their friend, you.

As you ponder and wonder and weave, cut and paste, add and subtract—realize that you are not simply adding fluff or frills, you are completing a creation, nothing less lofty than that.

Keep weaving, integrating, intermeshing, moving, sliding, changing—before you know it, you'll have a book right in front of your eyes!

This project is a spark, patiently awaiting its time. It waits more willingly and lovingly than you do. You wonder if it will 'happen.' It knows it will. It is already burgeoning, just below your day-to-day routine, with unrealized strength."

"It waits patiently? Well, tell it to grab my head and infuse it with some of that unrealized strength."

"Expect inspiration. There is sudden and there is evolutionary. You can expect some of each. Inspiration from within and without—both the same. Oh that sweet surprise of 'sudden' inspiration, the joy when the light bulb turns on. The wonder of the newness of a thing just discovered is awesome. One can remember the feeling later but never repeat the immediacy of the experience."

"Yes, I know. But this work requires a lot more honest sweat than inspiration. I have asked myself on more than one occasion: why don't you do it? I'll be happy to take the credit for it."

"Because you need to do the writing, not I. It is true that I can dictate this book for you, if you wish, word by word. But in so doing, you and I would not end up in the same 'mental place' at the completion of the work. What, then, would we have gained by our extended acquaintance? The process is not fully a process unless it happens to and through someone—like you, or whomever."

"We will end up in the same mental place? You and I? A surprising statement. Are you giving me an incentive? I don't need one, O, I am enjoying this work. I am finding little treasures in our conversations and rediscovering my old thoughts with fascination. What a 'work in progress' I am, though, aren't I? Man.

Through someone? Whatever process you have in mind—here, I offer myself to you. Do your thing."

"I have waited for this surrender—even in the form of a joke. For us to use you, you do not have to become like a hollow tube

into which we pour ourselves. You keep your judgment, we pass
through it."

"Fine. Come. And don't procrastinate, come now. In my
now."

Having fun is so healthy

*"Have you considered the newness we could find in one
another?"*

"A thousand times already."

*"Remember, universal reality has a 'real' sense of humor. Join
in and lighten your load. Are you having fun yet? Let me know."*

"Yes, I'm having fun."

*"Fun, yes, fun—it is so healthy for you (and everyone else) to
have fun! This is how Einstein found relativity, and Jung found
the collective unconscious—by having fun! Now they are almost
symbols for their 'kind of thinking.'*
*You can learn from them, you know. While their bodies are
gone, the pool into which their spirits dipped while living is still
'here,' available to anyone willing to follow set steps. I can talk to
them (their spirits) at will, and so can you. It's easy. Just believe
that it's possible. The same is true, of course, for anyone else.*
*Those two were (are) not alone, as you are not alone. They
both tapped the collective unconscious."*

"You mean that public library in the sky? Yes, well, I don't
seem to have my library card yet. Show me where the thing is
and I'll go apply for one."

*"The record is within you and outside of you, and if it didn't
exist, neither would human civilization."*

"Interesting. But I need to be able to access it, not just talk about it."

"That's easy: first read your night dreams, then your daydreams. Just look right at them and decide what, if anything, they mean to you."

"And that will get me there? I will try.

'Einstein found relativity by having fun!'—such an appealing statement.

In the meantime, how about doing something practical, like expanding on some old topics for this book? There must be a dozen 'more on this later' promises in these pages. What about bilocation? Some technical details would surely make fascinating reading and provide me with some welcome thrills—and add some credibility to your assertions. Maybe."

"Split yourself and prove it—you'll be a rich man, in spite of yourself."

"That's for damn sure. Very funny."

"As I have said before, you need only do what comes most naturally to you, to do your kind of fun. The creation will roll out, not be dragged out.

Keep moving . . . The way to get to the end of the road is one step at a time! Don't look ahead to the whole trip, just deal with the part you're in.

Maybe you should take up the violin instead—by the time you master it, your Earth time should all be spent."

"Good idea. Then I'll come play it in your blue neighborhood and drive you nuts. Now that would be fun! My kind of fun."

"I love you."

"I love you, too, you merciless, meatless, wonderful something, you. I really do. This has been some trip."

"*Continue to do as you are doing—bravo—good—yes. But take that stance of relaxed anticipation I told you of in the very beginning. You are much more relaxed in your approach to meshing this whole thing into a coherent whole.*"

"I just plow on, happily working for you guys. I am your indentured servant, and loving it."

"*Do not be my servant, be my guide.*"

"Right. I guide you now to a place where you no longer neglect to give me everything I ask for. Follow me there, now."

"*Of course. Schwab, let's be comrades in spirit—working together, not for the good of mankind, but just for the fun of it! I implore you, let us next write a book about fun.*"

"What a thought. You'll be the first skinless author to write about fun. Or maybe not? I wonder.
But find a better, more direct way so we can speed things up."

"*Let's meet on the computer screen. Now that you are a believer, it should be easy.*"

"Now that truly is a gorgeous notion! That would be a first, wouldn't it? I love it."

"*This is a good time for you, a time wherein you have the right to stand in judgment, and stand in judgment you must. Don't be afraid to be ruthless. Cast out the trite, keep the time-tested.*"

"Stand in judgment of what? Cast out what trite?"

"*In reading, in writing, in work, in play, in prayer, in flight, in friendship, in changes in life.*

Your job is to separate the wheat from the chaff in your crazy, over-informationalized world! Learn to scan. Use radar to find jewels and discard the rest, even as you are doing with the book."

"I'm sure I'm already doing it to some degree, in some areas. But now that you put it so bluntly—hmm. I need to think about it.

Let's get back to that library up there. The very idea that all that information is there drives me crazy. It's all there? Available?!"

"Yes, the true reference library in the sky, the place where the encyclopedia of wisdom of the levels up to and including the causal plane is stored. Not so much stored as kept for handy access by newcomers and quick reference by old professionals in this arena."

"But why do I need to learn how to get there? I have you, and you know how!"

"You remember the story about learning to fish?"

"Unfortunately, yes. So teach me how to get there."

How to get to the library

"Stay awake in your dreams."

"Orifi, are you withholding information? What's up?"

"All you ever have to do is tell me exactly what information you desire and I will give you all I have available. Try me."

"Try you? The initiative has to come from me? OK, here goes: when I lie in bed about to go to sleep, what exactly do I do to stay awake during the falling-asleep process?"

"Focus on a spot up and between your closed eyes. Listen for block-out sounds, internal sounds that block out the outside world when you sleep. Do not let their rhythmic sound lull you to sleep. Just continue to listen. Sometimes you'll feel yourself drifting under. When you do, look at the spot again and start over.

One of the first things you'll notice is the volume of your own breathing changing to louder. Its character will change also, to a raspier sound. Again, don't let yourself be lulled to sleep. What you're actually seeking is some particular point between sleep and wakefulness. Experiment consciously and you will learn. It's something you need to play around with. Try this for a while, then come back to me for more specifics.

You know, some of your shamans spend a good part of their earth lives in this special place between sleep and wakefulness. They learn to carry information both ways—into their dreams and out of them. They have far more consciousness of that 'record' from which they take and to which they give. It's strange how little man experiments with this mysterious world called sleep."

"Yes, it is strange. But this human is going to start practicing this very night! And you will be busy from now on providing specifics, I promise."

"Good luck and God speed . . ."

Dream: A ladder

It was early morning. Dressed in suit and tie, briefcase in hand, I was walking on a narrow, paved road to catch a train to work. Others were doing the same. After a while, I turned off the paved road and followed a dirt road which soon turned into just a grassy path. I wondered how this could be if everyone used this way to get to the train station, although I seemed to be alone now. This made me a little uneasy, but I continued.

Then I found myself slowly climbing up a wooden ladder that was attached to, or even partially embedded in, an almost

266

vertical rock and earth surface. I wondered again how this could be the normal way to get to the train.

The rungs looked very old and totally unused. I inspected one closely, noticing with great clarity the finest details—the weathered surface, the coloration, what looked like tiny lichen in the cracks. On I climbed, until I stopped because the rung before my eyes had an ant colony in it. There were many holes and it was partially covered by dirt the ants had piled on it. Only a few were visible, moving very slowly, as if even they were ancient. I watched for a while, entranced by the improbable scene. Then it occurred to me that this rung wouldn't hold me, and I was worried. So I raised myself on tiptoe, stretched my left arm up, and grabbed the next higher rung, intending to pull myself past the weakened one. But what my hand touched felt different. I looked up and saw to my surprise that the ladder changed to a solid, all-metal, much newer and safer one, and there wasn't much farther to go. I heard voices and could sense the train on the platform above. This filled me with satisfaction, because I realized that now there was nothing ahead of me that could keep me from catching it.

The narrow, but smooth and easy, road at first. Then off on a rougher, rarely used one, then onto an overgrown path, and finally a steep, precarious climb on steps not taken for ages.

The ants? Maybe old fears and doubts eating away the stuff that has to hold me? Not to worry! The moldy rung is right in front of my eyes as long as I keep them open. And I don't have to kill the ants. Even if I got them all, including the ones gnawing deep inside, it wouldn't do a thing to reverse the weakness. I just need to reach a little higher and pull myself over the weak spot. As soon as I make that decision, new solid support awaits unexpectedly. Maybe all the student has to do is keep his eyes open and recognize what's before him, and what he needs will be there?

Three cheers for the dream designer.

O

33 Taste the Honey Now

"So here we are, dear O."

"Yes, here we are.
As you now know, Schwab, there is no easy transition from one level of reality to another. You'll find no answers on a silver platter. Answers, you know, are not spun out in a philosopher's study but in the deep of the universe—yes, in fact in its essence, which, of course, is your essence.

But strive mightily and surely absolutely nothing will ever defeat you! Stumbling blocks will fall away from your path. Old shattered dreams will reconstruct themselves and give you back the hopes of your youth.

The gulf between your selves has surely narrowed and you are learning to allow your spiritual convictions to splash out over all areas of your life. Bread of the spirit is beginning to surpass bread of the body in your quest for health. Things that now you can only yearn for will be yours."

"I don't know about 'splashing.' But I do feel as solid as an oak inside. I feel healthy."

"Yes, you are beginning, if still only subconsciously, to deepen your personal relationship with your creator. Soon you will gain courage sufficient for the conscious realization of this fact."

"I have no inkling what that might be like."

"Actually, you still dream that you must indulge in a decisive battle. In fact, you need only be moved by the momentum of your own personal history. And, also, do not reject the notion of being swept away by spectacular events.

Remember, there are infinite areas of life where reason is not the final court of appeal. Things that are quite obviously irreconcilable in rational experience can be perfectly reconciled in intuitive experience. I know you know this now. You are invited to step aside and allow the balanced functioning of each. In terms of your ultimate purpose, this balance must be achieved."

"Yes, but the intuitive aspect is still such a wild and untamed business. It comes and goes as it pleases. It bowls me over with rich and creamy stuff at unexpected times, and then leaves me high and dry when I'm craning my neck to get a specific response. No, I wouldn't call this a balanced functioning yet."

"And even when the balance has been achieved, always leave space, in the end, for things beyond any human possibility of explanation. Although your understanding will clarify what is 'knowable,' remember that no one can ever view this universe free of distortion and limitation. But being often highly perplexed is in no way contrary to growth, understanding, or development. The more positive your assertions are, the less likely you are to be seeing 'the whole picture.'

After giving up your attempt to give detailed answers to questions no man can answer, you will proceed on with new friends who will help you to answer those questions that can be answered.

An open attitude about reality is a soothing, healing approach, leaving room for wonder and amazement. No adherence to some set of rules will ever move a human out of the ordinary and into the extraordinary.

Remember, you are powerless to resist the energy's effect. Acknowledge your part in transcending the visible veil and uncovering the invisible aspect. And do enjoy yourself as each new step confronts you."

"All right, Orifi. You're sounding more and more human, you know. Better watch out. What will your friends think?"

"We are all in this together, remember?"

"Yes, but only you know this from experience. I only know it in my head."

"Small, simple truths implode into your consciousness—surely more proof that you have not been left to your own devices.

Your time is ripe. Greet it enthusiastically. Embrace it with open arms. Such spectacular experience is closing in.

Do what you will and do what you must, but by all means, enjoy! Have fun, loosen up, flow . . .

See images in the clouds
Eat a blade of grass
Feel the sun on your face
Work physically
Sweat profusely
Smell the wet soil
Taste the honey
Touch the bark on a tree . . .
. . . then see behind the physical reality and hear the rhythm of the universe."

O

34 So Long, Bear

Dream: I did it

I was standing on a hard surface of two to three inches of frozen snow. All around was a stark wintry scene of gently rolling hills, barren as far as I could see, no trees, no bushes. I was looking at the sharply defined paw prints of a huge bear, following them with my eyes to where they disappeared over the top of the nearest hill. My belly felt nervous and tight as I surveyed the white emptiness, fully aware that should the bear appear over one of the many low rises, there would be no escape this time. There was no place to hide.

My invisible companion was with me, behind my right shoulder, saying things that I don't remember.

I could have turned around and hurried back to where I came from. But not this time. A mixture of fear and anger and a 'that's it, I've had it!' rebellion grew into a new calmness and determination. I made up my mind and started walking alongside the bear's tracks, knowing that if I caught up with him, that would be it for me. But that's what I wanted—to face him, to get it over with. Whatever he would do to me, he would do to me. The longer I walked, the more feisty I became.

While all these things were going on inside my dream head, it seemed that there was another me watching the me that was experiencing the dream, watching with what felt like great interest, seemingly not concerned at all about any danger but only about what I was doing.

My shadow and I reached the top of a hill. Below us lay a good-sized pond nestled between snow-covered mounds. A very pretty picture, but my attention was drawn to about a dozen people playing on the opposite side of the frozen pond, both on it and off it. Some had cleared a small area of snow and were skating while others on the shore were toasting them with drinks in their hands. I decided to go down to warn them. When I reached the pond, I hollered and waved my arms and, to my relief, they started walking up the slope.

Just then my compadre said something. I looked over my left shoulder, and there, standing on the crest of a nearby rise, was my nemesis of so many dreams—the Bear! I stared at him, and I knew that those tiny pig eyes were watching me. My stomach was churning, but more from excitement than fear. Here he was, and here I was, and something had to happen now that would change things.

A plan grew in my head. I knew what my only chance was and started walking, then running, around the neck of the pond. When I reached the other side, I walked out onto the ice and began shouting and waving my arms to get him angry and, so I thought in the dream, keep him from thinking. The Bear responded immediately as hoped and came storming down the hill, hitting the ice at a gallop. He didn't get far before I heard the most welcome sound—that of cracking ice! How sweet it was to watch my tormentor slowly sink and then disappear under the ice! I was ecstatic, delirious with joy. I jumped around on the ice, shouting my triumph to the quiet hills.

"Hey, Orifi, the bear is dead! I killed him! I did it! Did you see it?"

"Walking on ice has always been easier than walking on water. Isn't it nice to know that you can do either?"

"What? I didn't walk on water. Come on, say more. No riddles. I am overjoyed by this dream. Some fear structures were dismantled. I can't wait to see what changes I will become aware of in my waking state."

"Have confidence in your opinions. They are just as valid, sometimes more so, than anyone else's, including mine."

"I do. This dream was a biggie. I expect to see some really delicious effects from it in my conscious thoughts. I will stop dragging that heavy sled around with me. I weigh less now, Sweet Sage—I hope the wind doesn't catch me as I bounce into the next day. How's that?"

"Never again pass a mirror without smiling at yourself."

O

35 Ahead into the Past

"I'm going to end this book now. Do you agree?"

"Absolutely."

"Then I think it's only proper that you have the last word, don't you?"

"Absolutely. How about we return to one of your pet topics, Fredo?"

"Uh-oh . . . And what is that, Sweet One? Be kind to me now. I deserve some kindness now."

"Indeed you do. No, seriously, how about a few words about those 'aliens' you so love to read and talk and think about? In other words, how about a dose of your cherished thrills? Just for the fun of it?"

"I'm going to kiss you one day soon."

"I can't wait. So let me begin.

Your roots are not altogether earthly

Your civilization is just now beginning to reach ahead into its own deep past. Your science begins to place you on the brink of 'discovering' new knowledge—that is actually ancient truth. I say your pompous modern technology only whispers a hint of technologies past. You love to call your

> *Today's puzzling perplexities are tomorrow's casual comments.*

fancy world scientific, while you refuse to call your deep past anything but science fiction—for now.

Look everywhere at Earth's surface and you'll see markings from your own real, not mythological, past. This past remains, to a great degree, cryptic to you still. Some large markings talk to your 'physical' alien brothers to a far greater extent than your technological attempts to reach life elsewhere do. In Peru, on the high plains, there are ancient airstrips that you have read of many times. They have permanently scarred the earth as a reminder to your psyches and a sign to all visitors."

"Were these the Sumerian and Egyptian gods I've been reading about (Zacharia Sitchin's books)?"

"Of course. And Greek, and contemporary.

Your own roots are not altogether earthly, as I have told you before. Modern man is indeed mainly a hybrid, a creature born, originally, of two worlds. That same "original sin"—interbreeding between earthlings and "outerlings"—was also the deep root beginning of human civilization. The notion that intelligent (i.e., self-conscious) life was planted should surprise no one.

Today's puzzling perplexities are tomorrow's casual comments. Such is history, progress, or whatever. You shall see.

To remember your deep past, psychology and hypnotism etc. would really have to regress past multitudinous births!"

"How far back? How did it start?"

"*Once upon an ancient dream, man took flight and was joined with Earth. When man enters sleep and takes flight, part of his exhilaration is straight excitement, but more of it is racial memory of a kind. You return more often to sleep seeking flight than seeking rest. Or, better put: though your body seeks rest, your spirit desires flight. Your memories of flying machines and your memories of flying dreams are inextricably intermeshed in your psyche. Your culture describes departing spirits as 'flying' to heaven. So does the mythology of many other cultures. This is not by chance! You will remember, in the very beginning of our journey together, I described mythology as the 'saving place' for new and old truths that can't presently be held comfortably in man's consciousness, but which, by their true nature, need to be saved.*

But we spoke not only of ancient mythology. We also once spoke of modern movies. They, too, preserve information that consciousness cannot comfortably contain right now (you could become a movie critic with a totally new approach, haha). And what of children's books and comic books? This stuff is everywhere, camouflaged in myth for your comfort, but oozing out everywhere just the same. Hidden, but, of course, not altogether. The obvious everyday world you view is brimming with secrets of the past and of the future. It is more exciting, in fact, than any movie or book. As you learn bi-vision—seeing more than one reality simultaneously—you will 'see' more and more, and your world will be less and less cryptic."

"What a rich, exciting vision. 'This stuff is everywhere . . .' You make it so hard to sit and brood. ' . . . brimming with secrets . . . ' This is not news, as you always point out. But the way you put it is so exhilerating. ' . . . oozing out everywhere . . .' Love it.

So bring me bi-vision. Bring it to me or me to it."

"*One platter of 'double vision' coming up! Remember the 3D posters with hidden pictures at the mall? The picture is always there, but you have to look at it a certain way if you hope to see the 'secret.'*"

"Yes, I've been practicing with those. Frustrating at [...] now easier—and strangely thrilling when the hidde[...] emerges. But say more about our distant home."

"Your home isn't in the distant stars, only your patriarchy is—that is, your ancient fathers were visitors, but, ahh, your mothers were always of Earth. Thus, 'Mother Earth.'"

"You are so sweet—'... your mothers were always of Earth... '—Reassuring. Satisfying. But I have a question: in all these ancient mythologies, why was it always 'the sons of gods cavorting with the daughters of men?' Why not the other way around? Men might have liked to cavort with the daughters of gods, you know. I know I might have had such a thought—assuming, of course, that 'gods' implies some attractiveness. They weren't lizards, were they?"

"That's just the way it happened, Schwab. In any case, the males were so wrapped in fear that they couldn't have 'gotten it up' even if the occasion had presented itself, which it didn't."

"Haha! Such an earthy remark from my fleshless sage, out of the blue. Warms my heart. And yes, I can see how that could have been true.

From far reaches of many universes

And now something about the present that I hesitate to ask, knowing your limitless wretchedness: are there any among us now? I know I asked you this before, years ago, seeking thrills, but now I really want to know."

"Ah yes, there are indeed aliens among you now—physically, not just mentally—from far reaches of many universes."

"That is so fantastic . . . How I love it. What a magnificent world I live in.

277

Now the next question may be a little odd, but it has occurred to me, so here goes: do they all know that they're aliens?"

"Some do, absolutely, but most do not. You don't, do you?"

"Stop it. Be nice. Introduce me to an alien who knows he/she is one. Pretty please, O, I want to meet one, maybe have a cup of coffee, play a game of chess, talk about 'far reaches' . . ."

"I'm telling you that your own ancient ancestors were aliens. You want to see one now, today? Take one very long hard look in the mirror."

"Stop it, will you? Introduce me to one, wise guy guru of mine."

"I know more than one. We'll get together soooooooooon."

"Oh no. Another Orifian soon. If I count the number of o's and multiply by a thousand, that puts us in the year . . . you're beautiful, but your sooooons are not.

Nothing wrong with a little stroking

There's just one more little topic and then that'll be it, really. It's not directly related to aliens, but not altogether unrelated. Recently I've been enjoying some articles having to do with the age of our universe. Here is a chance for you to say something incredibly brilliant and thereby endear yourself to some scientific types, maybe. I would love that. What do you say?"

"Endear myself? We both know who has a need to endear himself. Or, better, to stroke his intellect with some hard scientific 'facts,' yes? Schwab . . . But, OK, I did say that you deserved something.
When your scientists guesstimate the age of the solar system, the universe, etc., they don't account sufficiently for the cooling-off

278

time, which was in fact longer than the entire time they have allotted to date."

"You mean after the Big Bang?"

"Yes."

"Is that theory correct?"

"Partially correct, yes. Off base in the timing. Again, it took far longer than calculated."

"Were there other big bangs? To start those parallel universes you've talked about? Those lovely infinite intermeshed continuums?"

"Yes, of course. And their opposites, the implosive collapses."

"Wonderful. I can't wait for one of those. What about that problem of the missing matter? They say that all the visible, detectable matter in our universe is nowhere near enough to satisfy the mathematical equations. Is there more stuff?"

"Yes, black matter. It is the inside-out version, the mirror reflection, of white (visible) matter. Balance is essential to the preservation of physical matter, somewhat like the equal and opposite forces in the laws of motion."

"Is it measurable?"

"Absolutely not. It is detectable only by surmise of its necessity."

"Fascinating. Is this related somehow to the propulsion systems of the alien crafts?"

"Now you begin to understand how they seemingly 'hop' in and out of your 'real' material world."

"I understand nothing. But it's so interesting . . .

I read also how some scientists are beginning to look longingly at Einstein's fudge factor again, that cosmological constant he invented to make the equations make sense. He discarded it and called it a big mistake, but now it seems that maybe he shouldn't have. You know?"

"Yes, yes, but they will tire of ending up in the vast empty center of all matter, because there is no 'math' that can bridge the physical to the metaphysical."

"Too bad. That would be so satisfying."

"Yes. Let's close this discussion of the age of the universe etc. by going back to this old question: is there any noise in the forest when a tree falls and there is no one there to hear it? Likewise, is/ was there any 'time' before there was anything or anyone there to 'sense' it?"

"No time when there is no one to sense it! Wow. The implications . . .

I know I should stop wasting time thinking about such things, but it's so hard to stop."

"Schwab, I want you to know, again, that it's okay to ponder the universe, but in the end you must leave the understanding thereof to the one who created it. I'm serious. Who is the goldfish to explain his watery world?"

"Hmm. A tough one to swallow."

"Nothing wrong with your sense of humor, I see.
And relax."

Anything can teach you everything

I came across a marvelous article recently about a very special bird, the emperor penguin.

Other penguins do as all reasonable birds of cold c
They lay their eggs and hatch their offspring as early ii
as possible to give the little guys a chance to grow fat
so that they can hit the ocean (or the airways, as th
be) as self-sufficient adults before winter returns. The emperor,
however, is a big bird, and the antarctic summer is much too
short to allow time for incubation and development. Solution?
These amazing creatures simply lay their eggs in the middle of
the harshest winter on earth! They waddle many miles inland,
huddle together in one tightly packed, warmth-giving blob, and
go about the business of breeding and hatching in—60°F and
raging storms! Unbelievable. How can this be?

Nothing to it, say the invisible engineers. We'll give them a
fold in their well-padded bellies just above the legs into which
they can stick an egg or chick, we'll give them the ability to
store enough fat to go nine weeks without food, and we'll teach
them the proper behavior to survive the cold. You see, after the
eggs are laid, the fathers coax them away from the mothers and
take over the incubation task. The mothers make the long trek
back to the sea and don't return for nine weeks! By that time
the males have lost one third of their body weight. But how can
they survive for so long under those impossible conditions?
Via another ingenious behavior variation: While packed tightly
together, the blob is in a constant state of flux, with the perimeter
emperors who serve as windbreaks never staying there for long.
They cycle back into the interior for warmth in a never-ceasing
life-giving shuffle! What an image. How I would love to see it. A
thousand big male emperors, each with a chick tucked under his
belly, all behaving in the only way that makes survival possible
for them: as one body of interdependent individuals.

It's all one big mystery, isn't it? Penguins, aliens—what's the
difference? Equally unfathomable. That stuff is all around us,
oozing out everywhere.

And so, the idea of aliens is no more unacceptable to me
now than some bird that lays her egg on the South Pole. Same
with an invisible sheepdog who nudges us in the direction we're

supposed to be moving in. Or that there is such a direction. All one big mystery.

And I love the fact that I'm alive in the midst of all this, befuddled and happy.

I will continue relentlessly

"I love being alive, Sweet Big One, do you know that?"

"Yes, Schwab, I know. Perhaps now you see what I meant, so long ago, when I talked about the happy, fertile soil you have provided for our seeds?

Your world is indeed miraculous. As your conscious awareness of it grows, your interactions with it fill your heart with ever-growing wonder—and you find yourself a participant!

Every daybreak is a renaissance for you, each morning a promise. The stark light of noon is a presentation of reality. Afternoon's amber glow bathes you in its warmth. Dusk beckons you to find your own peace here. Twilight whispers eternal mysteries in your ear. Moonlight kisses your cheek softly, not unlike the way the morning dew kisses the earth. Twinkling starlight dazzles your eyes and your heart. Again dawn creeps up to you quietly, rinsing away your sleepiness with its light.

Now open yourself to your own beauty. Stand mystified and awestricken in your own precious presence. Love of the most vast persuasion is entering your life and continually becomes more real to you.

My message can literally reach across this page and grasp you and transform your mind, your very being. Expose yourself fully to my message."

"You know that I have, in my own way, exposed myself to your words over these twenty plus years, and allowed them to change my thoughts in myriad ways. I wish I had done it more intensely, and more consciously, and more smartly, and more fully, and and and . . . I did what I did, and so here we are. Or is it there? Ha.

Orifi, I want to tell you, once again, how much I appreciate your presence in my life. I am really glad that we met. Do you mind if I get a little mushy here as I look back on these many pages? I want to thank you for the lessons, even the most wretched ones, that you so cleverly designed to clean out my conceits and fears, and for the thrills you provided, as necessary, to keep me interested and happy. I want to thank you for renewing my sense of wonder about myself and my physical world. I want to thank you for encouraging me to look inside for answers and to trust what I find there. And for a dozen other things."

"And how, if not through you, would I know of the magnificence of the physical experience? Oh yes, I assure you once again that I, too, benefit from this relationship and I, too, feel the need to say thank you.

Earth life, Schwab, is a beautiful blend of the seen and the unseen, designed to force you to squeeze the truth out of every inward and outward experience. I will show you from every point of view that I have to offer. I will borrow examples from every area of your life. I will continue relentlessly—and you will understand."

O

Epilogue: A Letter to a Son

I, too, intended to continue, for sure, wherever it might lead. But with the book essentially finished, it was time for a break.

I decided to send a copy to Mike, not without some trepidation. Would he think his father had gone over the edge? No, my fears proved unfounded: he called to tell me how deeply it moved him, that he was reading it to his wife on the beach, and also sharing it with a friend. Wonderful words.

My thoughts then turned to John and how I would love to share it with him, too. A sadness seeped into my spirit and my joy lost some of its sweetness. Then I remembered that O had once suggested that I write a letter to him. I never did, but now the thought came to me: why not?

On a cool fall day I drove to the little cemetery in the woods where his grave lies. There, under the long sweeping branches of an old white pine, I sat on the polished stone bench that has a carving of a waterfall and his name on it, and started writing.

Hello, fruit of my loins. How the hell are you? What's it like where you are? How I miss your presence in my physical world. I don't know what I long for more, to be where you are or to have you back here. I want to continue this physical existence. But I also want to wake up on your side and explore the wonders there with you.

It's a glorious day here on earth, John, one of those crisp, clear, sunny fall days when the New York trees are glowing in soul-feeding colors that make one stop and stare and drink deeply and think unusual thoughts. And it makes me wonder—why are we so deeply touched by beauty? Are our psyches responding to something beyond the reach of our conscious minds? Is the awe I feel an invitation, a nudge, to look deeper? I think so.

For a long time I felt myself tightly wrapped up in a cocoon like a caterpillar, each thread of this solid barrier a belief or fear of some kind. But lately, I feel sections are frayed away, some strands are broken, the wall is no longer solid and impermeable. I see the gooey thing inside squirming and wiggling, and it is exciting—I am full of hope. Can you see it? Maybe you can make yourself useful and unwind a couple of yards of thread? Hey, I coached your soccer team for years, so how about doing something for Papa now?

I know, I know, no one can ripen for us. We are like apples. The farmer can prune and nurture the tree to ensure a good crop, but only the apple itself can ripen. Can you see me hanging there? A magnificent, scrumptious Golden Delicious? Unaware of its state of ripeness?

"Yes I can, and it's a sight, let me tell you."

Oops, I am starting to make up responses. But that's OK. Orifi said if I can't hear your side of the conversation, I should talk for both of us.

John, I finally accept that my life experience is as unique and valid as anyone else's. Can you believe how long it has taken me to realize this? It's such a huge change for me. A lack of confidence in my own worth, in my legitimate place in this universe, has been a ruling aspect of my life for as far back as my awareness reaches. But not any more. Now I trust that my roots are deep and strong and healthy. They thrive in the same mystery as everyone else's, as valid as any.

Remember the Desiderata poster we had hanging in the kitchen? 'You are a child of the universe,' it said, 'no less than the trees and the stars. You have a right to be here.' It seems that such reminders are always around us, speaking to us from kitchen walls and a myriad of other places, but we don't hear until we're ready. I have a right to be here. Amazing.

And those so-called aliens, John—including our ancestors, according to Orifi—they have to be growing out of the same life stuff as we, no matter how different they may be. I bet our ideas about them appear absurd to you now, but don't forget that everything has a purpose, including the state of our ideas about everything.

Why, I bet you're cavorting with their nonphysical selves right now!

I wonder what role human consciousness plays in *their* development? And theirs in *ours*? I believe that everything is connected. We are not alone, they are not alone. I learn, you learn, they learn. It's all one big classroom.

But do you know what all this developing and growing and ripening and cocooning is all about? I don't. Not in my head, anyway. I think the most we can ever see is the next inn along the way, and that's it. Even where you are. You guys don't know where this journey goes, either.

I recognize that we don't know what's real, John. Perception truly determines our reality, and what we perceive seems to depend on our individual state of readiness. The Bard knew that when he said, 'Readiness is all.'

Maybe the conscious mind is like a cell of our bodies: The receptors in the cell walls admit only those proteins from the surrounding blood soup that have the correct shape for the intended use, and no others. Like Lego pieces, they must fit precisely. Maybe the relationship between thoughts and our minds is like that—maybe the world is filled with billions of thoughts, and only those that fit our unique individual belief structures are admitted. Maybe the ideas we 'think' are not really 'ours,' but merely those that fit the receptor configuration.

Maybe every experience, every dream—every physical and nonphysical event that touches our conscious and unconscious minds—changes our belief structures, our Lego shapes. That is, we learn. Old thoughts then no longer fit, new ones are admitted, and we are wiser. This may take a long time, but it always happens.

What do *you* think? Does it work that way where you are? Do you still 'think?' And what does O mean by ' . . . John is not busy doing, he is busy being . . . ?' What are you doing when you are being? (See? The meaning of this statement will remain a mystery to me until my belief shapes change.)

I think everything about human growth obeys the principle that I used to resent so much: when the student is ready, the teacher appears. Now, it seems absolutely appropriate that it should be that way.

In any case, I trust now that you hear me. You're not dead. The physical person I knew is dead, and I miss *that* you, so much. But this physical world is only the surface, of that I am now convinced. The essence of the John I knew continues, and so does the love you felt.

What is love, John? Have you learned more about it? Orifi says it's the most important aspect of reality for us to learn while we're physical. But what is it? It feels like some kind of flux or energy that is beyond our understanding. In those precious moments when I *feel* it, at varying levels of intensity and clarity, all other aspects of myself—my reason, ego, fears, hopes, pains and joys, even what I call understanding—seem like foam on top of deep waters.

Maybe love *is* us, maybe it is the life energy itself. This I know: when I let it take me, when I allow myself to stop thinking—then I feel connected, and real, and strangely aware. And so maybe that's what Orifi means by surrendering. And appreciating.

John, I wish you would tell me about these things from your new perspective, with your new eyes. Can you? Maybe there are no Lego pieces in my conscious mind into which your thoughts would fit, but still I'd like you to try.

You know, I really don't know, after all this time, who or what Orifi is. His reality is simply unfathomable to me, but just for fun consider this: if we design our own reality at some level of our total selves, as he has said so often, then he could only appear in my life if I invited him, and it is I who arranged for his many words. Why did I do that? Perhaps because, due to some uniqueness of my inner makeup, I find it acceptable to receive input this way. Maybe my superconscious reaches my conscious mind via 'his' words. So, therefore, maybe it is I who have taught myself to trust and love myself? And Orifi's last name is Schwab? Ha! Funny. I don't think so—but what do I know?

What are *you* learning now? Anything? I hope you're not spending your time thinking and philosophizing. Do they play soccer there?

"On a level you would never believe—unless, of course, you were here, too! But don't rush. You have lots of work left to do, Papa."

Work? What work? I'd rather come to where you are and play soccer with you.

"Your work is your writing, and much more."

My writing? I am writing this book to share Orifi's gifts to me, and their effects on my reality over these many years. But beyond that—I don't know, John.

Listen, am I really hearing you, or am I making these words up in my mind?

"The crazy thing is, Papa, that you're the old hand at this stuff, and yet you are the one who doesn't believe we really speak—as we do right now."

It's just so hard to accept.

"Yes, it's harder for you, right now, than it is for me. Remember, too, that as long as we speak, I remain tied to our earth and all that I was, even if I might need to move on. This is the supreme test of a parent: first the loss, then letting go."

Do you want to move on?

"I don't really know now, but the 'time' will come when I will need to."

I won't hold you.

"I know, Papa . . . because—you really love me."

O